Making Character Bears

MAKING CHARACTER BEARS

VALERIE TYLER

GUILD OF MASTER CRAFTSMAN PUBLICATIONS LTD

First published 1998 by
Guild of Master Craftsman Publications Ltd,
166 High Street, Lewes,
East Sussex BN7 1XU

Reprinted 1998

ISBN 1 86108 069 7

Photography by Dennis Bunn

Line drawings by John Yates

The publishers and author can accept no legal responsibility for any consequences arising from the application of information, advice or instructions given in this publication. The bears featured are made for collecting, not as toys for young children. If bears are made for young children, care must be taken to conform to British Standards and EC regulations on safety, or equivalent requirements in other countries.

Designed by Ian Hunt Design

Typeface: New Aster

Printed in Hong Kong by H & Y Printing Ltd

For John, with love

Measurements

Although care has been taken to ensure that imperial measurements are true and accurate, they are only conversions from metric. Throughout the book instances may be found where a metric measurement has slightly varying imperial equivalents, because in each particular case the closest imperial equivalent has been given. Care should be taken to use either imperial or metric measurements consistently. (See also Metric Conversion Table, page 178.)

Suppliers

Good craft shops or haberdashers can supply most of the materials for bear-making, and there are mail-order firms which advertise in specialist craft magazines. The materials used for the projects in this book were supplied by Oakley Fabrics, 8 May Street, Luton, Beds., LU1 3QY.

Contents

PART TWO: THE BEARS

INTRODUCTION

As with many children, Teddy was my first friend and I whispered all my hopes and fears to him. It did not matter that he was slightly balding and his eyes had long since fallen out. We had resisted my mother's attempts to put them back: Teddy would not have been Teddy with eyes!

Technically Teddy was my sister's bear, so when I grew up and left home Teddy naturally remained with her. By way of compensation, however, she bought me another. I named him Wellington. Teddy and Wellington were not at all alike. Teddy was a 1940s bear made of mohair, with long limbs and a fat stomach. Wellington was a 1970s bear with man-made fur fabric, a short snout and short limbs.

It could have been that I was older, or perhaps it was the feel of Wellington's fur, or his slimmer waistline, but although I loved him he was not as cuddly as Teddy. He was less approachable, more aloof. What was the difference? I began studying other bears and sure enough I noticed distinct characteristics. Eyes slightly too large for the head seemed to stare, while eyes too close together gave a shifty look. However, if the eyes were placed further apart and slightly down the head, an air of innocence was achieved which was far more appealing.

My interest increased when I discovered 'collector' bears. Antique bears have longer snouts, longer limbs, buttons in their ears, humps on their backs and a whole wealth of characteristics apparently forgotten by modern manufacturers. The heartbreaking part was the price range. With four young children and a teacher husband, the 'collector' bears were totally beyond my pocket.

Then the summer of 1992 happened. It was meant to be a walking holiday, but it rained, and rained, and rained! Eventually, wet and miserable, we descended upon my parents. Could we dry off with them? Four children in the house and endless rain might seem a nightmare for some grandparents, but not for my mother. She decided that we would make teddy bears. My children, aged from seven to fourteen years, joined in enthusiastically. As soon as the furry face of my first bear began to take shape it seemed to come to life. His expression and character were so individual and personal. All the children, boys included, completed a bear and I completed two. We still treasure them today. I returned home via my mother's fabric supplier, having taken my first step into the world of character bears.

Teddy, a 1949 Chiltern Hugmee. Photographed by kind permission of Mrs Carolynne Adam.

Carolynne (aged 2) and Teddy.

I soon started to develop the different techniques needed for the specific expressions I had observed for so many years in antique bears. I experimented with the positioning of the eyes, longer snouts and limbs, and even the hump on the back. I used different fabrics to make a bear look young or old and developed techniques for reducing the size of a bear to just 13cm (5⅛in). As I discovered, it is not just a case of shrinking the pattern.

The positions of the eyes and ears proved to be vital for producing specific expressions, but I began to feel that the bears needed more than just an expression. To give a complete effect they needed clothing or accessories. I have seen dressed bears, but unless they are mascot bears, when the clothing can be highly relevant, the point for me is very largely missed if a bear is fully dressed. So I set out to choose appropriate accessories to round off the character of each bear I made. It can be quite a challenge to select the one or two items that complement a particular bear, but that is part of the fun.

We live side by side with my bears. In fact, they are gradually taking over the house. Some of them live on the stairs, with one or two bears for each step. More of them live in the fireplace (we do not use the fire!) and Tommy has his own chair. Guests are frequently surprised by bears popping up in odd places.

This book contains all the instructions needed to make your own 'character' collector bear. Although a basic knowledge of sewing will help, you need not have had any previous experience in making soft toys. I certainly had none when I began. There is a certain amount of equipment that you will need and this is clearly set out in Chapter 2. If you are used to sewing you will probably have much of this already.

Chapter 4 explains in detail how to make the basic bear and this chapter will need to be carefully used alongside the specific instructions for each bear in the second part of the book. As you become more skilled at making bears you will no longer need to refer back to Chapter 4. A photograph of each bear is shown alongside the instructions, so you can see exactly what you are aiming for.

The patterns for each bear are given in a separate section towards the back of the book. You will see that every bear is slightly different. All patterns are shown full size, so there is no need to alter any of the patterns unless it is your choice to change something.

When you have made enough of my bears I hope you will develop ideas of your own and want to experiment. The variations are endless and I hope you have tremendous fun exploring all the different styles and expressions a bear can have.

Wellington, a 1971 Wendy Boston.

Part One
Essential Information

1 A Brief History of Bears

Toy manufacturers have been making bears for more than a hundred years. The originals were not the soft toys we know today, however, but clockwork reproductions of the real thing which could dance. Other bears stood on all fours and could be pulled along on wheels by a string. It was not until the turn of the century that an unexpected event in the United States of America gave us the inspiration for the Teddy Bear as we know it today.

Teddy's Bear

In November 1902 Theodore Roosevelt, the 26th president of the United States (who was affectionately known as Teddy), was in Mississippi negotiating the disputed boundary between that state and Louisiana. For a little light relief a hunting party was organized and on 14 November President Roosevelt was near the Little Sunflower River with his hunting party. We can only assume that the hunting was poor, for in an attempt to please the President his hosts captured and stunned a bear cub. This unfortunate bear was tied to a tree so that the President could shoot him easily. It is reassuring to note that the President did not appreciate the offer and is reputed to have said, 'Spare the bear!'

According to a report in the *Washington Star*, 'The President . . . refused to make an unsportsman-like shot.' Clifford K. Berryman, the *Star*'s political cartoonist, immortalized the event with a cartoon depicting the bear as an innocent, child-like cub and the President turning away from it, holding up his hand in a noble gesture of refusal. The caption read, 'Drawing the line in Mississippi'. The cartoon caught the imagination of the American people and the bear became a regular feature of Berryman's cartoons right through Roosevelt's successful election campaign of 1902.

At this time Morris Michtom, a Russian émigré, was anxious for publicity. His wife, Rose, made a toy bear which he displayed alongside newspaper cuttings in his shop window. He named it 'Teddy's Bear'. The bear created a great deal of interest and by the end of 1903 the Michtoms had found financial backing and formed The Ideal Novelty and Toy Company which made their fortune.

Steiff

Meanwhile, on the other side of the Atlantic Ocean, someone else had come up with a similar idea. Margarete Steiff was born in Giengen, Germany. Having contracted polio as a small child she was confined to a wheelchair and became a seamstress in order to earn her living. At first she visited people in their homes, but later began a mail order business called The Felt Mail Order Company. Unwilling to waste the felt cut-offs, she used them to make elephant pincushions from a commercial pattern. These proved such a success that she widened her range of animals and fabrics until in 1892, well before the Roosevelt incident in America, she produced the first Steiff catalogue showing bears made of mohair. These bears were representations of wild bears, standing on their hind legs with no moveable joints. In 1893 the company was renamed The Felt Toy Company.

By the end of 1902 the company had started making a plush bear with moveable joints designed by Margarete's nephew, Richard. This bear was initially a failure because it was regarded as being too big and heavy and not at all appealing to children. Nevertheless, at the Leipzig Toy Fair, it was noticed by Hermann Berg, who promptly ordered 3,000 bears for a large department store in New York. Steiff now found themselves leading the market in America and ideally positioned to exploit the 'Teddy's Bear' phenomenon.

Richard Steiff redesigned his bear, adapting it to look younger and more appealing. He also used kapok instead of wood wool (wood shavings) for the stuffing, thus making the bears softer and more cuddly. The Steiff company tried to patent the name 'Teddy Bear', but failed to do so and had to accept the growing competition. In order to make Steiff bears instantly recognizable another nephew, Franz, suggested putting a button in one ear. This button and the words 'Button in the ear' were patented at the end of 1904 and are still in use today.

Other Early Developments

Now that the teddy bear had been established as a toy, it was to be exploited in other ways and 1907 was a year of great innovation. For the first time an animated teddy bear cartoon was produced in America, called *Little Johnny and the Teddy Bears*. It was also the year in which Dean's Rag Book Company in England published a book by Alice Scott entitled *Teddy Bear*. Probably one of the most enduring celebrations of the teddy bear should be attributed to J. K. Bratton who wrote 'The Teddy Bear Two Step'. When the words were added to the tune 23 years later, it became 'The Teddy Bear's Picnic'. The following year J. K. Farnell made the first British plush, jointed teddy bear and Dean's Rag Book Company advertised its first 'cut-out-and-sew' rag teddy bears.

Fig 1.1 *The Chef (see pages 90–2) owes much of his appeal to the longer snout and limbs characteristic of the older style of bear.*

The War Years

The First World War (1914–18) brought changes even to the teddy bear world. Steiff and other German manufacturers had their factories turned over to war work. This meant that there were no more imports and countries who had previously relied on Germany for teddy bear supplies had to expand their own soft toy industries. During these war years many famous names developed, including the British Chad Valley and Chiltern Toy Works. Other countries had to wait until after the war and it was not until the 1920s that the emergence of both the French and Australian teddy bear industries took place.

As the restrictions on raw materials caused by the war eased, the British companies expanded fast. In 1921 Daphne Milne bought an inspired first birthday present for her son Christopher: a British-made Alpha bear who became Winnie-the-Pooh.

The United States of America was relatively untouched by the war in terms of raw material restrictions and here the teddy bear industry continued to boom until the Great Depression, which forced many manufacturers to make cheaper, mass-market bears. Richard Steiff left his native Germany to oversee the American side of the business. Nonetheless, even with their most successful designer on the other side of the Atlantic, the German toy industry was back on its feet by the early 1920s.

The years between the wars saw a golden age for the teddy bear. In 1919 Alcock and Brown took British-made teddy bear mascots on the first nonstop flight across the Atlantic. In the same year 'Bobby Bear', Britain's first comic-strip teddy bear, appeared in the *Daily Herald*, and 'Rupert Bear' soon featured in the *Daily Express*.

By 1924 Walt Disney had produced the first colour animated film to feature bears, called *Alice and the Three Bears*. Arguably the most celebrated of all teddy bears, Winnie-the-Pooh, first appeared in print in A. A. Milne's books in 1926. In 1930 the Merrythought soft toy company went into production in England and is still manufacturing today.

On the other side of the world the Chinese unknowingly started a new fashion when a giant panda arrived at Chicago zoo in 1937. It is noticeable that during this time the teddy bear designs moved away from reality and concentrated on becoming more appealing. Glass eyes were introduced, humps disappeared and fillings became softer.

Post-war Changes

After the Second World War (1939–45) it took a long time for the teddy bear industry to recover. In order to survive at all there had to be changes and the most significant change was the use of man-made fibres for fabrics and stuffing. This not only reduced the cost of the finished product, but had the added advantage of making the toys more suitable for washing. This was a feature the public was increasingly demanding.

In 1954 the British manufacturer Wendy Boston, who had already patented the lock-in safety eyes some years before, now introduced the fully washable teddy. This decade also saw Sooty appear on British television and the arrival of Michael Bond's Paddington Bear.

Traditional manufacturers found it increasingly hard to compete with the Far East, which flooded the market with cheap, synthetic, mass-produced toys in the 1950s and '60s. The traditional soft-toy industry, with its emphasis on quality and expensive hand-finishing, could not compete with such low material and labour costs. Australian firms were particularly badly hit, as were companies in Great Britain, France, Germany and the United States. Steiff led the fight back from Germany and in 1951 Richard Steiff's bear was redesigned with a flatter and rounder face and with shorter and straighter limbs.

Revival

The late 1960s and early '70s were dark days for the teddy bear, although Disney apparently saw hope for the future. In 1960 Disney bought rights to Winnie-the-Pooh and made the first full-length Pooh Bear feature film in 1975. Others also played their part in the revival and adults who had owned and loved bears in their youth began to demand them once more. Peter Bull said on American television that he 'had a distinct sense of bereavement' when, as a boy, his mother had given away his teddy bear to a jumble sale. He received over 2,000 letters of support and this prompted him to write a book on the subject. *Bear With Me* (the title was later changed to *The Teddy Bear Book*) was published in 1969 and was an immediate success. After that, adult demand for collectable, traditional bears increased steadily.

In 1979 the 'Great Teddy Bear Rally' was held at Longleat House, home of the Marquess of Bath. More than 18,000 people and their bears attended. Further interest was generated when in 1981 Evelyn Waugh's novel *Brideshead Revisited* was serialized on television. Peter Bull's bear, Delicatessen, was used as Aloysius, the teddy bear companion of one of the central characters, the flamboyant Sebastian Flyte. Old bears had now become collector's items.

New bears are now made in 'limited edition' designs and these are eagerly bought by today's collectors. Old established firms also produce special bears to celebrate their anniversaries and major auction houses hold regular sales of classics. The story of the teddy bear continues and, who knows, the character bears you make now may one day command high prices at auctions.

2 Materials and Equipment

Everything you will need for making each bear is listed below. Also included are further details on specialist items such as fabric, joints and stuffing. It is best to assemble everything you need before starting on your first bear, to avoid the frustration of suddenly finding you need another joint or piece of felt after the shops have closed for the evening. Good craft shops or haberdasheries should be able to provide you with most items, or you can try the mail order suppliers listed in craft magazines. Optional equipment for making some of the accessories is detailed in Chapter 3.

The Essentials

- Sewing needles – strong, sharp and not too fat
- Small pair of sharp, pointed scissors
- Dressmaking pins, preferably with coloured heads so they can be seen easily
- Tape measure
- Wooden spoon to push the stuffing in
- Small wire or teasel brush suitable for brushing pile fabric
- Medium felt-tip pen for drawing round patterns
- Paper for tracing patterns
- Card for templates (old cereal packets work well)
- Fur fabric or mohair (see page 6)
- Felt or suedette for paw pads (see page 6)
- Strong sewing thread (normal cotton will break) in black, beige or grey depending on the colour of the fur
- Black or dark brown embroidery wool, or fine, three-ply knitting wool for the nose and mouth (see page 7)
- Plastic safety eyes (one pair per bear, see page 7)
- Plastic joints with washers (five per bear, see page 8)
- Polyester stuffing (see page 8)

Fig 2.1 Essential equipment: sewing needles, small sharp scissors, dressmaking pins, wire brush, felt-tip pen, paper, card, strong sewing thread, tape measure, wooden spoon and joint fixing tool.

Fig 2.2 *The different types of man-made fur fabric: long and short pile, dark and light colours, and a crushed effect.*

Fig 2.3 *Various mohair fabrics: short pile, light and dark shades, crushed and uncut.*

Fabric

There is an enormous range of fabric on the market to suit most tastes and pockets. However, the fur fabric or mohair that is suitable for quality bears is usually only stocked by specialist suppliers. Many suppliers will welcome a personal visit, but be strict with yourself. It is easy to become carried away and spend far more than you intend! If you prefer, most stockists are prepared to send samples through the post on receipt of a stamped addressed envelope. These suppliers should stock everything you need and they often provide a mail order service. I would recommend that you check craft magazines or the telephone directory for those most local to your home.

All my bears are made from fur fabric (see Fig 2.2) or mohair (see Fig 2.3). The fur fabric can be inexpensive and is ideal for the first-time bear maker. Some of my favourite bears are made from this. As my skills have developed, however, it has become apparent that mohair bears are very special. Unfortunately they are also expensive and I cannot afford to work exclusively in mohair, delightful though it would be. Suitable fabric of both types is usually sold in 137cm (54in) widths. In each set of instructions I give details of the fabric I have used for the bear shown in the photograph, but it is a personal choice and is only intended as a guide for you.

Whether you choose man-made or mohair fabric, the length of the pile is also something to be considered. The word 'staple' refers to each 'hair' of the fabric. A long staple fabric is suitable for larger bears but is usually not recommended for smaller bears due to questions of proportion. There are, of course, exceptions when a particular effect is required. A short staple will suit bears of all sizes, but sometimes a large bear is not so cuddly if the staple is very short (see Chapter 5). The staple will vary from approximately 6mm (¼in) to 2cm (¾in).

Features

Paw pads

The paw pads are often made from good quality felt (see Fig 2.4). It must be strong as normal strength felt will lose shape quite quickly. Suedette, a man-made material that looks and feels like suede, is also ideal for paws and this is what I normally use these days. I like the softness, and on the finished bear suedette always seems to look more 'professional' than felt. It comes in a good range of suitable shades for paws.

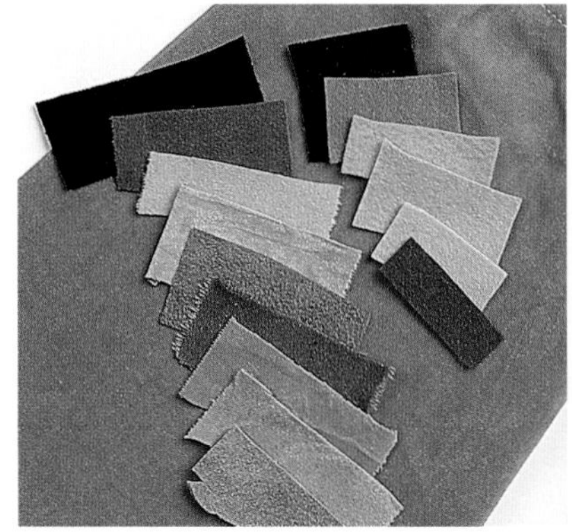

Fig 2.4 *Felt and suedette pieces for paw pads.*

Noses and mouths

I never use plastic noses or mouths for my character bears. It is a matter of preference, of course, but antique bears always had wool noses and mouths and this is the effect I want to emulate. Plastic noses come in different sizes and are secured in a similar way to eyes. The benefit of using plastic noses is that the finished article is prepared and shaped for you and it can be quite difficult to make the hand-sewn noses look the way you want. Plastic noses are mass-produced, however, and much character can be lost this way (see Chapter 5). Difficult though it may seem at first, I would recommend that you persevere with the hand-sewn method, using black or dark brown embroidery wool, or fine knitting wool if you prefer (see Fig 2.5). General instructions for creating a hand-sewn nose are given on pages 14–15.

Fig 2.6 *Plastic safety eyes.*

Fig 2.5 *Black and brown embroidery wool for handsewn noses and mouths.*

Eyes

Eyes vary in size and colour. All my bears have either amber or deep brown eyes. The smaller eyes are approximately 5mm (3/16in) in diameter and the largest eyes I use are 1.2cm (½in) in diameter. Make sure that you buy safety eyes which have a round metal washer at the back (see Figs 2.6 and 2.7).

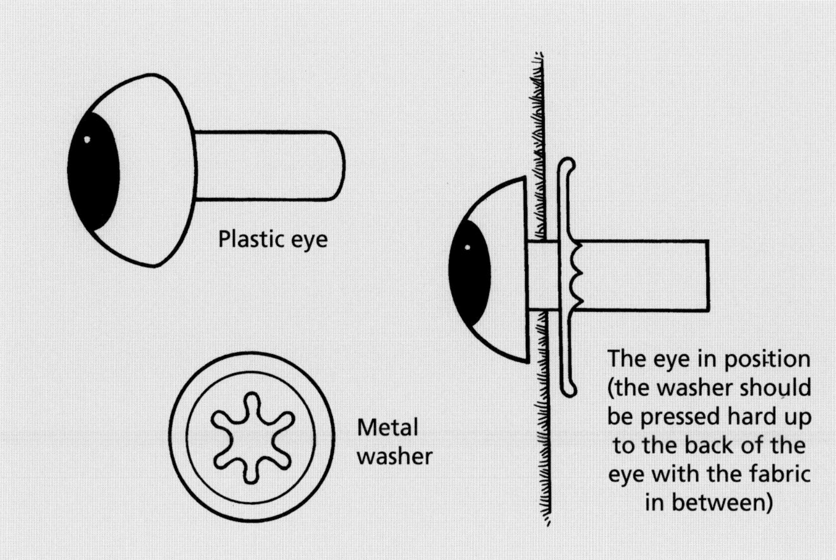

Fig 2.7 *How to attach an eye to the fabric.*

Fig 2.8 *Plastic joints.*

Joints

Usually five joints are needed for each bear, one for the neck joint and two each for the arms and legs to attach them to the body (see Fig 2.8). Plastic joints are shaped like a toadstool with a washer for the middle and a locking ring that fits tightly over the shank of the toadstool. A short metal rectangle measuring about 10 x 4cm (4 x 1⅝in) with a hole in the middle gives you something to push against when fixing the joint. Once the joint has been fixed together (see Fig 2.9) only great determination and strength can prize it apart. Joints range in size from 2.7cm (1¹⁄₁₆in) to 4.5cm (1¾in) in diameter, with the length of the shank being in proportion to the diameter. The size of joint depends on the size of bear being made. The instructions for each bear state which size is best.

I have never found a joint small enough to suit my miniature 13cm (5⅛in) bears and so I use large eyes for their joints instead. Of course there are no locking rings, but they seem to do the job. The bears are so small that the joints never seem to work themselves loose. Perhaps we are gentler with the smaller bears.

Stuffings

In the past wood wool was used to stuff bears. This is just another term for wood shavings. Wood wool can still be bought today from good suppliers, and although it is rarely used as the main stuffing, some people do use it for the snout. I always use polyester stuffing for my bears as it is lighter, easier to handle and more readily available.

I have heard of people using kapok or fleece clippings with some success, but those who are allergic to natural fibres should avoid such things. Some of the traditional, cheaper stuffings such as foam chippings and cut-up tights are generally unsatisfactory. They tend to cause lumps which spoil the shape of the finished bear. Whatever you do, steer clear of the springy stuffings which are specially designed for making cuddly toys. Collector bears need a much firmer filling. If you are uncertain about the differences between stuffings, ask for advice from your stockist.

Safety

Make sure that you go to a reputable stockist who can assure you that all fabrics, joints and eyes conform to minimum safety standards. It is, however, important to note that the bears in this book are designed to be collector bears and not toys for young children.

If you intend to make bears to sell, you must comply with various safety regulations. Again, good stockists will be able to give you full details of the British Standards and EC regulations in force at the time.

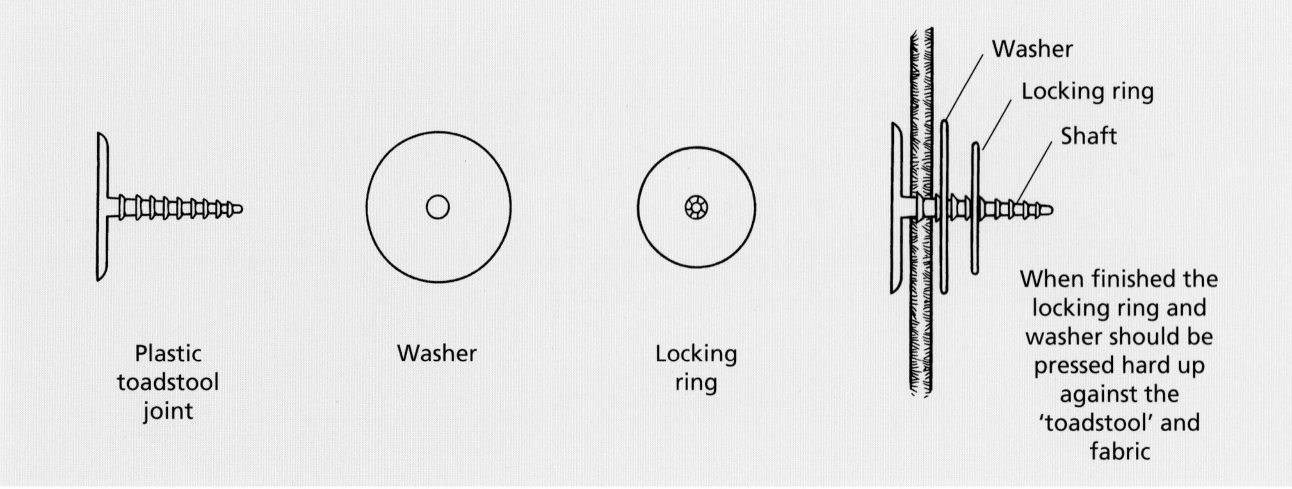

Fig 2.9 *The correct assembly of a joint.*

3 Accessories

The bears featured in this book are set apart from the average teddy bear by their individual characters. Their accessories are an important element of this characterization, encapsulating a pastime, or celebrating a particular occasion. Accessories can be made or collected. I do both. Obviously, home-made accessories are less expensive, so I usually prefer this method, but sometimes the only way to find the perfect item is to search the darkest shelves in the most unlikely shop.

Choosing Accessories

When deciding on accessories for a bear, the first question you must answer is, 'How little can I use while still making the character absolutely clear?' For the Ballet bear a tutu says it all. The Policeman needs a truncheon and a helmet. Normally I try to avoid masking bears' ears with hats, but in this case the accessory is vital.

It is essential not to overburden your bear with accessories. Ninety per cent of the charm will be the bear's own, while the accessories are simply the icing on the cake. Rule 1 is to try to limit yourself to two distinctive items. Never go over three.

The next problem may well be working out how to make the accessories. Rule 2 is 'never despair'. There is always a way to achieve what you have in mind. It may take time to deliver, but there will always be a way.

Rules are made to be broken. Rule 3 is 'never say never'! The mascot

Fig 3.1 *A selection of accessories used for the bears in this book, including the guitar and the doctor's stethoscope.*

Fig 3.2 *Cricketing bear – an example of a fully-dressed 'mascot'.*

Fig 3.3 *Minimal accessories are often best. All the Fisherman really needs is his rod.*

bears in this book break just about every rule. The Cricketer is totally dressed (see Fig 3.2). The only thing I have resisted is a hat, but I think the effect is successful.

Usually it is an item of clothing that helps the character most. Collars are effective, as are waistcoats or even boots. Sometimes other items are the key to success. The Fisherman, for example, needs no clothing because a fishing rod sums up his pastime (see Fig 3.3). The picnic basket was my daughter's suggestion and a blanket, though not really necessary, adds to the general air of comfort. A large umbrella would be another suitable accessory for a fisherman.

Skills and Equipment

A range of skills is needed to make all the accessories in this book. It is important to note, however, that if you can make a teddy bear there should be no problem with the accessories. Clear instructions for making the accessories are included with each bear. The skills needed include simple knitting, crochet, sewing, embroidery and papier-mâché.

Apart from the basic sewing kit that you need for the bears you will also require knitting needles, a crochet hook and some glue. There are no other vital pieces of equipment. A sewing machine may be helpful for the waistcoats and a small embroidery frame for the embroidery, but neither is essential for a good result. Embroidery should be worked on specialist cross stitch fabric and most good craft shops will sell this in small enough quantities.

Storage

I find that I need to store various bits and pieces for my bears. The large sides of empty cereal packets are cut and saved for making any patterns that I need to use regularly. I store them in washing powder boxes cut down to make magazine racks. Ribbons are never thrown away, but are stored in old biscuit tins in a cupboard.

In my workroom my husband has put on the wall six racks of small plastic drawers that are designed for storing nails, screws and so on. I find them invaluable for buttons, safety pins, plastic eyes, beads, strange buckles, old leather watch straps, chains, earrings – you would be amazed at what I keep in there, all collected over the years as possible accessories. I store such things by size and colour and usually go to the correct drawer first time.

Collecting

Odd scraps of material will also be immensely useful; nothing will go to waste (see Fig 3.4). The Bridegroom's stock and cravat (see page 41) are made from an old muslin nappy and the Teacher's waistcoat (see page 81) from an old pair of trousers. I never buy any material for dressing my bears. This said, you must accept that you cannot keep everything. I must admit that I am notoriously bad at this, but frequently have to force myself to go through all my stock and throw things away. It can be guaranteed that the very next week I will want something that has gone, but if I keep too much and exceed my allocated space allowance the family, quite rightly, complain. It is also the case that if I keep absolutely everything then I can never find what I want because there is too much to search through. The key is to be discerning.

Collecting a variety of odd items is also a good way of kitting out your bear with accessories other than clothing. I often find what I need in a most unlikely shop. Trophy shops often keep interesting things. It was from just such a shop that I found the Musician's guitar (see page 58) while on holiday in Wales. A family trip to Hampton Court Palace provided me with a pewter spirits measure which became the tankard for the Real Ale bear (see page 47). The Teacher's books (see page 79) belonged to my grandmother.

The best advice I can give is that you should be inventive. The accessories featured in this book are only a springboard for other ideas. I have used what I could find, and you may find something better or more suitable for your particular bear. Do not be daunted if you have to search; the right thing will turn up eventually.

Fig 3.4 *Even the smallest scraps of left-over material can be turned into a suitable accessory for one bear or another.*

4 Making a Basic Bear

The following step-by-step instructions apply to all the bears featured in this book (although the 'mascot' sporting bears on pages 63–9 are made in a slightly different way). You will need to turn back to these guidelines each time you make a new bear, until you are confident with the method. Before making your first bear, read right through the instructions to familiarize yourself with the steps you will be following. Specific instructions for each individual bear are, of course, given in Part Two.

Preparation

Fabric

Spread out your chosen fabric on a table and inspect it. Stroke it carefully with the flat of your hand and decide which way the pile lies. It should lie downwards on the finished bear. All the patterns in this book have an arrow to show which way the pile should lie.

> **TIP**
>
> Never press or iron fur fabric.
>
> Never use a sewing machine as the fabric will move as you sew.

Patterns

First trace the patterns from the book on to paper, being careful to mark on all instructions. Trace accurately: a careless pattern will produce a poor quality bear.

Then cut out the paper pattern and place it on the wrong side of the fabric, taking great care to follow the arrow which should be pointing down the lie of the pile. It is wise to fit all the pattern pieces on the material *before* drawing and cutting, so that you are certain you have enough material. If you are going to use the pattern again it makes sense to transfer it on to card, which also makes it easier to draw round. I use old cereal packets.

Draw around the pattern with a felt-tip pen, marking the slits on the head where the ears will be fixed, and the points for eye and limb position.

Remember, you will need the following parts for each bear:

- Two heads (one in reverse, see Fig 4.1)
- Two bodies (one in reverse) – sometimes there are three body parts
- Four arms (two in reverse) *or* two arms (one in reverse) depending on the pattern
- Four legs (two in reverse) *or* two legs (one in reverse), depending on the pattern
- Four ears
- Two leg paw pads (of felt or suedette – sometimes one is in reverse)
- Two arm paw pads (of felt or suedette – one in reverse)

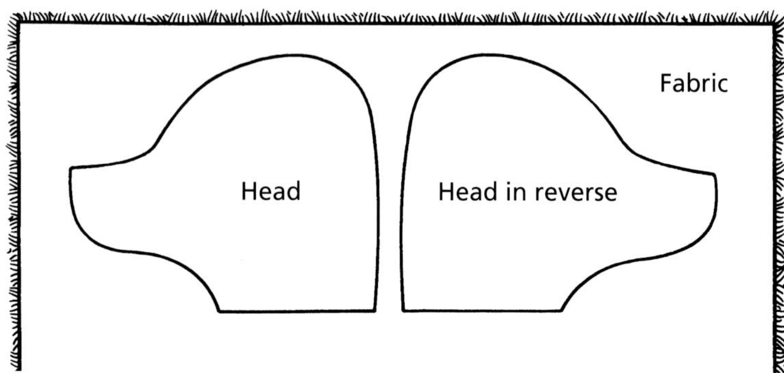

Fig 4.1 *The head pattern transferred to the wrong side of the fabric and ready for cutting. Note that one head outline is in reverse.*

Cutting Out and Sewing Together

Small, sharp scissors work best for cutting out pieces of fur fabric. Snip the back of the fabric with the tips of the scissors, using short cuts so that you do not snip through the pile.

Before sewing, put the fabric right sides together and pin (see Fig 4.2). You can tack the pieces together if you find it useful. It is important to push all the pile to the right side of your work with a needle before sewing, so that none of the pile shows on the wrong side of the completed seam. This will ensure a neat, almost invisible seam when it is finished.

Backstitch (see Fig 4.3) is used for most seams, although some bear makers prefer to use stab stitch (see Fig 4.4). All patterns include a 3mm (⅛in) seam allowance. Handsewing the seams will produce a far more accurate result than trying to use a sewing machine, as the pile on the fabric will cause it to move about too much in the machine.

For each part of the body you need to leave a section of seam unsewn to allow for stuffing later. The relevant sections are indicated on each pattern and mentioned in the instructions for each bear as appropriate.

TIP

Always fasten off very strongly, with four stitches in the same place. Seams that come apart will ruin a finished bear.

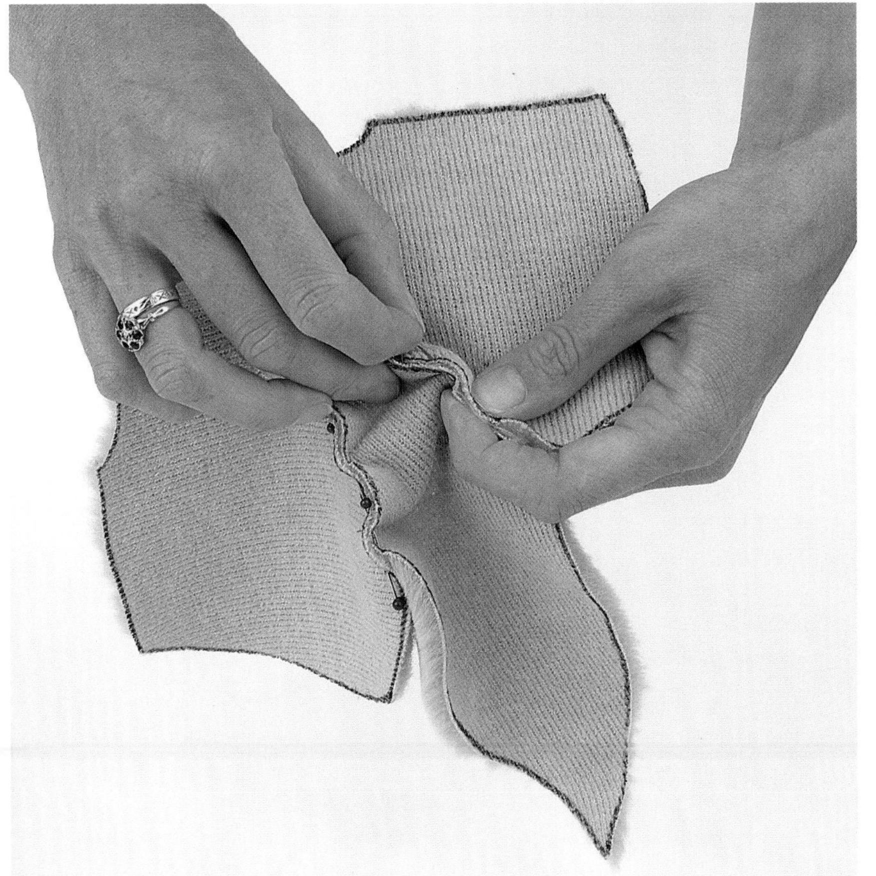

FIG 4.2 *The head pieces being pinned with right sides together.*

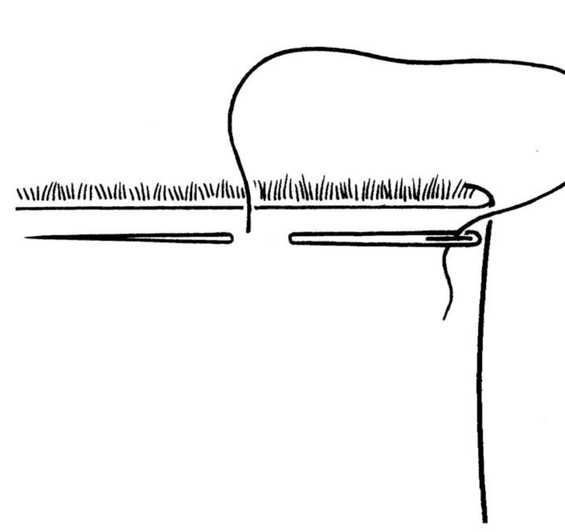

FIG 4.3 *Backstitch.*

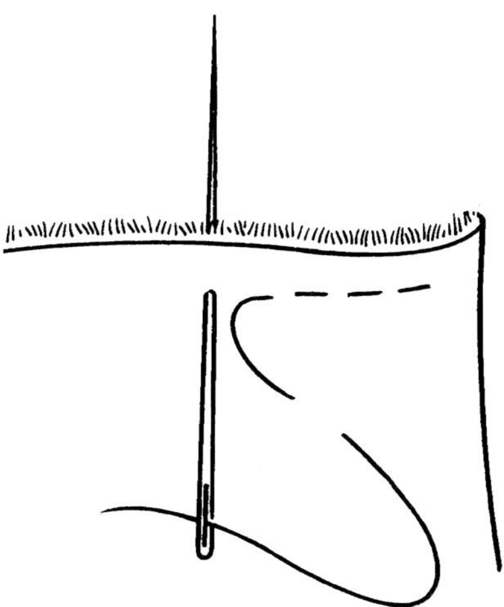

FIG 4.4 *Stab stitch.*

Ears

Ears will be sewn into a slit which is on the top and towards the side of the head. They are usually sewn into place with over stitch (see Fig 4.5). The ear slits are clearly marked on every pattern. After the ears are sewn and turned right sides out they should be carefully

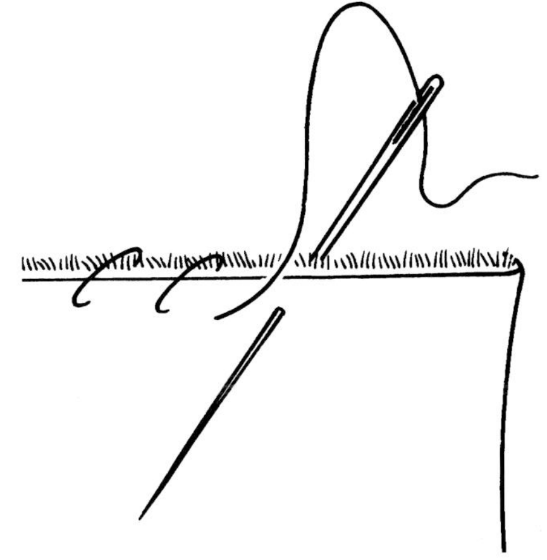

FIG 4.5 *Over stitch.*

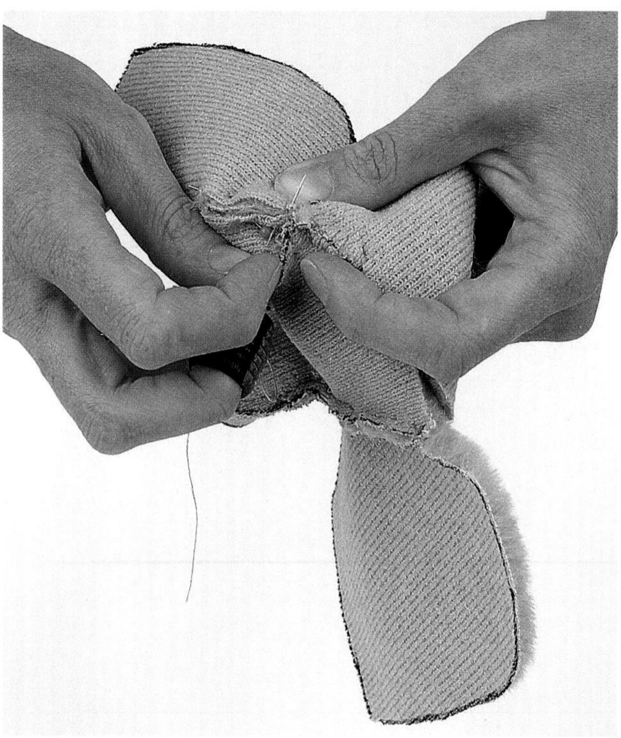

Fig 4.6 *An ear being sewn into place on the wrong side of the head.*

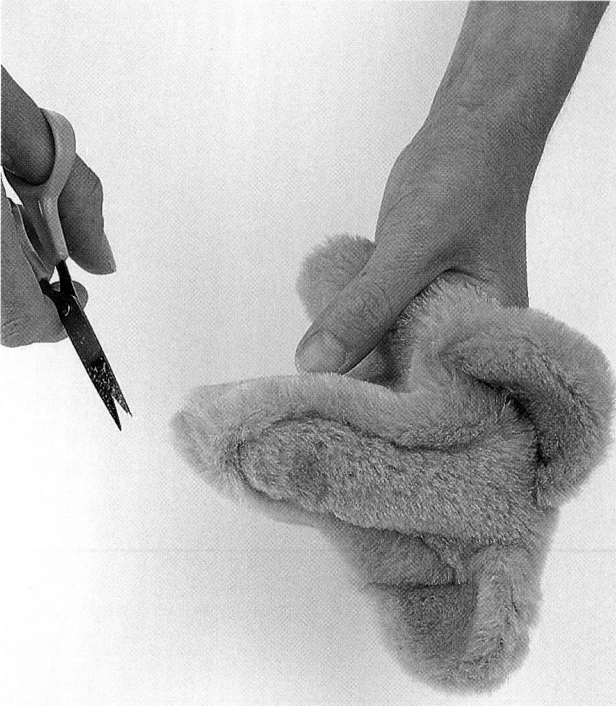

Fig 4.7 *The head, now sewn together, having the pile round the snout trimmed before the nose is sewn.*

inserted into the marked ear slot and oversewn into position on the wrong side (see Fig 4.6).

It is a sad fact, but bears are often picked up by their ears, as they are easily grabbed handles. Bearing this in mind, sew the ears very firmly in place to avoid accidents later on.

Nose and mouth

When the bear's head has been stitched together (but not stuffed) it is time to create the character. Advice and techniques for giving a bear character are dealt with in detail in Chapter 5.

The nose is the first thing to add. It is important to do this before inserting the eyes so that they can be positioned correctly in relation to the nose, depending on the effect you wish to achieve.

Put a little stuffing in the head, just to get the idea of its shape, then hold the face in your hand and study it carefully. Choose the exact place and shape of the nose and mouth, bearing in mind that the only rule is that the three-way join on the end of the snout must be covered.

It is a good idea to trim away all the pile directly under the planned position for the nose (see Fig 4.7). This will make the sewing easier and no hairs will poke through the finished nose.

To stitch the nose, first use a single thread of wool to sew an initial triangle across the three-way join at the end of the snout (see Fig 4.8). Using the triangle as a guide, sew the nose in the same wool with a double thread. Use bold, straight, vertical stitches, taking care that each one lies close to the previous stitch and that the guiding triangle is completely covered (see Fig 4.9).

Do not be disheartened if your first attempts do not turn out as you would like. Carefully cut the wool, pull it out and start again. It is worth getting it right and sometimes it takes me two or three attempts to achieve the effect I want.

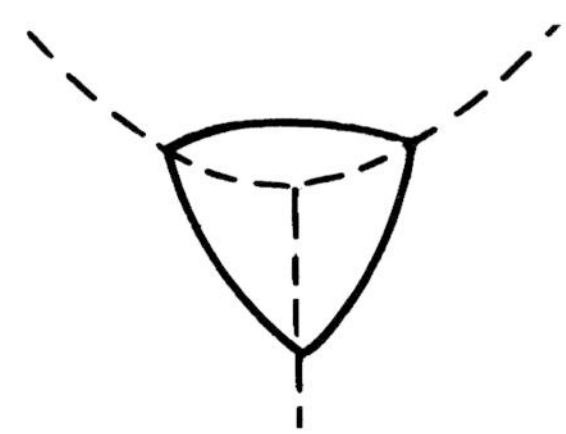

Fig 4.8 *The preliminary triangle sewn across the three-way join on the snout to give the nose its basic shape.*

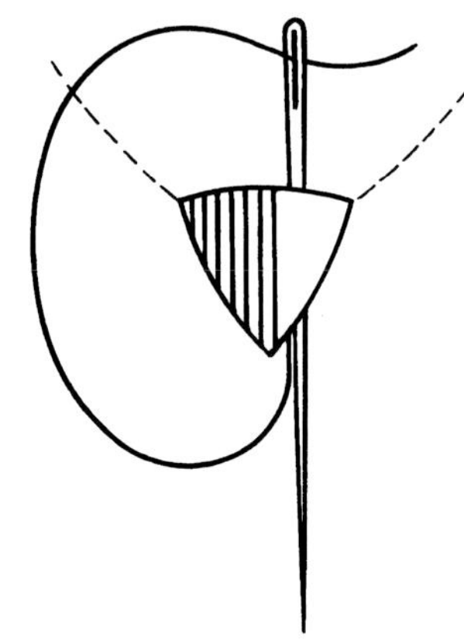

Fig 4.9 *The nose is sewn with long, straight stitches over the preliminary triangle.*

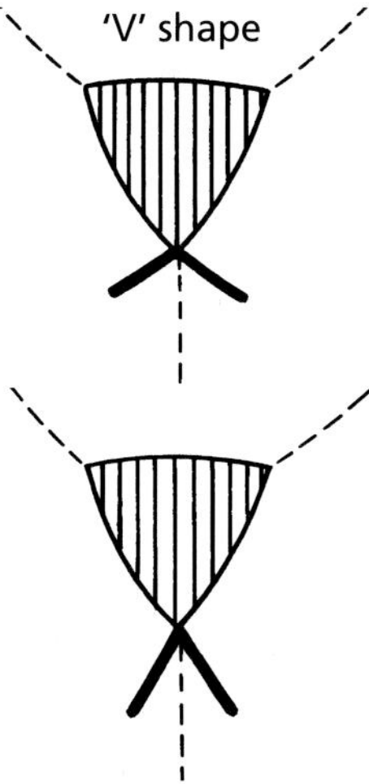

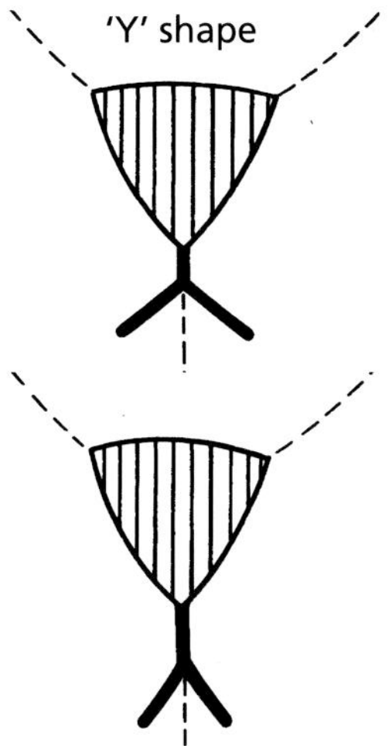

***FIG 4.10a and b** The positioning of the mouth using upside-down 'V' and 'Y' shapes.*

The mouth is also best stitched with double thread. Sew an upside-down 'V', with the point of the 'V' touching the base of the nose (see Fig 4.10a). The shape of the mouth can drastically alter the character of the bear (this is explained further in Chapter 5). An upside-down 'Y' shape can be used instead of the 'V' (see Fig 4.10b). Experiment as much as you need. Cast off very securely as nobody really wants a bear whose nose and mouth have unravelled.

Some bears will need the pile of the fabric clipped further around the snout when the nose and mouth are finished. Trim very carefully with the tips of your scissors. Remember you can always cut more off, but you can never stick it back on. When you reach the edge of the clipped section, grade the trimming so that the short pile gradually merges with the long.

Eyes

The eyes will usually be placed just outside the gusset seam (see Fig 4.11). The distance from the nose will alter according to the pattern and the character of the bear. The instructions will give you the correct distance in each case but, generally speaking, the lower the eyes the younger the bear will look. The size and colour of the eyes is entirely up to you, depending on the effect you wish to convey.

Use glass headed pins to mark the position of the eyes to begin with (remember the pins are usually very much smaller than the eyes will be). Now is the time when you can experiment with the expression until you are happy (see Chapter 5).

When you are sure about the position, make tiny holes for the eyes with the point of some small, sharp scissors. Be careful not to push the scissors through too roughly, for this will result in too large a hole. Don't panic if this does happen, as the hole can be stitched up on the wrong side, as long as you make sure that all the pile is on the right side of the fabric before sewing. This mend will not show if it is done carefully.

Insert the eyes into the holes and check they are in the correct position before securing (see page 7). This is your last chance to change them if you are not happy with the result. They can be taken out and the holes sewn up on the wrong side once again. The eyes can be repositioned two or three times if necessary and it will never show on the finished bear if you always take care to keep the pile to the right side of the fabric when sewing and finish the thread off securely.

Make sure the eyes are fixed in very firmly. The metal washers on the back must be pressed on as hard as you can manage. This is not only for cosmetic purposes but also for safety, in case the bear is kept within reach of any children. If the eyes are correctly fixed it should be very difficult to pull them out.

***FIG 4.11** The nose, mouth and eyes in position on the head.*

Assembling the Bear

It is vital to make certain that all the joints are very firmly pressed together when assembling the bear. You must always use the washers provided as this helps to keep them secure. Use the special washer-fixing tool (see page 8) to make the joints really firm. It can be useful to have a helping hand at this stage, and my husband is always the one to check the joints for me, as his fingers are stronger. When the bear is completed, the joints will loosen off a little as the bear is moved, so you should make them as stiff as possible to start with.

First of all, you need to gather up the neck opening on both the head and body with a running stitch (see Fig 4.12), using double thread for

Fig 4.13 The head being attached to the body with a joint.

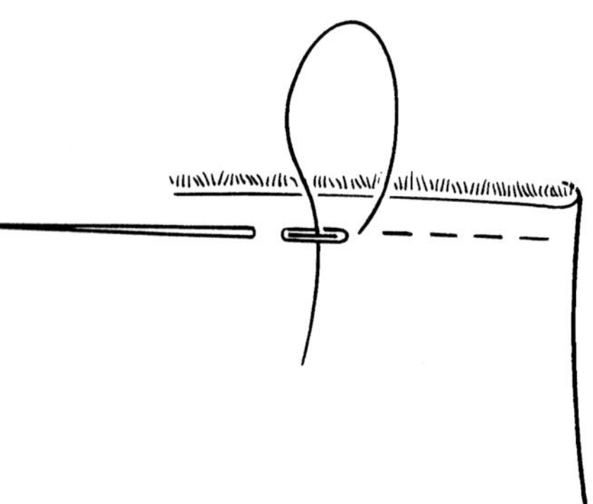

Fig 4.12 Running stitch.

strength. Fasten off the thread securely, leaving a small hole just big enough for the shank of the joint to fit through. Insert the shank from the head downwards into the body and fasten together below the neck as firmly as you can (see Figs 4.13 and 4.14). Once properly attached, any raw ends will completely disappear from view.

Now make small holes (as for the eyes) on the legs, arms and body ready for the positioning of the limbs. The exact position of the holes is clearly marked on each

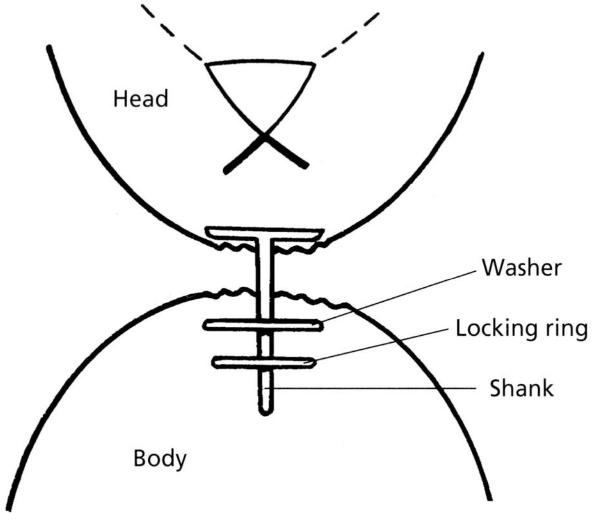

Fig 4.14 The position of the joint in head and body.

pattern. Insert the joints with the shank facing into the body and check that the positions of both arms and legs are to your satisfaction before securing in place as firmly as possible (see Fig 4.15).

Stuffing

Now that the bear is assembled you must insert the stuffing. This should be done a little at a time for best results. I find it useful to use the handle of a short wooden spoon to push the stuffing in really hard. The bear should be solid and the general rule is that if it is at all possible to push in a little more stuffing then you should do so. A poorly stuffed bear will lose its shape over time. The table below will give you an idea of the amount of stuffing you are likely to need.

Approximate amounts of polyester stuffing

SIZE OF BEAR	WEIGHT OF STUFFING
50cm (20in)	740g (26oz)
40cm (16in)	530g (19oz)
20cm (8in)	80g (3oz)

TIP

Never be tempted to use the points of scissors for stuffing as they invariably slip and go right through the fabric. Although you can sew up the hole without any real harm, it is best to avoid the problem.

First stuff the head, taking particular care to make the snout very firm indeed. If the snout changes shape due to poor stuffing, the face soon loses its character entirely. Wood wool can be used for the snout as it is more solid and holds its shape better than other stuffings (see Chapter 2).

Fig 4.15 *Fixing the legs on to the body.*

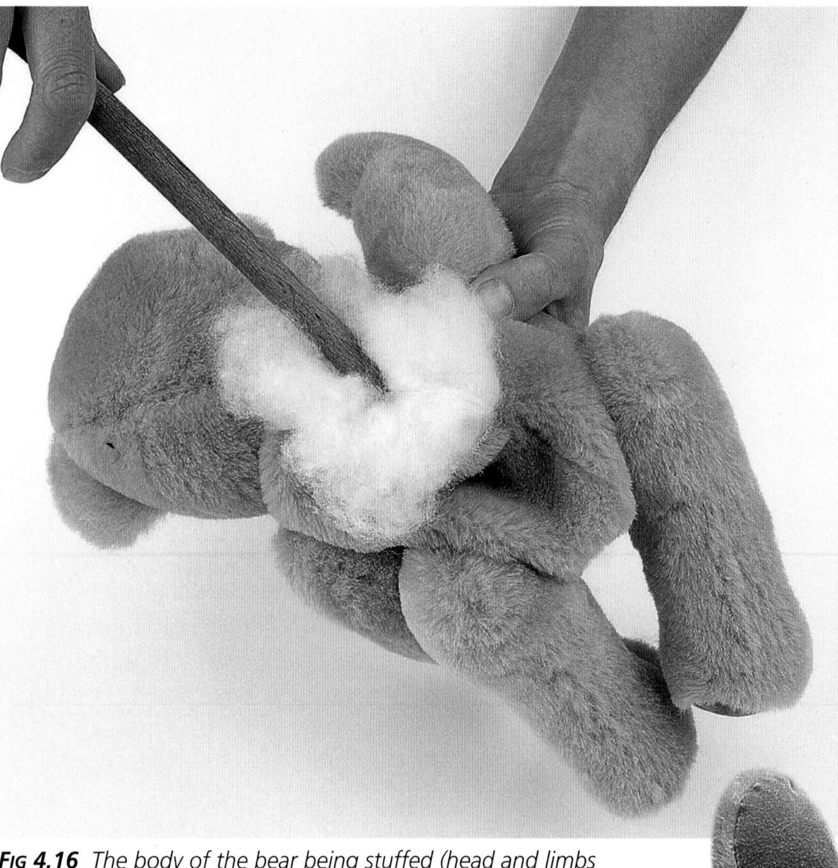

Fig 4.16 *The body of the bear being stuffed (head and limbs already stuffed).*

The legs and arms should be stuffed next, and it is important to make sure that the paws are extra firm. The body should be stuffed last of all (see Fig 4.16).

Sew up all openings (immediately after stuffing each piece) with ladder stitch (see Fig 4.17), using double thread to ensure that it does not break when pulling the stitches tightly over the stuffing. The seam can be hidden by using a wire or teasel brush to release any of the pile that may be trapped inside the seam or under the stitching.

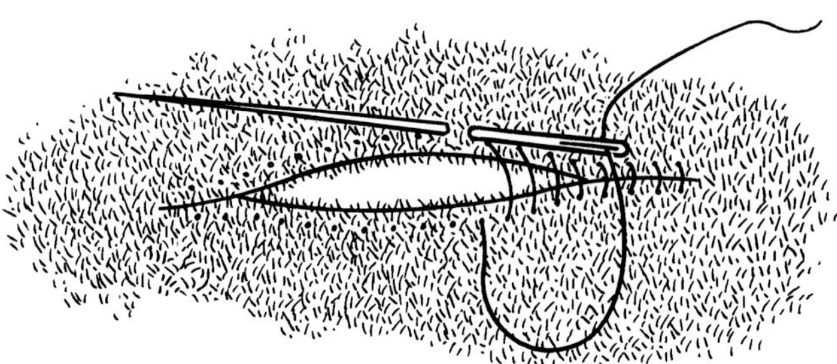

Fig 4.17 *Ladder stitch.*

Finishing Off

Assembled, stuffed and sewn up, the bear is still not quite finished. You now have to manipulate the body into its final shape, which might involve squashing down the head or flattening the sides of the face. It is possible to dramatically change the bear's character in this way. Once done it stays and you will not have to do it again. Do not worry if you are a little rough: as long as your seams are strong enough, the bear will not be harmed (see Fig 4.18).

Fig 4.18 *The completed bear.*

5 Giving a Bear Character

Technically all my bears are made in the same way, as described in the previous chapter: they all have two arms, two legs and a head. So why are they all different? How is it they are such individuals? What is it that gives them their character? In this chapter I want to share with you some of what I have learned about making a character bear. I am sure you will have ideas of your own once you have tried out a few of the bears in this book, just as I quickly started to experiment with the different possibilities once I realized what could be done.

Specific details on how to achieve different effects are given below, but generally speaking a very cuddly bear will need long staple mohair, a large stomach, a rounded snout, ears towards the side of the head, big (but not staring) soft, brown eyes and a wide, V-shaped mouth. At the other extreme, the more severe bear will need short staple fabric, a slim-line stomach, long limbs, a long snout, ears towards the top of the head, small eyes (taking care that they do not look 'piggy') and a narrow mouth. There are many alternatives to explore between these two distinct types.

Choice of Fabric

Deciding whether to use man-made fur fabric or mohair often depends upon how much money you can afford to spend, but it does also have an effect on the character of the finished bear. Mohair is luxurious, softer and generally more pleasing to touch, so if you wish to cuddle your bears this is something to consider. To my mind a short staple on an average-sized bear makes him less 'approachable', but it also gives a smart, no-nonsense quality, which is why the Policeman and City bears have short fur (see pages 87 and 93).

In contrast, the Bride and Groom are made from luxurious long staple mohair (see pages 37 and 39). They feel very warm and soft to the touch, and the mohair gives them both an air of quality. The Bride is made in dark mohair to contrast with the white wedding veil. The Bridegroom, who I must confess is one of my favourites, is truly distinctive. He has a look of nobility and is surely a bear of considerable consequence.

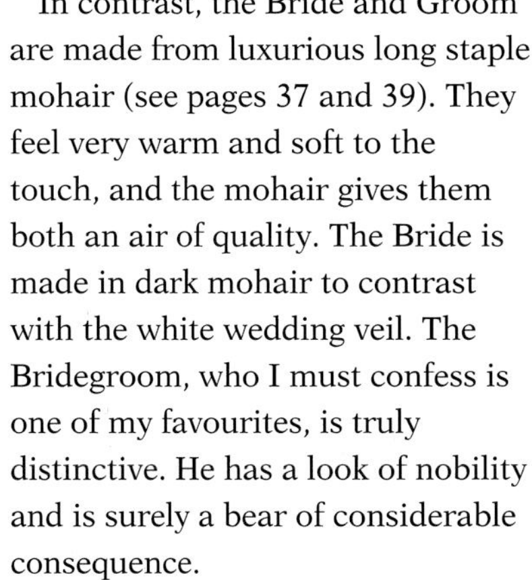

Fig 5.1 *The Fisherman and his son are made from the same fabric, but both give very different impressions due to their size.*

If you want to age your bear, then crushed mohair is ideal. The Teacher (see page 79) is the same age as all the others but has the look of an older bear. The Real Ale bear is also made from crushed fabric, but this time it is man-made. The fabric does make him look older, but being man-made it also seems to make him look slightly less well kept, as if the beer has got to him (see page 47).

The Doctor is made from uncut, loom state mohair – fabric straight from the loom, with no chemicals, dyes or finishes, just a latex coating on the back to make it strong enough to use. The pile is still looped, and this gives the Doctor an individual look all of his own (see page 84). The Chef has that look of a lovable rogue because his man-made fibre is slightly shaggy (see page 90).

The same fabric on a different size of bear can imply a completely different character. The Fisherman and his son are both made from man-made fibre with a medium length staple (see Fig 5.1). On the Fisherman it looks very traditional, whilst on his smaller son it looks unkempt, which suits a young and boisterous bear cub. The National bear and the Musician are both made from the same medium length, man-made fibre. Look at them and decide for yourself the difference the size of bear makes (see pages 96–7 and 58).

While differently sized bears in the same fabric can create certain effects, it is also the case that the same bear made from different fabrics can completely alter the appearance. The Christmas bears are a good example of this (see later in this chapter and pages 34–5).

Fig 5.2 *The lengths of the legs on the Ballet and Gardener bears are appropriate to their characters.*

Size and Proportion

We have already looked at the length of staple compared to the size of bear. Size is also important in order to suggest a particular character. Tiny bears are very appealing. Look at the Christmas bears: who could resist their charm? Each one is properly proportioned, with limbs and head an appropriate size. Tommy's baby bear (see page 27) is also small, but her head is proportionally larger which makes her look very young.

The Policeman and Ballet bears are long limbed (see pages 87 and 49), making them less cuddly, but these proportions give a more mature, serious look. If the Ballet bear were short and fat she would become comical. With a different character, such as the Gardener (see page 51), short limbs give an elderly appearance and fit in with the general effect (see Fig 5.2).

The size of the stomach also gives clues to a character. The Policeman watches his weight, whereas the City bear suffers from too many executive lunches. Real Ale bear's stomach is so large it is easier to stay sitting down. A good rule to remember is this: the larger the stomach, the more cuddly the bear.

Faces and Expressions

The position of the facial features is the main factor which determines the expression and thus the personality of a bear.

Ears

The Doctor has ears high up on the head and eyes fairly low down. This gives a rather wide-eyed and innocent look. (I think I was influenced by all those 'Doctor in Charge' books I read in my youth.) I see him as a young doctor, rather out of his depth but doing his best. The Chef's ears are very far forward, which reduces the size of his forehead and makes him look slightly quizzical. It has the added bonus of giving enough room behind the ears for the hat. The alert position of City bear's ears in contrast (see Fig 5.3) make him look far more busy and intelligent. The Policeman's ears are a bit too big which, together with the long, pointed snout and head tilted forward, gives him a look of authority. The Real Ale bear's ears are quite low down, and while this makes him look younger, his fabric tends to age him, so I think he looks like a young bear who has been loved and cuddled by several generations and is no longer in the best condition.

Eyes

The Fisherman's son has eyelids made of felt, which gives the impression that he is dozing off while his father fishes. Large eyes also tend to convey youth, whereas eyes that are too small may look 'piggy'. Solid black eyes can seem to stare (as can eyes that are too big). I usually use eyes with proportionally large black pupils outlined by colour. I prefer the colour to be dark brown, hazel or sometimes

Fig 5.3 *A close look at the heads of the City bear and the Chef shows what a difference the placing of the ears can make.*

orange. I never use blue eyes because, however attractive they may look on dolls, I feel they do not work on bears. Soft brown eyes are most consistently successful.

Tommy's baby has eyes which are shut. No plastic eyes are used here, just thread. With her head to one side and the position of her paws on her ear and in her mouth, she looks as if she is asleep.

Mouth

The mouth can also say much about your bear. If you refer back to Fig 4.10 on page 15, you will see four differently shaped mouths. A wide, V-shaped mouth gives an amiable expression, and, generally speaking, the narrower the mouth the more severe the character. The National bear and the Gardener show this clearly (see pages 96–7 and 51). A Y-shaped mouth is more traditional, but once again the wider the mouth is, the more agreeable will be the expression you achieve.

Head and snout

The tilt of the head is vital. The Policeman's head is angled downwards, as if he is talking to a young bear. The Real Ale bear's head droops on his large tummy (indicating how much he has drunk, perhaps), whereas the Fisherman's head is erect and alert.

The Gardener has a pensive look as he ponders the wonders of nature. He also looks comfortable with life and this is only partly achieved by the set of the head. Soft brown eyes and a mouth turned up at the edges give a contented expression. While the snout is trimmed on top, it is left long underneath to produce the effect of a beard, yet another characteristic that makes him look a little older.

If a younger look is desired then a good, general rule is not to trim the snout at all, although if the staple is very long you may need to trim a little. The Teacher's snout is not trimmed, which would generally make him look younger, but the crushed mohair and fusty accessories age him. In this case I left the snout fur long so as to soften his character and prevent too stern an expression (see Fig 5.4).

A Range of Characters

The Christmas bears are excellent examples of all I have said in this chapter. There are ten of them, all made from the same pattern but all very different. Six of them are made from the same short staple mohair. As you will see from Fig 5.5, placing the head on one side and looking slightly down gives a most appealing, innocent expression.

Fig 5.4 *Much depends on the angle of the head and the way the snout is trimmed. Such small touches can create big effects, as with the Teacher, the Bridegroom and the Gardener shown here.*

Fig 5.5 *The Christmas bears show off a whole range of possible characteristics. Here are six of them, all very distinct, all made from short staple mohair.*

The slightly raised head and smiling mouth of one of the other bears gives a playful look. One of the seated bears looks older because her eyes are smaller. The standing bear in the green and white scarf has a more pronounced nose and larger eyes, which give him (or maybe her) a comical appearance.

Turning to the bear with the multicoloured, striped jacket (see Fig 5.6), we see large eyes, nose and mouth which have a 'cartoon' look. This is a bear who is always getting into mischief! The one in the stripy jumper is made of the same fabric, but has smaller, more regular features and consequently has a far more traditional look. These two bears are made from short staple, man-made fabric.

The remaining two bears are made from medium staple fabric, the standing one being of a man-made fibre. The one holding the other end of the scarf is something of a ragamuffin. He is made from mohair, but because the staple does not sit well on such small limbs he looks unkempt and probably badly behaved. With the smallest of bears it is often necessary to make the bear in a specific fabric before being able to discover exactly what the character will be. I had no idea that the bear on the left would end up so scruffy.

As you can see, no single feature determines the character. Each bear is a mass of characteristics which together reveal a particular disposition. You may disagree with some of my observations and prefer to decide on your own, trying out the different possibilities for yourself. If you have never made a bear before, it is wise not to begin with the Christmas bears as they are quite fiddly. Once you have established your skills with some larger bears, however, you might find it useful to make a range of such small bears and experiment with different features in order to discover a whole range of individual expressions.

FIG 5.6 *The other four Christmas bears.*

Part Two
The Bears

6 Occasional Bears

Tommy

Bride and Bridesmaids

Bridegroom and Pageboys

Christmas bears

Tommy

A Bear for All Seasons

TOMMY

A BEAR FOR ALL SEASONS

Tommy stands 41cm (16in) tall. He was made for my husband. He had never owned a bear of his own, and now in his middle years I felt he deserved one. I made Tommy for his birthday and my husband was delighted. With so many bears in the house it was good to have one of his own. At Christmas Tommy joined in the celebrations by holding a Christmas stocking and on each wedding anniversary I took to making something for Tommy to hold, proclaiming how many years we had spent together.

It soon became a tradition for me to make something for Tommy so he could share in all our family celebrations. When our eldest son started driving lessons, Tommy also carried 'L' plates. When our son passed his 'A' levels, Tommy received a certificate too. Tommy now has so many accessories that to have included them all would have been a book in itself, so I have included just a few to get you started.

MATERIALS

BEAR

- Long staple mohair 70 x 70cm (27½ x 27½in)
- Suedette 17 x 13cm (6¾ x 5⅛in)
- 1 pair of deep brown plastic safety eyes 1.2cm (½in) in diameter
- Strong sewing thread to match fabric
- Black wool (for the nose and mouth)
- 5 joints 4.5cm (1¾in) in diameter
- Polyester stuffing 550g (20oz) approx.
- Velcro (soft side) 8cm (3⅛in) – match to the colour of Tommy's paw if possible

ACCESSORIES

CHRISTMAS STOCKING

- Green and red double knitting wool – just scraps are needed, less than 25g (1oz) of each
- Set of 4 double-ended needles size 3¼mm (No 10)
- Velcro (hooked side) 1cm (⅜in)

CERTIFICATE

- Good quality cream paper 15 x 20cm (6 x 8in)
- Narrow red ribbon 15cm (6in)
- PVA glue
- Small piece of salt dough (or genuine wax seal)
- Velcro (hooked side) 1cm (⅜in)

'L' PLATES

- Card 15 x 7.5cm (6 x 3in)
- White felt 15 x 15cm (6 x 6in)
- Red felt 10 x 5cm (4 x 2in)
- White wool 50cm (20in)
- Matching red and white cotton thread

ANNIVERSARY CUSHION

- Squared graph paper
- White or cream Aida embroidery fabric (14 squares to 1in) 10 x 10cm (4 x 4in) – this will give you extra at the edges
- Lining material suitable for backing the cushion 8 x 8cm (3⅛ x 3⅛in)
- White or cream lace 2cm (¾in) wide, 60cm (23⅝in) long
- Embroidery cottons – pink, yellow, orange, green and 2 shades of blue
- Handful of polyester stuffing
- White or cream sewing cotton
- Velcro (hooked side) 1cm (⅜in)

PARTY WAISTCOAT

- Printed cotton material 50 x 40cm (20 x 16in)
- Matching cotton thread
- Embroidery cotton (optional)

GET WELL SOON BANDAGE

- White cotton material 75 x 7cm (30 x 2¾in)

WELCOME TO YOUR NEW HOUSE

- Made-up wallpaper paste 15g (½oz)
- Plain white flour 125g (4oz)
- Table salt 125g (4oz)
- Water 60ml (2 fl oz)
- Ribbon 60cm (24in)
- PVA glue
- White cotton material 5 x 5cm (2 x 2in) (optional)
- Ribbon 2cm (¾in) wide, 50cm (19¾in) long
- Range of acrylic or poster paints
- Spray-on clear acrylic lacquer (available from car accessory stockists)
- Variety of shaped cake icing cutters
- Garlic press

NEW BABY

- Short staple mohair 30 x 30cm (12 x 12in)
- Suedette or strong felt 7 x 7cm (2¾ x 2¾in)
- Black wool (for eyes, mouth and nose)
- Strong sewing thread
- 1 joint for the head 3.4cm (1⅜in) in diameter
- 4 pairs of eyes for the arm and leg joints 1.4cm (⅝in) in diameter
- Printed cotton material 15 x 15cm (6 x 6in)
- White lace 1cm (⅜in) wide, 60cm (24in) long

Making the Bear

TIP

Until you are familiar with the techniques of bear making you will need to refer regularly to the general instructions given in Chapter 4.

1 Using the patterns from the back of the book (see pages 104–7), cut out all the pieces. Remember to mark on all the relevant points such as ear slits and joint holes.

2 Take the two head pieces and the head gusset. Cut the ear slits on the head gusset from point A to K, and on the head from point A to B.

3 On both head pieces pin together the dart marked E to D (right sides facing). Backstitch the dart, taking care that all the pile is on the right side.

4 With the right sides together pin the head pieces on to either side of the head gusset, from C to A, and stitch in place.

5 Take the four ear pieces and pin them right sides together for both ears. Sew around the long curved edge from H to H and turn right sides out.

6 Insert the ears into the slot marked B to K and pin. Overstitch the ears very securely in place.

7 Now pin and stitch one side of the head only with right sides together from point A to G (leaving the other side open for stuffing). Then pin and sew from C to F and turn the head right sides out.

8 Sew the nose and mouth with the black thread. As you will see from the photograph, Tommy's mouth is wide and smiling upwards.

9 The eyes should be added next, positioned approximately 5cm (2in) from the tip of the nose.

10 Pin two of the leg pieces together and sew from point L to M and from J round the top of the leg and down to K. The section J to L will be left open for stuffing. Repeat this for the second leg. Do not turn right sides out.

11 Take the sole of one foot cut from suedette. With the right sides facing inwards, pin on to the bottom of the leg, matching points K to K and M to M. Stitch and turn right sides out, repeating for the second leg.

12 Now take the arm pieces. Snip the fabric as shown at P. Cut out the paw pads from suedette and sew a 2cm (¾in) patch of Velcro (the soft side) on to one of them. You will need to decide whether you want Tommy to be right-pawed or left-pawed. Pin a paw pad on to each arm piece, matching P to P and Q to Q. Sew from P to Q.

13 Fold each arm piece over right sides together and sew from S to P and from R to N. Turn right sides out. The section R to S is left open to allow stuffing.

14 Pin together the two side body pieces, right sides together, and sew from T to V and from U to W, leaving the section V to U open for stuffing. Take the front body and match Z to Z and W to W, right sides together. Pin and sew, then turn right sides out

TIP

Take special care when trimming the snout. Tommy's snout is only slightly trimmed, as far up as the eyes and around the nose.

15 Assemble the bear as explained in the general instructions (see pages 16–18).

ACCESSORIES

Christmas stocking

1 Using four double-ended needles size 3¼mm (No 10) and the green double knitting wool, cast on 29 stitches, making sure that there are 13 stitches on the first needle and 8 each on two others.

2 Work 10 rows in rib (knit 1, purl 1) around the needles. The rest of the stocking is made in stocking stitch (1 row knit, 1 row purl) as follows.

3 Change to the red wool and work 2 rows. Then change to the green wool and work 4 rows.

4 Repeat step 3 three times. Continue with the green wool for the rest of the stocking, working 8 rows on the needle with 13 stitches. This forms the heel. Break the wool.

5 Now return to the other 16 stitches. Rejoin the wool and work 4 rows on these stitches, picking up a new stitch along the edges of the heel at the end of each row. There should be 20 stitches on these needles.

6 Working on all three needles (33 stitches) work 4 rows, knitting together 2 stitches at both edges of the heel. Each time the edge stitch of the heel should be one of the two stitches knitted together (25 stitches). Continue on these stitches for 8 rows.

7 Then knit 2 together 12 times, knit the final stitch (13 stitches). Finally knit 1 row.

8 Thread the wool through the 13 stitches and pull up tightly on the wrong side of the sock. Fasten off with 3 neat stitches. Turn the stocking right sides out and thread the loose strand of wool at the rib edge through on to the wrong side to hide it. Sew a small piece of Velcro (hooked side) at the top of the stocking.

TIP

If you do not wish to knit a stocking, why not buy a red or green baby's sock instead?

Certificate

1 Take the paper and carefully roll it up along the long side. Wrap the red ribbon around it and glue in place (you may need to hold it temporarily with an elastic band). Cut a 'V' shape into the end of the ribbon.

2 Make a small ball of salt dough (see instructions for 'Welcome to your new house' below) and flatten to form a seal. Dry it out for 48 hours in the airing cupboard until the seal is brick hard. Paint it deep red and varnish, leave to dry and then stick on to the red ribbon. If you have real sealing wax and a seal, use that instead.

3 Glue a small square of Velcro (hooked side) on the back of the rolled certificate.

'L' plates

1 Cut the card into two pieces measuring 7.5 x 7.5cm (3 x 3in). The card must be slightly smaller than the white felt and may need a little trimming.

2 Cut four pieces of white felt slightly bigger than the pieces of card.

3 Using the pattern on page 107 cut out two 'L'-shaped pieces in the

red felt. Pin these on to the centre of two of the white squares of felt. Sew them on using blanket stitch (see Fig 6.1) and the red cotton thread.

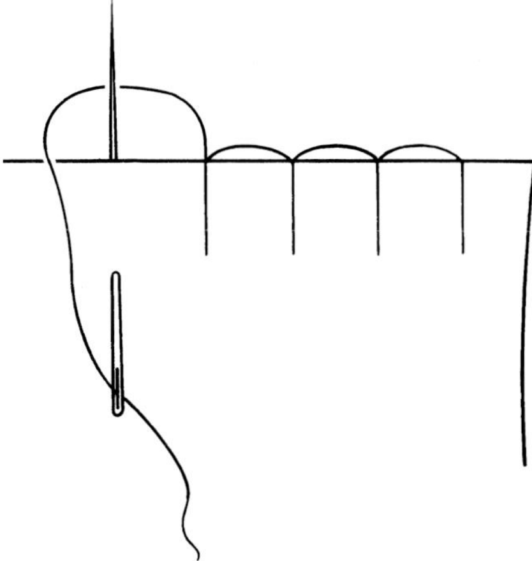

FIG 6.1 Blanket stitch.

4 On either side of one piece of card put a plain white felt square and a square with the red 'L' on it. Oversew these together using the white cotton thread. Do the same with the other 'L' plate.

5 Sew the 'L' plates together with the white wool, leaving a 15cm (6in) length of wool between them so that they can be hung over Tommy's arm.

Anniversary cushion

1 First you need to chart your own design on the squared paper. The pattern of bells and flowers shown on page 108 can be the basic design, but you will need to overlay the number and names relevant to you. Patterns for appropriately sized numbers and letters are also included on page 108. You may have to adapt my patterns a little if your names are longer or shorter than mine. Colour in each square of the chart to match your planned colour scheme, or if using only a pencil give a different symbol for each colour of embroidery cotton.

2 When your design is complete, embroider it in cross stitch and backstitch on the Aida fabric. Before starting to sew, fold the fabric into four so that you can find the centre of the fabric. Match this with the centre of the pattern and begin your embroidery in the middle. This way you will not run off the end of your fabric.

3 When the embroidery is completed, gather the lace and pin it on to the edge of the cushion so that the raw edge of the lace lies alongside the raw edge of the Aida fabric and the neat edge of the lace faces into the middle of the cushion (remember that the Aida fabric is larger than you will need and larger than the backing material). Tack into position (see Fig 6.2). Lay the

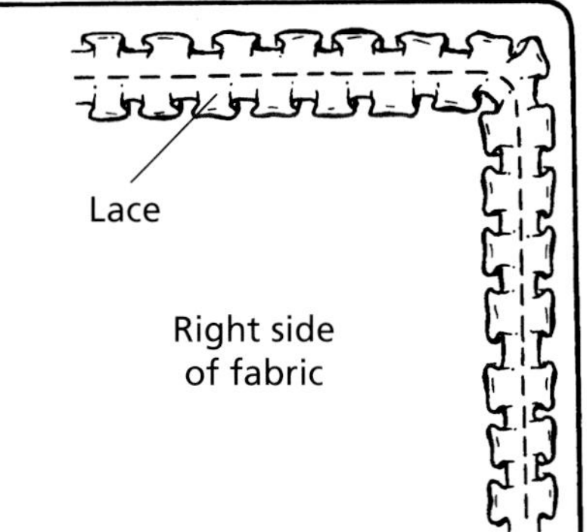

FIG 6.2 The position of the lace on the anniversary cushion.

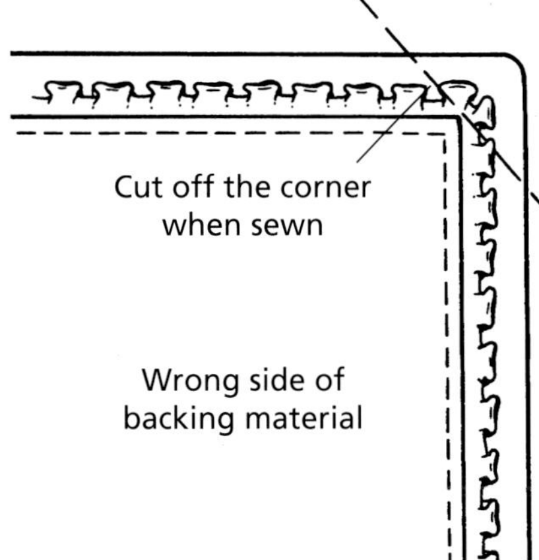

FIG 6.3 Sew the cushion together (leaving one side open for stuffing) and cut off the corners for a neater finish.

backing material on top and sew through all three thicknesses around three sides of the cushion and through just the lace and the Aida on the fourth side, to leave a gap for stuffing. Snip off the corners (see Fig 6.3).

4 Turn the cushion right sides out and stuff lightly. Sew up the gap with ladder stitch.

5 Lastly sew 1cm (3/8in) of Velcro (hooked side) on to the back of the cushion.

Party waistcoat

TIP

Try the waistcoat on Tommy regularly while you are making it.

1 The pattern for the waistcoat is on page 109. Fold the printed cotton in half and pin the pattern on to the material, taking care to place the back of the waistcoat on the fold of the material. Cut out the front and back. Repeat. Do not try to fold the material into four layers and cut out all the pieces at one time as the material 'walks' and you will not get a true pattern. You should end up with two back pieces and four front pieces (two in reverse). One of the back pieces and two of the front pieces will form the lining.

2 Mark the darts on all the pieces. Pin and sew with backstitch on the wrong side from J to K on the front pieces. Do the same on the back pieces from M to N and P to R. Press the side darts downwards and the back dart to one side.

3 If you wish to embroider or decorate the front of the waistcoat, do so now.

4 With right sides together, pin together the shoulders of the front and back from A to B on the waistcoat and then on the lining. Use backstitch or a sewing machine to fasten them together. Press.

5 With right sides together, now put the lining on to the waistcoat and stitch with a sewing machine or backstitch from the front side seam C, through D then on to E, A and P. Continue along the back of the neck and through the shoulder at A, through E, D and across to C.

6 Trim the seam close to the stitching, turn right sides out and press.

7 Fold the rough edges in on to the wrong side of the material around both armholes. Pin and slip stitch together (see Fig 6.4). Do the same along the back hem from C to C.

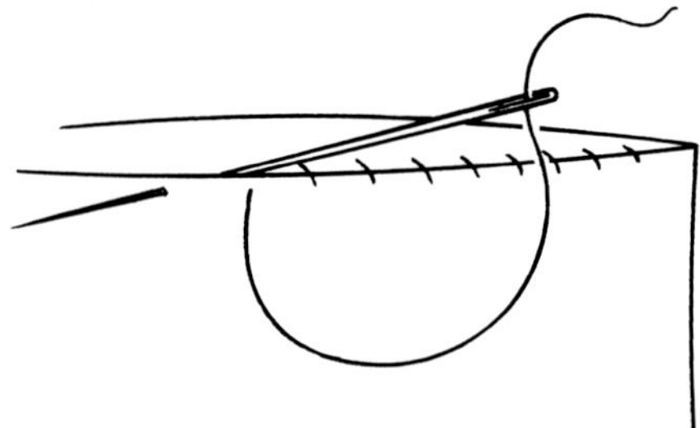

Fig 6.4 Slip stitch.

8 Stitch the front to the back under the arm from H to C on the wrong side with backstitch. Press.

Get well soon bandage

1 Fold the rough edges of the material inside along the long edge of the bandage and iron flat.

2 Put the bandage under Tommy's arm as a sling and tie in a reef knot behind his head, or you could bandage the relevant limb.

Welcome to your new house

> **TIP**
>
> To stick the pieces of dough together always use water brushed on with a pastry brush. 'Build' your house on baking parchment placed on a baking sheet so that it does not stick when baking.

1 First make the dough by mixing together the wallpaper paste, flour, salt and water. Knead for six minutes.

2 Roll out the dough to approximately 6mm (¼in) thick. Trace the house template from page 109, place it on the dough and cut round with an ordinary dinner knife. Cut out the windows.

3 Roll out a sausage shape approximately 1.5cm (⅝in) thick from the spare dough and attach to the bottom of the house.

4 Roll out a very thin sausage and stick this above the upstairs windows to give the line for the roof. For decoration indent with the end of a ball point pen along the line of the roof. The roof tiles are cut using 1cm (⅜in) rose petal icing cutters. You will need approximately 30 tiles and these are stuck to the roof beginning at the bottom and working up. Arrange the points of the 'petals' upwards.

5 Use another thin sausage of dough to make the window sills.

6 For the steps leading to the door you will need three more sausages of dough (decreasing in size). The bottom step should be 3cm (1⅛in) wide and the top one 2cm (¾in) wide. All three steps together measure 2.5cm (1in) high. The front door is 2.5cm (1in) tall and 2cm (¾in) wide. With a knife mark planks from top to bottom. A tiny ball of dough is stuck on for the handle.

7 Fix a triangle of dough over the door and cover with seven tiles as for the roof.

8 The balustrades are made from 6mm (¼in) thick dough, 5cm (2in) long and 2cm (¾in) wide, narrowing to 1.5cm (⅝in). Fix this on either side of the steps, curling the wide end back on itself at the bottom. Two balls of dough are stuck on the balustrades as flower pots.

9 Squeeze a ball of dough the size of a table tennis ball through a garlic press. Cut off neatly with the knife and stick the strands on either side of the balustrade to make the plants. A variety of cake icing cutters can be used to make the pink blossom, the creeper up the side of the house and the flowers in the flower pots.

10 When completed, put the house and baking sheet into the oven at the lowest heat possible. It will need to bake for between four and six hours. Test the house carefully every hour with your finger. When it is brick hard, turn the house over to ensure that the back is cooked as well as the front to prevent mould. When the dough is cooked, store it in the airing cupboard until you are ready to paint it as this will ensure that it stays very dry.

11 Use acrylic paints or poster paints to decorate the house according to personal taste, or you could copy the colours on my house. The roof is painted with a mixture of brown, yellow and red, with each tile painted individually

in a slightly different combination of colours. You can always add a little green to represent moss.

12 After the paint has dried, spray with two or three coats of the clear lacquer. Make sure that each coat is dried between applications.

13 Finally glue the ends of the ribbon on to the back and then glue the white cotton fabric over the end of the ribbon. This gives a neat edge and will ensure that the ribbon is secure. Place over Tommy's head. (This stage is optional.)

> **TIP**
>
> You cannot keep your finished house in damp conditions or it will revert to dough. A centrally heated house is fine, but I once wintered a salt dough house in an unheated conservatory and you can guess the rest! The completed house can be restored if only slightly damaged by leaving it in the airing cupboard for several days.

New baby

> **TIP**
>
> Until you are familiar with the techniques of bear making you will need to refer regularly to the general instructions given in Chapter 4.

1 Using the pattern from page 110, cut out all the pieces.

2 Take the two head pieces and the head gusset. Cut the ear slits marked on the head gusset from B to C and on the head from A to B. Then with right sides together pin and stitch the head pieces on either side of the head gusset from D to B.

3 Take the four ear pieces and pin right sides together for both ears. Sew around the long curved edge from V to V and turn right sides out.

4 Insert the ears into slot C to A and pin. Oversew securely into place.

5 With right sides together, pin and stitch one side of the head only from B to E (leaving the other side open for stuffing). Then pin and sew from D to W. Turn the head right sides out.

6 Sew the nose and mouth in the shape shown in Fig 6.5. Do not trim the snout, keeping the soft look of the full pile.

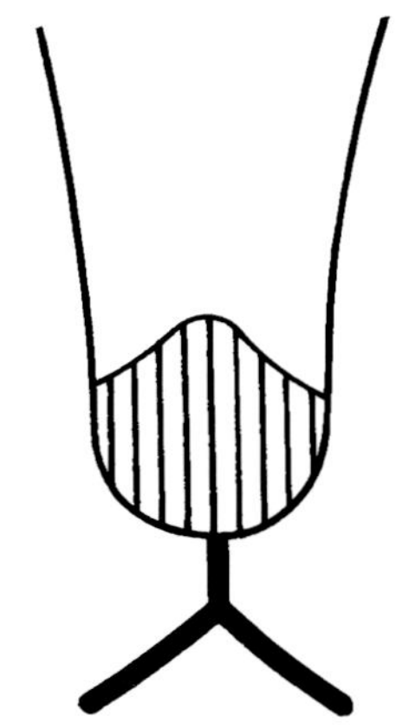

FIG 6.5 The shape of the baby bear's nose and mouth.

7 Sew the eyes in the place marked on the pattern with double wool and one straight stitch. Fasten firmly on the wrong side of the fabric.

8 Fold over one of the leg pieces with right sides together and sew from F to G. Leave H to Y open for stuffing. Repeat for the second leg. Do not turn right sides out yet.

9 Cut out the two soles for the paws in suedette (or felt). With right sides facing inwards pin each one on to the foot, matching Z to Z and G to G. Sew and turn right sides out.

10 Now take the arm pieces and snip the fabric as shown at L. Cut out the paw pads in suedette (or felt), match points L to L and M to M, then pin and sew from L to M.

11 Fold the arms over with right sides together and sew from O to N and M to L, leaving M to N open for stuffing. Turn right sides out.

12 Pin the two body pieces right sides together and sew from S to R and from Q round the bottom and up to P, leaving open R to Q for stuffing. Turn right sides out.

13 Assemble the baby bear as set out in the general instructions (see pages 16–18).

14 For the baby's blanket, take the cotton fabric and sew a 3mm (⅛in) hem all round it and then slip stitch the lace edging on to the hem.

15 With a small stitch just catch the baby's left paw at her mouth and the right paw at her ear. Pull the blanket through the gap between face and paw.

Christmas Bears

Most people have a star or an angel at the top of their Christmas tree. I have a teddy bear! In fact I decorate the whole tree with teddy bears as well as the more traditional tinsel and baubles.

The Christmas bears are just 13cm (5⅛in) tall and are made from a variety of fabrics. As well as making delightful seasonal decorations, they are quick to make and can be useful if you want to experiment with some different facial expressions. Be warned, however: they are rather fiddly to make and might be frustrating for the first-time bear maker, so wait until you have a little experience before embarking on these little charmers.

MATERIALS

BEAR

- Mohair or fur fabric (short to medium staple) 15 x 30cm (6 x 11¾in)
- Suedette 5 x 8cm (2 x 3⅛in)
- 1 pair of plastic safety eyes 6mm (¼in) in diameter
- Strong sewing thread
- Black wool (for nose and mouth)
- 5 plastic safety eyes (for the joints) 1.2cm (½in) in diameter
- Several handfuls of polyester stuffing

ACCESSORIES

- 1 pair of knitting needles size 3¼mm (No 10)
- Double knitting or 4-ply wool (odds and ends will do)

MAKING THE BEAR

TIP

Until you are familiar with the techniques of bear making you will need to refer regularly to the general instructions given in Chapter 4. The Christmas bear is very small and therefore more difficult to make. If you are a first-time bear maker, it will be best to try out your skills on a larger bear before tackling this more fiddly project.

1. Using the pattern from page 111, cut out all the pieces.

2. Take the two head pieces and the head gusset, and cut the ear slits on the head gusset from A to B and on the head from A to C.

3. With right sides together, pin and then stitch the head pieces on either side of the head gusset from D to A.

4. Now take the two ear pieces and pin right sides together. Sew around the long curved edge from G to G and turn right sides out. Repeat for the second ear. Insert the ears into slot C to B. Overstitch the ears in place very securely.

5. Pin and stitch from A to F on one side of the head only (leaving the other side open for stuffing). Then sew from D to E and turn the head right sides out.

6. Sew the nose and mouth with the black thread in your chosen style, depending on the expression you wish to achieve (see pages 14–15).

7. Add the eyes next, positioned approximately 1.3cm (½in) from the tip of the nose.

8. Fold over one leg piece with right sides together. Pin and sew from H to I and J to K, leaving I to J open for stuffing. Repeat for the second leg. Do not turn right sides out.

9 Take one paw sole cut from the suedette and with right sides facing inwards, pin it on to the sole of the foot, matching M to M and H to H. Sew securely all the way round, then turn the leg right sides out. Repeat for the second leg.

10 Take one inner arm and a paw pad and pin right sides together, matching P to P and Q to Q. Stitch in place, then open out the paw pad and pin the inner arm to the outer arm, right sides together and matching R to R and S to S. Sew from R right around the arm to S, leaving open the section R to S for stuffing. Turn right sides out and repeat for the other arm.

11 With the right sides of the body pieces facing, pin them together and then sew from T to U and from V round to W. Leave open U to V for stuffing.

12 Assemble the bear as described in the general instructions (see pages 16–18).

Accessories

Scarf

1 Cast on eight stitches then knit the scarf using garter stitch (plain knitting) throughout. The length is up to you; simply keep knitting until the scarf is long enough to wrap around the neck of the bear. You can make the scarf all one colour, or try knitting four rows of one colour followed by two rows of a contrasting colour.

2 Make a fringe by using 5cm (2in) lengths of wool. Fold each length in half and with a crochet hook push the loop through the edge of the knitting and put the raw ends through the loop (see Fig 6.6), pulling tightly. When the fringe is complete, trim to neaten the ends.

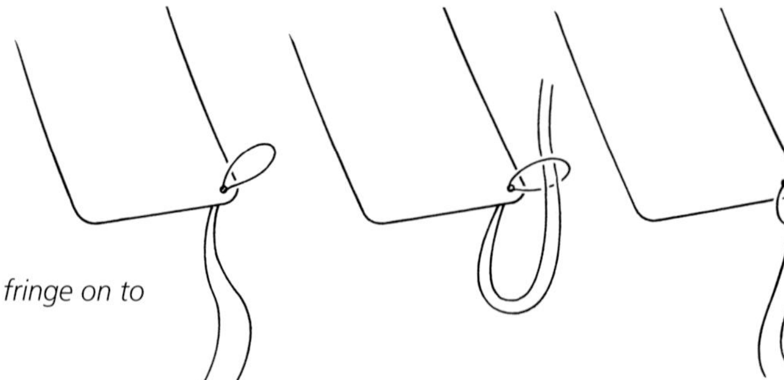

Fig 6.6 *Adding the fringe on to the knitted scarf.*

Jacket

1 Cast on 20 stitches and knit 10 rows. Garter stitch should be used for the whole jacket.

2 At the beginning of the next two rows cast on seven stitches then knit 14 rows.

3 Knit 13 stitches and turn. Knit 4 rows on these 13 stitches, decreasing one stitch at the neck edge on alternate rows.

4 Knit 4 rows, increasing one stitch at the neck edge on alternate rows.

5 Cast on 10 stitches across the front of the jacket and knit 14 rows.

6 Cast off 7 stitches at the arm edge, knit 10 rows and cast off. Rejoin the wool at the back of the neck and cast off 8 stitches.

7 Work the other side in the same way as the first, but in reverse.

8 Oversew under the arm and down the side seams on the wrong side, then turn right sides out.

9 Put the jacket on to the bear and sew up the front. Add small buttons or embroider buttons down the front.

Jumper

1 Cast on 20 stitches, then knit 3 rows of rib (knit 1, purl 1). Now knit stocking stitch (1 row knit, 1 row purl) for 14 rows.

2 Work 7 more stitches and turn. Work 4 rows on these 7 stitches, decreasing one stitch at the neck edge on alternate rows. Then work 4 rows, increasing one stitch at the neck edge on alternate rows.

3 Cast on 7 stitches across the back of the jumper, then knit 14 rows of stocking stitch and 3 rows of rib. Cast off.

4 Rejoin the wool at the back of the neck and cast off 6 stitches.

5 Work the other side in the same way as the first side, but in reverse.

6 Make the sleeves by casting on 14 stitches, working 3 rows of rib then 3 rows of stocking stitch. Cast off.

7 Sew the arms on to the jumper in the middle of the side seams, with right sides together.

8 Pick up 20 stitches around the neck with right sides facing. Work 2 rows in rib and cast off.

9 Oversew under the arms and down the side seams on the wrong side, and turn right sides out.

10 Put the jumper on the bear and sew together down the back using ladder stitch and the same colour of wool.

TIP

If you wish to make multi-coloured jumpers or jackets, use contrasting colours to make simple stripes.

THE BRIDE

Brides should be at their best on their wedding day and this bear (standing 38cm (15in) tall) had to be made from quality mohair. To make a striking contrast with the white wedding veil, I chose a long staple, dark mohair.

MATERIALS

BEAR

- Long staple mohair 60 x 68cm (24 x 27in)
- Suedette 20 x 16cm (8 x 6¼in)
- 1 pair of deep brown plastic safety eyes 1.2cm (½in) in diameter
- Strong sewing thread
- Black wool (for the nose and mouth)
- 5 joints 4.5cm (1¾in) in diameter
- Polyester stuffing 550g (20oz) approx.

ACCESSORIES

- White net or lace 2.5 x 0.5m (3 x ½yd)
- White sewing cotton
- Variety of small artificial flowers (white and pink) no more than 1cm (⅜in) across

Making the Bear

TIP

Until you are familiar with the techniques of bear making you will need to refer regularly to the general instructions given in Chapter 4.

1. Using the pattern from pages 112–14, cut out all the pieces.
2. Cut the ear slits on the head gusset from C to B, and on the head from C to A. With the right sides together, pin and stitch the head pieces on either side of the head gusset and stitch from D to C.
3. Take two ear pieces and pin right sides together. Sew around the long curved edge from G to G and turn the ear right sides out. Repeat for the second ear.
4. Insert each ear into slot A to B and pin. To shape the ear slightly, bend points G towards the centre front by 1cm (⅜in). Overstitch each ear in place very securely.
5. Now pin and stitch on one side of the head only from C to F (leaving the other side open for stuffing). Turn right sides out.
6. Sew the nose and mouth with black wool, then position the eyes approximately 4.5cm (1¾in) from the tip of the nose.
7. Fold over one leg piece and pin together. Sew from Q to P. The section M to N will be left open for stuffing. Repeat for the second leg. Do not turn the legs right sides out yet.
8. Take the sole of one paw cut from suedette and with the right sides facing inwards, pin and sew on to the bottom of one foot, matching R to R and Q to Q. Turn right sides out and repeat for the second leg.
9. Now take the arms and snip the fabric as shown on the pattern at H. Take the paw pads (cut from suedette) and match H to H and L to L. Pin and sew from H to L.
10. Fold each arm over with right sides together and sew from K to J and from I round the paw to H. Turn right sides out, leaving J to I open for stuffing.
11. Pin together the two body pieces, right sides together, and sew from V to W and from X round to Z, leaving W to X open for stuffing.
12. Assemble the bear as shown in the general instructions given on pages 16–18.

TIP

Trim the snouts of the Bride and Groom to match each other.

Accessories

Wedding veil

1. Using running stitch, gather up one of the long sides of the white net or lace so that it measures 15cm (6in). Oversew to secure the edge and round off the two remaining corners with sharp scissors.
2. Twist together a 20cm (8in) length of white flowers and oversew these to the gathered edge of the veil.
3. Attach the veil firmly behind the Bride's ears with small stitches (oversewing is best).

Bouquet

Tie together a bunch of the white and pink flowers and stitch these on to the Bride's paw. If you prefer you could use Velcro to attach the flowers, as with Tommy (see page 30).

Bridesmaids

The Bride's helpers are made from the same patterns as the Musician (see pages 137–8) and the Rugby player (see page 143). Their head-dresses and bouquets are simply smaller versions of the Bride's.

THE BRIDEGROOM

The Bridegroom (43cm (17in) tall) is one of my very favourite bears. All distinguished bears should be made of mohair and I chose a light colour to contrast with the Bride. For an extra touch of class I also thought he should wear a collar and cravat in the style of the early nineteenth century.

MATERIALS

BEAR

- Long staple mohair 60 x 68cm (24 x 27in)
- Suedette 20 x 16cm (8 x 6¼in)
- 1 pair of deep brown plastic safety eyes 1.2cm (½in) in diameter
- Strong sewing thread
- Black wool (for the nose and mouth)
- 5 joints 4.5cm (1¾in) in diameter
- Polyester stuffing 550g (20oz) approx.

ACCESSORIES

- White muslin 60 x 35cm (24 x 14in)
- Iron-on Vilene 26 x 7cm (10 x 2¾in)
- White sewing cotton

Making the Bear

TIP

Until you are familiar with the techniques of bear making you will need to refer regularly to the general instructions given in Chapter 4.

❶ Using the pattern from pages 115–17, cut out all the pieces.

❷ Cut the ear slits on the head gusset from A to C, and on the head from A to B.

❸ On both head pieces pin together the dart E to D (right sides facing), and backstitch, taking care that all the pile is on the right side.

❹ With the right sides together, pin and stitch the head on either side of the gusset from F to A.

❺ Take two ear pieces and pin with right sides together. Sew around the long curved edge from H to H and turn right sides out. Repeat for the second ear. Insert the ears into slot B to C. To give the ears shape, bend just the edges (H) towards the front middle of the ear, no more than 1cm (⅜in). Overstitch each ear in place very securely.

❻ Pin and stitch the head to the gusset on one side only from A to G (leaving the other side open for stuffing). Sew from F to I and turn the head right sides out.

❼ Sew the nose and mouth with the black wool and then position the eyes approximately 5cm (2in) from the tip of the nose.

❽ Pin two leg pieces together and sew from L to M and from J round the top of the leg and down to K. The section J to L will be left open for stuffing. Repeat for the second leg. Do not turn right sides out.

❾ Take the sole of one paw cut from suedette. With the right sides facing inwards, pin and sew on to the bottom of the leg, matching K to K and M to M. Turn right sides out and repeat for the other leg.

❿ Now take the inner arms and the paw pads (the paw pads should be suedette). Match P to P and Q to Q, pin and sew from P to Q.

⓫ Pin together the inner and outer arms (right sides facing) and sew from S through P, around the paw and on through Q, over the top of the arm and down to R. Leave the section R to S open for stuffing. Turn right sides out and repeat for the second arm.

⓬ Pin together the two body pieces (right sides together) and sew from T to V and from W to Z, leaving V to W open for stuffing. Turn right sides out.

⓭ Assemble the bear as described in the general instructions (see pages 16–18). Take care to ensure that the Groom's chin is slightly lifted, as shown in the photograph on page 39. The pattern was designed with this in mind and it should be achieved quite easily as long as the head is sewn together and joined to the body very carefully.

TIP

Take special care when trimming the snout. The Groom is an immaculate bear and the grading from very short fur on the snout to the longer fur on the rest of the head has to be perfect. Do not be alarmed by this! Take care to snip very small amounts of fur at any one time. Use the tips of the scissors and where the short fur should merge into the long fur just snip very gradually. Practise on a spare scrap of fabric if you are nervous. Take your time and keep inspecting the result.

ACCESSORIES

Collar

NOTE

The Groom's collar would normally have been attached to his shirt, but the bear has no shirt, so the collar stands on its own.

1 Using the pattern on page 118, cut out two collar pieces in white muslin. Place right sides together and sew from 1 through 2, 3, 4, 5, 6, 7, 8 and down to 9, using either handsewn backstitch or a sewing machine. Do not turn right sides out.

2 Cut out the interfacing in iron-on Vilene (pattern on page 118). Iron the interfacing on to the inside of the collar, matching the numbers. Take care not to have the stiffening overlapping the seams as this will give a bulky effect when the collar is turned out. Turn the collar right sides out and press.

3 Fit the collar on to the Bridegroom, turning the rough edge under so that it is hidden. Sew the collar together at the back of the bear's neck with several neat stitches on top of each other.

Cravat

1 The cravat is simply made from a rectangle of muslin 115cm (45in) long and 12cm (4¾in) wide. I actually had to make a seam halfway up the long edge as my material was not long enough.

TIP

Do not use machine stitching, as this would not be in keeping with the period.

Neatly hem the edges all around the rectangle, taking care to keep the turnings and the stitches very small.

2 Iron the cravat, then carefully pleat the fabric with your fingers lengthways along the middle of the cravat (do not iron the pleats as they should be left soft). Place the centre of the cravat at the front of the Groom's neck, cross it round the back, then bring forward again and tie in a soft bow. Gently pull the collar up as it should be stiff to give the Groom a slightly haughty look.

Page boys

The page boys are made in the same way as the Walking and Swimming bears (see pages 55–7 and 61–2). The bow ties are made from 15cm (6in) of 1.2cm (½in) wide navy blue ribbon, with a bow on one end and a popper used as a fastening.

7 Hobby Bears

Fisherman and son

Real Ale bear

Ballet bear

Walking bear

Musician

Gardener

Fisherman and Son

Fisherman and Son

The Fisherman (who stands 40cm (15¾in) tall) and his son (who stands 20cm (8in) tall) are both made from the same medium staple, man-made fur fabric. However, on the son it looks longer because he is so much smaller. The lids on his eyes droop as he feels himself falling asleep. However he just manages to keep an eye on the fly at the end of his father's rod.

MATERIALS FOR FISHERMAN

BEAR

- Medium staple, man-made fur fabric 60 x 68cm (24 x 27in)
- Suedette 20 x 15cm (8 x 6in)
- 1 pair of deep brown plastic safety eyes 1.2cm (½in) in diameter
- Strong sewing thread
- Black wool (for the nose and mouth)
- 5 joints 4.5cm (1¾in) in diameter
- Polyester stuffing 550g (20oz) approx.

ACCESSORIES

- Crochet hook size 2.5cm
- Darning needle
- Blue, grey, beige and white 3- or 4-ply wool (scraps of each will be enough)
- Dark brown 3- or 4-ply wool 50g (2oz)
- Miniature picnic basket (mine is 10 x 7cm (4 x 2¾in))
- Long, straight stick 66cm (26in) (cut from an appropriate bush, or use a geranium stick or portion of bamboo cane)
- Black thread 50cm (20in)
- Fishing weight, or heavy, dark bead, or fly

Making the Bear

TIP

Until you are familiar with the techniques of bear making you will need to refer regularly to the general instructions given in Chapter 4.

1. Using the pattern from pages 119–21, cut out all the pieces.

2. Cut the ear slits on the head gusset from A to K, and on the head from A to B.

3. With the right sides together, pin and stitch the head pieces on either side of the head gusset from C to A.

4. Take two ear pieces and pin right sides together. Sew around the long curved edge from H to H and turn right sides out. Repeat for the second ear. Insert the ears into slot B to K, turning the edges of each ear (H) towards the centre front by 1cm (⅜in). Pin and overstitch both ears in place very securely.

5. Pin and stitch on one side of the head only from A to G (leaving the other side open for stuffing). Sew from C to D and turn the head right sides out.

6. Sew the nose and mouth with the black wool, then position the eyes approximately 5cm (2in) from the tip of the nose.

7. Pin two leg pieces together (right sides together) and sew from

L to M and from J round the top of the leg and down to K. The section J to L will be left open for stuffing. Repeat for the second leg. Do not turn right sides out.

8 Take the sole of one paw cut from suedette. With the right sides facing inwards, pin on to the bottom of one leg, matching K to K and M to M. Stitch and turn right sides out, repeating for the second leg.

9 Pin the paw pads (in suedette) to the arms, matching P to P and Q to Q with right sides together. Sew from P to Q.

10 Fold each arm over with right sides together and pin and sew from S to R and from I right around the arm and paw to N. Leave R to I open for stuffing and turn right sides out.

11 Pin together the two body pieces with right sides together and sew from T to V and from U to W, leaving open V to U for stuffing. Turn right sides out.

12 Assemble the bear as described in the general instructions (see pages 16–18).

Accessories

Blanket

1 The blanket is made from small crocheted woollen squares. To begin, make a small loop in the wool and crochet the foundation circle by working seven trebles after the fourth chain from the hook. Work all the trebles into the original loop, then fasten the last treble to the row of four chain stitches with a loop to make the foundation circle.

2 Crochet the second row into the gaps of the first row, making sure that two trebles are worked in the corners. Complete the row by looping the last stitch into the first.

3 Change the wool colour and work two more rows, then complete the square with one row of the dark brown wool.

4 When 99 squares have been made, crochet them together with single stitch in the dark brown wool to make nine rows of eleven squares. All the 'ends' which are left dangling should be sewn into the blanket with a darning needle.

5 Work two rows of trebles around the whole blanket.

6 Make the final row by working a single stitch into the first gap to anchor the wool. Miss two gaps and make eight trebles into the same gap, miss two gaps and anchor the fan with a single stitch. Continue in this way right around the blanket. Fasten off by anchoring the fan, then break the wool and sew the end into the blanket.

Fishing rod

1 Take the straight stick and simply fasten the thread on to one end by tying a knot. A dab of glue may be used to secure it.

2 Tie the weight, bead or fly on to the bottom end of the fishing line. It is a good idea to cut off the hook on any fly you use, so that there is no risk of accidents.

MATERIALS FOR FISHERMAN'S SON

BEAR

- Medium staple, man-made fur fabric 30 x 30cm (11¾ x 11¾in)
- Suedette 5 x 8cm (2 x 3⅛in)
- 1 pair of deep brown plastic safety eyes 9mm (⅜in) in diameter
- Scrap of dark brown felt
- Strong sewing thread
- Black wool (for the nose and mouth)
- 1 joint 3.5cm (1⅜in) in diameter
- 2 pairs of eyes 1.2cm (½in) in diameter (for arm and leg joints)
- Polyester stuffing 75g (3oz)

Making the Bear

TIP

Until you are familiar with the techniques of bear making you will need to refer regularly to the general instructions given in Chapter 4.

1. Using the pattern from page 122, cut out all the pieces.

2. Cut the ear slits on the head gusset from A to C, and on the head from A to B. With the right sides together, pin and stitch the head pieces on either side of the head gusset from D to A.

3. Take two ear pieces and pin right sides together. Sew around the long curved edge from G to G and turn the ear right sides out. Repeat for the second ear. Insert the ears into slot B to C and pin. Overstitch each ear in place very securely.

4. Pin and stitch on one side of the head only from A to F (leaving the other side open for stuffing). Sew from D to E and turn the head right sides out.

5. Sew the nose and mouth with the black wool.

6. Position the eyes approximately 2cm (¾in) from the tip of the nose. Then sew the eyelid (cut from felt) over the top half of each eye with slip stitch. Look at the angle of the eyelids in the photograph on page 19 to help you get it right.

7. Fold over one leg piece with right sides together and pin and sew from N to Q. Also join P to P (the section O to P will be left open for stuffing). Repeat for the second leg. Do not turn right sides out.

8. Take the sole of one paw cut from suedette and, with the right sides facing inwards, pin on to the bottom of the leg, matching P to P and Q to Q. Stitch and turn right sides out, repeating for the second leg.

9. Take each arm piece and snip the fabric as shown on the pattern at I. Take the paw pads cut from suedette and pin them on the arms, taking care to match I to I and J to J. Sew from I to J with right sides together.

10. Fold the arms over with right sides together, matching L to L and M to M. Pin and sew from H to L and from M to I. Turn right sides out.

11. Pin together the two side body pieces with right sides together and sew from R to S and from T to W, leaving open S to T for stuffing. Pin the front body to the side pieces, matching U to U and W to W with right sides together. Sew from U to W on both sides of the front body. Turn right sides out.

12. Assemble the bear as described in the general instructions (see pages 16–18).

Real Ale Bear

Real Ale bear is better off sitting down because his stomach is so large, but he is actually 36cm (14in) tall when standing straight. A pewter tankard full of good beer is never far from his side.

MATERIALS

BEAR

- Crushed 'mohair effect' man-made fur fabric 66 x 68cm (26 x 27in)
- Suedette 20 x 12cm (8 x 4¾in)
- 1 pair of deep brown plastic safety eyes 1.2cm (½in) in diameter
- Strong sewing thread
- Black wool (for the nose and mouth)
- 5 joints 4.5cm (1¾in) in diameter
- Polyester stuffing 550g (20oz) approx.

ACCESSORIES

- Pewter beer tankard (mine is actually a spirits measure)

MAKING THE BEAR

TIP

Until you are familiar with the techniques of bear making you will need to refer regularly to the general instructions given in Chapter 4.

1. Using the pattern from pages 123–5, cut out all the pieces.

2. Cut the ear slits on the head gusset from B to C, and on the head from B to A. With the right sides together, pin and stitch the head pieces on either side of the head gusset from D to B.

3. Take two ear pieces and pin right sides together. Sew around the long curved edge from G to G and turn right sides out. Repeat for the second ear. Insert the ears into slot A to C and pin. To give the ears shape, bend just the edges of the ears (G) towards the centre front of the ear, but no more than 1cm (⅜in). Overstitch the ears in place very securely.

4. Pin and stitch with right sides together on one side of the head only from B to E (leaving the other side open for stuffing). Next sew from D to F, then turn the head right sides out.

5. Sew the nose and mouth with the black wool, flattening out the mouth so that it smiles upwards (see photograph).

6. Position the eyes approximately 5cm (2in) from the tip of the nose.

7. Pin two leg pieces right sides together and sew from N to O and from P round the top of the leg and down to Q. The section P to O will be left open for stuffing. Repeat for the second leg. Do not turn right sides out.

8. Take the sole of one paw cut from suedette and with the right sides facing inwards, pin on to the bottom of the leg, matching N to N and Q to Q. Stitch and turn right sides out, repeating for the second leg.

9. On each arm piece snip the fabric as shown in the pattern at H. Take the paw pads (suedette) and pin to each arm, matching H to H and J to J with right sides together. Sew from H to J.

10. Fold each arm over with right sides together and pin and sew from K to L and from M to H. Turn right sides out.

11. Pin together the two side body pieces with right sides together and sew from S to T. Then take the back body and pin to the sides, matching R to R and T to T. Sew down one side only of the body back from R to T, leaving the other side open for stuffing. Turn right sides out.

12. Assemble the bear as described in the general instructions (see pages 16–18).

TIP

Other suitable accessories for a beer-drinking bear might include interestingly shaped glasses, beer bottles, or even a fine collection of beer mats.

Ballet Bear

This is the tallest bear in the book. Standing on the tips of her toes, she stands 50cm (20in) tall. She is made from 'antique pink' crushed mohair and her arms are bent so that she can be elegantly posed.

MATERIALS

BEAR

- 'Antique pink' crushed mohair 66 x 68cm (26 x 27in)
- Suedette 22 x 12cm (8¾ x 4¾in)
- 1 pair of deep brown plastic safety eyes 1.2cm (½in) in diameter
- Strong sewing thread
- Black wool (for the nose and mouth)
- 5 joints 4.5cm (1¾in) in diameter
- Polyester stuffing 600g (21oz) approx.

ACCESSORIES

- Salmon pink netting 2.5m x 15cm (3yd x 6in)

TIP

I bought my netting from a florist's shop, but you may find the right colour in a haberdashery department instead.

Making the Bear

TIP

Until you are familiar with the techniques of bear making you will need to refer regularly to the general instructions given in Chapter 4.

1. Using the pattern from pages 126–9, cut out all the pieces.

2. Cut the ear slits on the head gusset from B to C, and on the head from B to A. With the right sides together, pin and stitch the head pieces on either side of the head gusset from D to B.

3. Take two ear pieces and pin right sides together. Sew around the long curved edge from G to G and turn right sides out. Repeat for the second ear. Insert the ears into slot A to C and pin. To give the ears shape, bend just the edges of the ears (G) towards the centre front, but no more than 1cm (⅜in). Overstitch each ear in place very securely.

4. Pin and stitch on one side of the head only from B to E with right sides together (leaving the other side open for stuffing). Sew from D to F and turn the head right sides out.

5. Sew the nose and mouth with the black wool and flatten out the shape of the mouth so that it smiles upwards.

6. Position the eyes approximately 5cm (2in) from the tip of the nose.

7. Pin two of the leg pieces with right sides together and sew from N to O and from P round the top of the leg and down across the toe to Q. The section P to O will be left open for stuffing. Repeat for the second leg. Do not turn right sides out.

8. Take the sole of one paw cut from suedette. With the right sides facing inwards, pin on to the bottom of the leg, matching N to N and Q to Q. Stitch and turn right sides out, repeating for the second leg.

9. Pin a suedette paw pad to each inner arm, matching H to H and J to J (right sides together). Sew from H to J.

10. Pin an inner arm to an outer arm, right sides together, and sew from K right around the arm to L, leaving L to K open for stuffing. Turn right sides out and repeat for the other arm.

11. On each body piece, pin and sew the dart U to W on the wrong side. Pin the two body pieces together, right sides facing, and sew from S to R and from T through U and up to Y, leaving the section R to T open for stuffing. Turn right sides out.

12. Assemble the bear as described in the general instructions (see pages 16–18).

TIP

As Ballet bear is so large, give all the joints an extra push to make them as firm as possible.

Accessories

Tutu

1. Fold the netting in half lengthways and gather on the fold along the entire length.

2. Put this around the bear's waist and pull up the thread to make it the correct size. Remember to take into consideration the fact that the tutu needs to be pulled down at the front (see photograph).

3. Fasten the gathers off securely and sew the back together. Pull the tutu down at the front. The pile of the mohair will keep the netting in place.

THE GARDENER

THE GARDENER

The Gardener is one of the most friendly and cuddly of my bears. He stands 34cm (13½in) tall and wears an amiable expression. He loves his garden and is at peace with the world.

MATERIALS

BEAR

- Medium staple, man-made fur fabric 50 x 68cm (20 x 27in)
- Suedette 17 x 12cm (6¾ x 4¾in)
- 1 pair of deep brown plastic safety eyes 1.2cm (½in) in diameter
- Strong sewing thread
- Black wool (for the nose and mouth)
- 5 joints 4.5cm (1¾in) in diameter
- Polyester stuffing 325g (12oz) approx.

ACCESSORIES

- Dark green felt 13 x 15cm (5⅛ x 6in)
- Brown felt 12 x 14cm (4¾ x 5½in)
- Green and brown sewing thread to match
- Handful of gravel (can be bought from a garden centre), washed and dried
- A5 sheet of yellow cartridge paper
- A5 sheet of orange cartridge paper
- A5 sheet of white cartridge paper
- Light green and dark green felt-tip pens
- PVA glue
- Card 25 x 15cm (9¾ x 6in) (the cardboard back of a writing pad is ideal)
- 2 pipe cleaners
- Green florist's wire

MAKING THE BEAR

TIP

Until you are familiar with the techniques of bear making you will need to refer regularly to the general instructions given in Chapter 4.

1. Using the pattern from pages 130–2, cut out all the pieces.
2. Cut the ear slits on the head gusset from B to C, and on the head from B to A. With the right sides together, pin and stitch the head pieces on either side of the head gusset from D to B.
3. Take two ear pieces and pin right sides together. Sew around the long curved edge from G to G and turn right sides out. Repeat for the second ear. Insert the ears into slot A to C and pin. Overstitch both ears in place very securely.
4. Pin and stitch on one side of the head only from B to E (leaving the other side open for stuffing). Then sew from D to F and turn right sides out.
5. Sew the nose and mouth with the black wool, flattening out the mouth so that it is smiling upwards.
6. Position the eyes approximately 5cm (2in) from the tip of the nose.

7 Fold one of the legs with right sides together, matching P to P and O to O. Sew from N to O and from P round the top of the leg to Y. Then sew from W to Q. The section from P to O will be left open for stuffing. Repeat for the second leg. Do not turn right sides out.

8 Take the sole of one paw cut from suedette and with the right sides facing inwards, pin on to the bottom of the leg, matching N to N and Q to Q. Sew all round the paw and turn right sides out. Repeat for the other leg.

9 Pin the inner arms and the paw pads (cut from suedette) together, matching H to H and J to J with right sides together. Sew from H to J. Now pin the inner arms to the outer arms (right sides together) and sew from K right around each arm to L, leaving from L back to K open for stuffing. Turn right sides out.

10 Pin together the two front body pieces with right sides together and sew from S to T. Now take the back body piece and with right sides facing pin and sew together the dart from Z to T. Still with right sides together, pin the back body to the front body, matching V to V on both sides of the back and T to T. Sew down one side of the back body only, from V to T, leaving the other side open for stuffing. Turn right sides out.

11 Assemble the bear as described in the general instructions (see pages 16–18).

Accessories

Flower pot

1 Using the brown felt, cut out the pot following the pattern on page 133. Match the edges at points a and b, then oversew down the edge, keeping the seam flat.

2 Cut out the card according to the pattern, roll it up and slip into the flower pot to make a stiff cylinder.

3 Roll the top edge of the felt over on the outside of the pot to make a rim, cut out the flower pot base and oversew it on to the bottom of the pot. Cut out another base from card (slightly smaller all round) and place inside the pot.

Daffodils

TIP

If you do not have yellow or orange cartridge paper, colour white paper with a yellow or orange pen.

1 Following the pattern on page 133, cut out two of the large daffodil flower shapes and one of the small shapes from the yellow card. Score the flowers with paper scissors as indicated in Fig 7.1 and fold.

2 Cut three 7cm (2¾in) lengths of florist's wire and bend over one end of each by 3mm (⅛in).

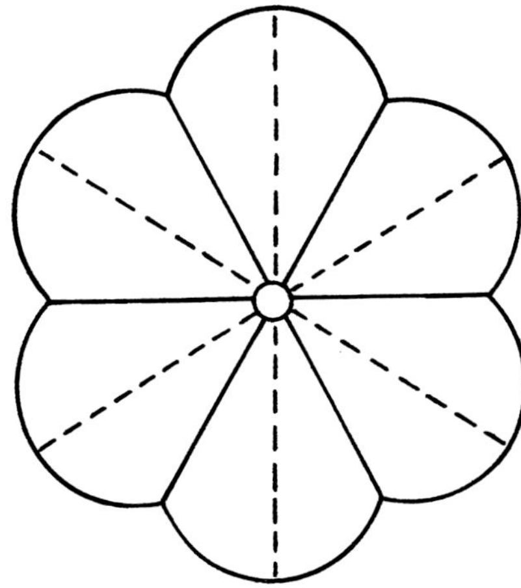

FIG 7.1 Score the daffodil petals on one side of the card along the dotted lines and fold. Then score the card on the other side along the unbroken lines and fold.

3 Cut out two large daffodil trumpets and one of the small trumpet from the orange card. Roll each one up to make a cone and glue. Use a dab of glue to stick the pointed end into the centre of each daffodil flower.

4 Push the wire through the centre of the flower, so that the folded end is inside the trumpet. Use a tab of glue to keep it in place. Leave to dry completely before fixing into the pot.

5 Make the leaves following the pattern on page 133. The white paper can be coloured in various shades of green with felt-tip pens. Stick on to the lengths of wire. It is important that the leaves are coloured on both sides. Leave to dry.

6 Fill the flower pot with gravel mixed with some PVA glue. Arrange the flowers and leaves, bending the wire if it is too long. Leave to dry.

Yucca plant

1. Fold one pipe cleaner in half and cover it with brown felt, oversewing along the top and the long edge.

2. Cut three or four leaf shapes from the white paper (using the pattern on page 133) and colour them in dark and light green stripes, making sure you cover both sides of the paper.

3. Glue one end of the three or four leaves on to the end of a 3cm (1⅛in) piece of wire. Leave to dry, then poke the wire end into the felt of the stem.

4. Make four more of these wired leaves and fix into the stem to make a second branch.

5. Fill a flower pot with gravel mixed with PVA glue as for the daffodils and fix the yucca plant in the pot, leaving the glue to dry.

Seed tray and trowel

1. Using the patterns on page 134, cut out the seed tray from the card and green felt. Score and bend the card from points A to A on all four sides.

2. Place the card on to the green felt and match points B to B. Oversew from A to B to form the inside of the tray. Now oversew from B down to C, making sure that the card is between the two layers of felt, to form the outside of the tray. Repeat on the remaining three corners.

3. Cut out as many seedlings as you want from the white paper coloured with green pens, using the pattern on page 134.

4. Fold the 8cm (3⅛in) pipe cleaner in half to form a handle for the trowel. With the bend in the pipe cleaner at the top, cover the whole thing with brown felt, oversewing along the top and down the long edge, but leaving 1.5cm (⅝in) unstitched at the bottom.

5. Using the pattern on page 134, cut out the trowel blade in card and bend it slightly so that it curves down the middle like a real trowel. Open out the bottom of the pipe cleaner handle and insert the trowel blade so that one end of the pipe cleaner is on top of the blade and the other underneath (see Fig 7.2). Use PVA glue to stick the blade and felt securely in place and leave to dry.

6. To complete the seed tray, fill with gravel mixed with PVA glue and then arrange the seedlings and trowel in the gravel. Leave to dry.

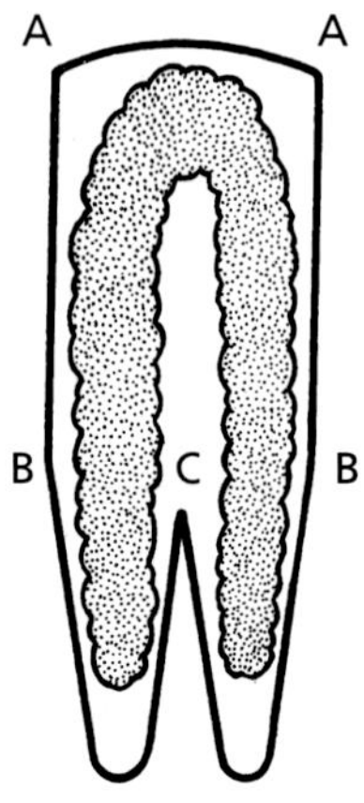

Fig 7.2 *The pipe cleaner for the trowel handle bent over inside the brown felt. Fold the felt over, matching A to A, and oversew across the top at A and down to B. Insert the card trowel blade into the handle at C and glue in place. Leave to dry.*

TIP

If you use grey card for the trowel blade you will not need to colour it. If not, you will need to use a grey felt-tip pen.

THE WALKER

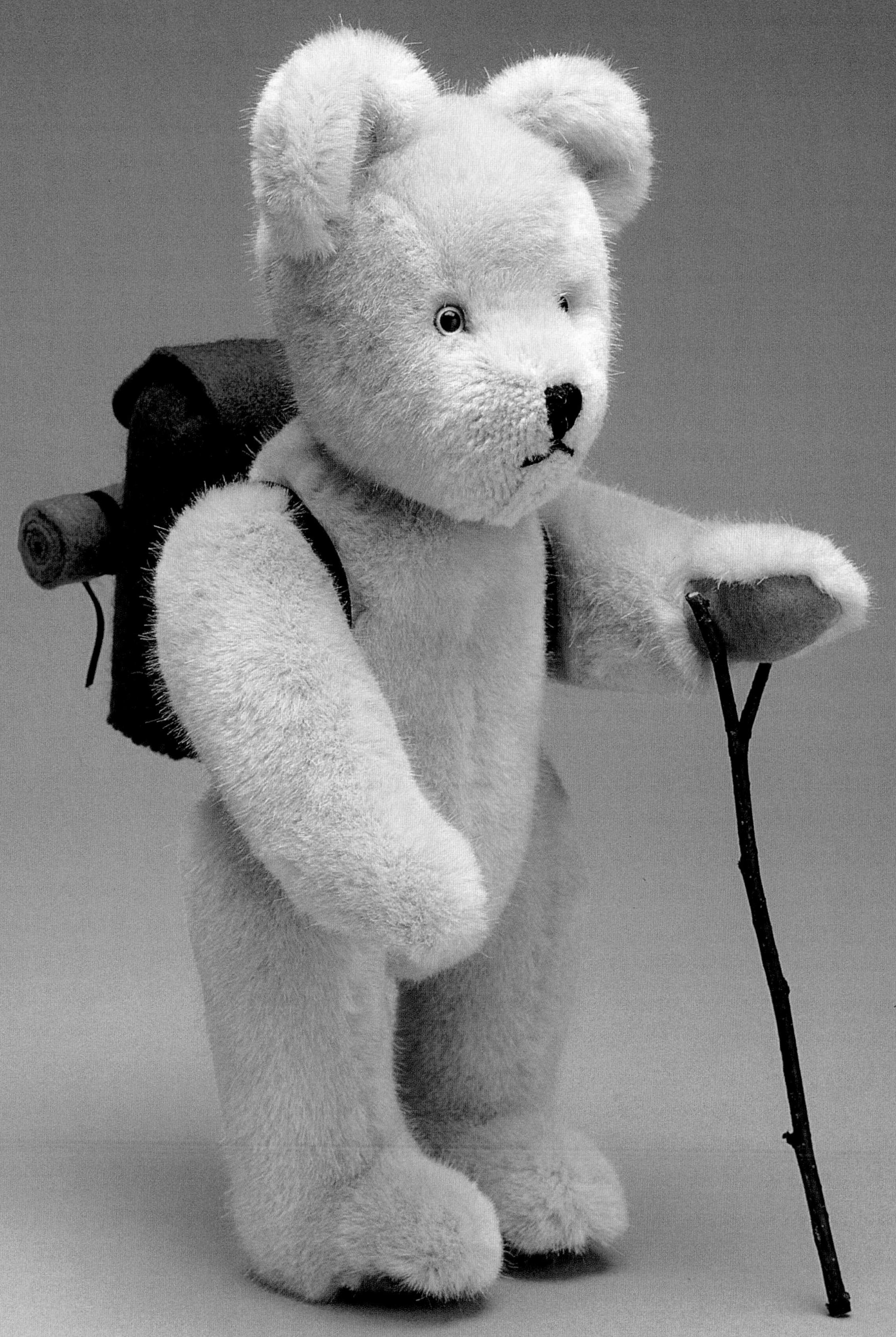

THE WALKER

The Walker is 30cm (12in) tall, a good-looking and trim figure with his short staple fur and bright eyes.

MATERIALS

BEAR

- Short staple mohair 30 x 68cm (12 x 27in)
- Suedette 20 x 8cm (8 x 3⅛in)
- 1 pair of pale amber plastic safety eyes 7mm (¼in) in diameter
- Strong sewing thread
- Black wool (for the nose and mouth)
- 5 joints 3.5cm (1⅜in) in diameter
- Polyester stuffing 175g (6oz) approx.

ACCESSORIES

- Dark green felt 15 x 15cm (6 x 6in)
- Mid green felt 7 x 15cm (2¾ x 6in)
- Dark green sewing cotton
- Black ribbon 5mm (3/16in) wide and 55cm (22in) long
- Black sewing cotton
- Handful of polyester stuffing
- Card 6 x 4cm (2⅜ x 1⅝in) – an old cereal packet is ideal
- Straight twig no more than 20cm (8in) long, with a forked top

MAKING THE BEAR

TIP

Until you are familiar with the techniques of bear making you will need to refer regularly to the general instructions given in Chapter 4.

1. Using the pattern from pages 135–6, cut out all the pieces.

2. Cut the ear slits on the head gusset from B to C, and on the head from B to A. With right sides together, pin and stitch the head pieces on either side of the head gusset from D to B.

3. Take two ear pieces and pin right sides together. Sew around the long curved edge from G to G and turn right sides out. Repeat for the second ear. To give the ears shape, bend just the edges (G) towards the centre front of the ear. Bend in no more than 5mm (3/16in). Insert the ears into slot A to C and pin. Overstitch each ear in place very securely.

4. Pin and stitch with right sides together on one side of the head only from B to E (leaving the other side open for stuffing). Sew from D to F and turn the head right sides out.

5. Sew the nose and mouth with the black wool, flattening out the mouth to smile upwards.

6. Position the eyes approximately 3cm (1⅛in) from the tip of the nose.

7. Fold over one of the leg pieces with right sides together and pin and sew from N right up the leg to O. Join the heel at Q. The section from P to Q will be left open for stuffing. Repeat for the second leg. Do not turn right sides out.

8 Take the sole of one paw cut from suedette and with the right sides facing inwards, pin on to the bottom of the leg, matching N to N and Q to Q. Stitch right around the sole of the foot and turn right sides out, repeating for the second leg.

9 Snip the fabric on both arm pieces as shown on the pattern at H. Pin the suedette paw pads to each arm, matching H to H and J to J (right sides together). Sew from H to J. Fold the arms over (right sides together) and pin and sew from M to K and from L to H, leaving K to L open for stuffing. Turn right sides out.

10 Pin together the body pieces (right sides together) and sew from S to T and from R to W, leaving T to R open for stuffing. Turn right sides out.

11 Assemble the bear as described in the general instructions (see pages 16–18).

TIP

Trim the snout only around the nose itself and then grade sharply.

Accessories

Haversack

1 From the dark green felt cut out a rectangle measuring 15 x 10cm (6 x 4in). Oversew the short edge in the form of a flat seam.

2 Cut out the base from the same felt, using the pattern on page 136, and oversew into position at one end of the cylinder. Cut out another base, this time in card fractionally smaller than the felt base, and place this into the bottom of the haversack.

3 Gather the top end of the haversack with running stitch and then fill with the polyester stuffing before drawing up the thread and finishing off securely.

4 Cut out the lid in the same felt (pattern on page 136) and position over the top of the haversack, sewing securely at the back.

5 Sew on to the lid 4cm ($1\frac{5}{8}$in) of ribbon, folding the edge under to keep it from fraying. Stitch the other end of the ribbon on to the haversack so that the lid is neatly closed.

6 Now take the mid green felt and roll up so that it becomes a bed roll 7cm ($2\frac{3}{4}$in) wide. Tie this up with some of the strong thread used for sewing the bear. Fasten the bed roll to the haversack with two 10cm (4in) strips of ribbon.

7 Lastly sew on the straps. You will need to allow approximately 15cm (6in) of ribbon for each strap. The top of each strap should be positioned approximately at the base of the lid on the back of the haversack. The bottom of each strap should be on the base.

Walking stick

Cut the twig down to an appropriate size if necessary, and rest one paw in the fork.

THE MUSICIAN

The Musician is 26cm (10in) tall, made from long staple, man-made fabric. I came across the guitar in a little shop we found on holiday, and because all my family play the guitar it was the ideal instrument for our Musician bear. With a bit of searching around, you should be able to find whichever instrument is most appropriate for the owner of your bear.

MATERIALS

BEAR

- Long staple, man-made fur fabric 30 x 68cm (12 x 27in)
- Suedette 14 x 7cm (5½ x 2¾in)
- 1 pair of deep brown plastic safety eyes 9mm (⅜in) in diameter
- Strong sewing thread
- Black wool (for the nose and mouth)
- 5 joints 3.5cm (1⅜in) in diameter
- Polyester stuffing 175g (6oz) approx.

ACCESSORIES

- Small guitar (or any musical instrument)

Making the Bear

TIP

Until you are familiar with the techniques of bear making you will need to refer regularly to the general instructions given in Chapter 4.

1. Using the pattern from pages 137–8, cut out all the pieces.

2. Cut the ear slits on the head gusset from B to C, and on the head from B to A. With the right sides together, pin and stitch the head pieces on either side of the head gusset from D to B.

3. Take two ear pieces and pin right sides together. Sew around the long curved edge from G to G and turn right sides out. Repeat for the second ear. Insert the ears into slot A to C and pin. Overstitch each ear in place very securely.

4. Pin and stitch with right sides together on one side of the head only from B to E (leaving the other side open for stuffing). Sew from D to F and turn the head right sides out.

5. Sew the nose and mouth with the black wool and position the eyes approximately 3.5cm (1⅜in) from the tip of the nose.

6. Pin one leg piece right sides together and match P to P, O to O and N to N. Sew from N to O and from P round the top of the leg to Q. The section P to O will be left open for stuffing. Repeat for the second leg. Do not turn right sides out.

7. Take the sole of one paw cut from suedette and with the right sides facing inwards, pin on to the bottom of the leg, matching N to N and W to W. Stitch all the way round and turn right sides out.

8. Snip the fabric on each arm-piece at H as shown on the pattern. Pin the suedette paw pads to the arm pieces, matching H to H and J to J with right sides together. Sew from H to J. Next fold the arms over (right sides together) and sew from K to L and from M to H, leaving L to M open for stuffing. Turn right sides out.

9. Pin together the two side body pieces with right sides together and sew from S to T. Take the front body piece and pin to the side pieces, matching R to R and T to T. Sew down one side only of the body front from R to T, leaving the other side open for stuffing. Turn right sides out.

10. Assemble the bear as described in the general instructions (see pages 16–18).

Accessories

Any musical instrument would be suitable for the Musician, so the choice is up to you. Another idea would be to photocopy down to an appropriate size a sheet of manuscript paper on which you have written some musical notes.

I punched out some silver paper with a hole punch and put some of the little discs in the guitar case as money.

8 Sporting Bears

Cricketer

Rugby player

Tennis player

Football Fan

Swimmer

Golfers

THE SWIMMER

The Swimmer is 20cm (8in) tall. Never without a bathing towel, he could be on the beach or by the swimming pool.

MATERIALS

BEAR

- Short staple mohair 33 x 33cm (13 x 13in)
- Suedette 9 x 6cm (3½ x 2⅜in)
- 1 pair of light amber plastic safety eyes 7mm (¼in) in diameter
- Strong sewing thread
- Black wool (for the nose and mouth)
- 1 joint 3.5cm (1⅜in) in diameter
- 4 safety eyes 1.2cm (½in) in diameter (for arm and leg joints)
- Polyester stuffing 75g (3oz) approx.

ACCESSORIES

- Piece of towelling 23 x 13cm (9 x 5in)

TIP

Immersing a bear completely in water will damage the fur fabric and the stuffing!

MAKING THE BEAR

TIP

Until you are familiar with the techniques of bear making you will need to refer regularly to the general instructions given in Chapter 4.

1. Using the pattern from page 139, cut out all the pieces.

2. Cut the ear slits on the head gusset from B to C, and on the head from B to A. With the right sides together, pin and stitch the head pieces on either side of the head gusset from D to B.

3. Take two ear pieces and pin right sides together. Sew around the long curved edge from G to G and turn right sides out. Repeat for the second ear. Insert the ears into slot A to C and pin. Overstitch each ear in place very securely.

4. Pin and stitch with right sides together on one side of the head only from B to E (leaving the other side open for stuffing). Sew from D to F and turn the head right sides out.

5. Sew the nose and mouth with the black wool and position the eyes approximately 2.5cm (1in) from the tip of the nose.

6. Pin two leg pieces with right sides together and sew from N to O and from P round the top of the leg down to Q. The section from P to O will be left open for stuffing. Repeat for the second leg. Do not turn right sides out.

7. Take the sole of one paw cut from suedette and with the right sides facing inwards pin on to the bottom of the leg, matching N to N and Q to Q. Sew all the way round and turn right sides out. Repeat for the second leg.

8. Take the paw pads (suedette) and pin to the inner arms, matching H to H and J to J (right sides together). Sew from H to J.

9. Pin the inner and outer arms right sides together and sew from K right around the arm through J and round the paw to H. Leave K to H open for stuffing. Turn each arm right sides out.

10. Pin together the body pieces with right sides together, and sew from S to T. Now sew from R to W, leaving T to R open for stuffing. Turn right sides out.

11. Assemble the bear as described in the general instructions (see pages 16–18).

ACCESSORIES

Towel

Make a small hem all around the towelling and simply hang over the bear's arm.

THE CRICKETER

This bear is fully kitted out for a cricket match. A compact 20cm (8in) tall, he is the ideal mascot for any keen cricketer. The Cricketer has no joints and is made in a slightly different way from many of the bears in this book.

MATERIALS

BEAR

- Short staple, man-made fur fabric 17 x 15cm ($6\frac{3}{4}$ x 6in)
- Suedette 7 x 4cm ($2\frac{3}{4}$ x $1\frac{5}{8}$in)
- White cotton fabric 18 x 14cm (7 x $5\frac{1}{2}$in)
- White felt 8 x 6cm ($3\frac{1}{8}$ x $2\frac{3}{8}$in)
- Card 7 x 5cm ($2\frac{3}{4}$ x 2in)
- 1 pair of amber plastic safety eyes 5mm ($\frac{3}{16}$in) in diameter
- Strong sewing thread
- Black wool (for the nose and mouth)
- Polyester stuffing 50g (2oz) approx.

ACCESSORIES

- White wool 25g (1oz)
- White felt 22 x 12cm ($8\frac{3}{4}$ x $4\frac{3}{4}$in)
- 1 pair of knitting needles size $3\frac{1}{4}$mm (No 10)
- Cable needle
- Ready-made miniature cricket bat (mine is 11cm ($4\frac{3}{4}$in) long and I bought it at a country fair)
- 3mm ($\frac{1}{8}$in) dowel 27cm ($10\frac{5}{8}$in) long
- 1 matchstick
- Polystyrene sheet 4.5 x 2.5cm ($1\frac{3}{4}$ x 1in)
- Red bead

Making the Bear

TIP

Until you are familiar with the techniques of bear making you will need to refer regularly to the general instructions given in Chapter 4.

1 Using the pattern from pages 140–1, cut out the head, head gusset, ears and two of the paw pads in fur fabric. Cut out the other two paw pads in suedette.

2 Cut the ear slits on the head gusset from B to C, and on the head from B to A. With the right sides together pin and stitch the head pieces on either side of the head gusset from D to B.

3 Take two ear pieces and pin right sides together. Sew around the long curved edge from G to G and turn right sides out. Repeat for the second ear. Insert the ears into slot A to C and pin. Overstitch each ear in place very securely.

4 Pin and stitch with right sides together on one side of the head gusset only from B to E (leaving the other side open for stuffing). Sew from D to F and turn the head right sides out.

5 Sew the nose and mouth with the black wool and position the eyes approximately 2.5cm (1in) from the tip of the nose.

6 Cut out the body and legs in white cotton fabric, making sure that the edge along points I, M and J is cut on the fold. This fold will be at the centre front.

7 With right sides together, sew from H through M and down to K, with a 5mm ($\frac{3}{16}$in) seam allowance. Use a sewing machine or handsewn backstitch. This seam will form the centre back. Turn the legs right side out.

8 Making sure that the fold is at the centre front and the seam at centre back, match J to K, M to M and I to H. Pin and sew from JK up to M using a machine or backstitch (you are sewing through both centre front and centre back). This forms the legs and they can now be stuffed.

9 The upper part of the white fabric (from M up to I and H) is the body and may also be stuffed now.

10 Sew the head to the body with strong ladder stitch (this neck is not jointed), ensuring that the neck of the cotton body has been turned neatly under. Stuff the head and neck firmly before sewing up the gap B to E with ladder stitch.

11 Cut out the shoe soles in cardboard and white felt and the shoe uppers in white felt. Match P to P, Q to Q and N to N, then oversew from Q, through N and on to P. Insert the card piece as stiffening and stuff the part of the shoes made by the uppers.

12 The centre bottom point of the legs (JK) should be joined to the shoes at R. Fit the legs to the shoes and oversew firmly into place. Extra stuffing must be added while the shoes are being sewn on to the legs, so that the ankles are strong enough to support the bear when he stands. Stuff the ankles a little at a time as you sew, making absolutely sure that they are firm enough before finishing off the stitching.

13 Match a suedette paw pad with a fur fabric paw pad and sew along the long edge from W to W. Turn right sides out and stuff, repeating for the second paw.

14 Cut out the arms in white felt and pin each one up, matching S to S and U to U. Oversew to make a flat seam. The flat seam should be put to the back of the arm and the paw pad joined to the wrist edge of the arm (S). Ensure that the fur fabric side of the paw is to the back and the suedette side towards the front.

15 Stuff each arm and oversew the top end in position on each shoulder.

16 Cut out the chest piece from the fur fabric and sew in place under the bear's chin.

17 Cut out the cuffs and the collar and shirt front from the felt. Fold over the collar along the line from V to V shown on the pattern and press. Place around the neck, matching Y to Y at the centre front. Oversew from Y to Z.

18 Fold the cuffs along the dotted line shown on the pattern and press. Oversew in place around the bear's wrists.

Accessories

Sleeveless sweater

1 Cast on 48 stitches with the white wool and rib (knit 1, purl 1) 4 rows.

On row 5 (knit 4, purl 1) four times, knit 8, then (purl 1, knit 4) four times.

On row 6 (purl 4, knit 1) four times, purl 8, then (knit 1, purl 4) four times.

On row 7 [knit 4 (*purl 1, put 2 stitches to the front on a cable needle, knit 2, knit the 2 stitches from the cable needle, purl 1**), knit 4, repeat from * to **], knit 8, repeat from * to **, knit 4, repeat from * to **, and knit 4.

Row 8 is the same as row 6.

Rows 5 to 8 make the pattern. Keeping to the pattern, complete row 10.

On the next row work 24 stitches, turn. These 24 stitches form the front.

2 For the armholes, cast off 2 stitches at the beginning of the next 2 rows.

Cast off 1 stitch at the beginning of the next 2 rows.

Work 9 stitches. Turn and reduce by one stitch at the neck edge on the next 8 rows.

Cast off. Repeat for the other side. Reverse.

3 Make the back by reducing the armholes as for the front and working the remaining 18 stitches. Cast off when the back matches the front.

4 Join one shoulder. Pick up 38 stitches evenly around the neck, rib 2 rows and cast off. Join the other shoulder seam and under the arm.

Batting pads

1 Following the pattern on page 00, cut out four pads in felt and two knee pieces (making sure that each knee piece is cut on the fold as shown in the pattern).

2 Oversew together two of the pads all the way around. The thickness of the felt will be sufficient so no extra stuffing is needed. Then use a sewing machine, or a very neat backstitch, and stitch as indicated by the broken lines on the pad pattern.

3 Keeping the knee pad folded, overstitch around the three open sides (again no stuffing is needed). Sew as indicated by the dotted lines on the pattern, as for the pad.

4 Now put the knee piece on to the pad with the fold at the top. The pattern shows exactly where it should be placed. Oversew the knee piece to the pad at both sides.

5 Make up the other pad in the same way.

6 The pads should be attached to the bear's legs with white wool. Sew a length of wool to the inside edge of the pad at all three points marked X. Sew through the centre joint and then take each length of wool round the back of the bear's leg, and attach the wool at the corresponding X on the outer edge of the pad. When complete there will be three separate lengths of wool around the back of the leg holding the pad in place.

Bat

Using thread which matches the colour of the cricket bat handle, place the bat on the bear's paw and oversew the handle to the paw, taking the thread right round the handle.

Stumps and ball

1 Cut the dowel into 9cm (3½in) lengths and cut a groove in the top of each stump for the bails. Press into the polystyrene sheet for the stumps.

2 Cut two lengths of matchstick to fit the top of the stumps.

TIP

If you do not have a red bead for the ball, try painting another bead red.

If you cannot find polystyrene sheet, balsa wood would work, but a hole should be made before pushing in the stumps.

THE TENNIS PLAYER

Like the Cricketer, the Tennis Player is 20cm (8in) tall and another ideal mascot.

MATERIALS

BEAR

- Short staple, man-made fur fabric 30 x 18cm (12 x 7in)
- Suedette 7 x 4cm (2¾ x 1⅝in)
- White cotton fabric either 63 x 8cm (25 x 3⅛in) or 45 x 12cm (17¾ x 4¾in) (this is used both for the body and the tennis skirt)
- 1 pair of amber plastic safety eyes 5mm (3/16in) in diameter
- Strong sewing thread
- Black wool (for the nose and mouth)
- Polyester stuffing 50g (2oz) approx.
- White felt 8 x 6cm (3⅛ x 2⅜in)
- Old white socks (you will need a length of 4cm (1⅝in) taken from the top of each sock)
- Card 7 x 5cm (2¾ x 2in)

ACCESSORIES

- White T-shirt material 18 x 20cm (7 x 8in)
- Strong garden wire 26cm (10in) (I used green, but the colour is up to you)
- Dark blue ribbon 6mm (¼in) wide, 15cm (6in) long
- Light blue ribbon 6mm (¼in) wide, 10cm (4in) long

Making the Bear

TIP

Until you are familiar with the techniques of bear making you will need to refer regularly to the general instructions given in Chapter 4.

1. Using the pattern from page 142, cut out the head, head gusset, ears and arms in fur fabric – there should be a rectangle of at least 18 x 9cm (7 x 3½in) left for the legs. Cut out the two paw pads in suedette.

2. Cut the ear slits on the head gusset from B to C, and on the head from B to A. With the right sides together pin and stitch the head pieces on either side of the head gusset from D to B.

3. Take two ear pieces and pin right sides together. Sew around the long curved edge from G to G and turn right sides out. Repeat for the second ear. Insert the ears into slot A to C and pin. Overstitch each ear in place very securely.

4. Pin and stitch with right sides together on one side of the head gusset only from B to E (leaving the other side open for stuffing). Sew from D to F and turn the head right sides out.

5 Sew the nose and mouth with the black wool and position the eyes approximately 2.5cm (1in) from the tip of the nose.

6 Cut out a rectangle 18 x 6cm (7 x 2⅜in) in white cotton fabric for the body. There should be a rectangle 45 x 6cm (17¾ x 2⅜in) left for the skirt.

7 Cut out a rectangle 18 x 9cm (7 x 3½in) in fur fabric for the legs.

8 Join the body and legs together at the waist (the 18cm (7in) side) using backstitch (remember that the pile on the legs should be lying down towards the feet). When stitched, open out and then sew the back seam with backstitch also, so that you end up with a cylinder.

9 Sew the centre front to the centre back, on the fur fabric only, to form the legs (see Fig 8.1). Legs and body should now be stuffed.

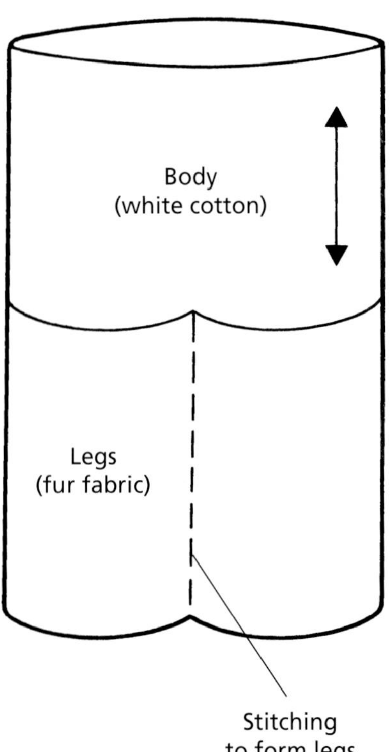

FIG 8.1 Sew up the centre front of the fur fabric to make the legs.

10 Sew the head to the body with strong ladder stitch (this is not a jointed neck). Stuff the head and neck firmly before sewing up the gap from B to E.

TIP

When sewing the head to the body, it will help to turn the raw edges of the cotton body under and gather the neck of the body.

11 Cut out the sole of the shoes both in cardboard and white felt and the shoe uppers in white felt. Take the two felt pieces and match P to P, Q to Q and N to N and pin. Oversew from Q, through N and on to P. Insert the card and stuff the part of the shoes made by the uppers.

12 Fit the socks on to the ends of the legs and slip stitch into place. Oversew the socks to the shoes where they meet. Ensure that any raw edges are turned under. Insert extra stuffing into the ankles as you go. The bear will only stand up well if the feet, ankles and legs are firmly stuffed. If you wish, stitch a bow from white embroidery thread on the shoes.

13 Now take one inner arm and one suedette paw pad. With right sides together match H to H and J to J. Pin and sew from H to J. Flatten out the arm and place it on to the outer arm with right sides together. Sew from K, around the paw, over the top of the arm and on to M. Leave open K to M for stuffing. Repeat for the second arm.

14 Trim off the fur pile for 3cm (1⅛in) at the top of the arms. The T-shirt goes over this part and the full pile might appear too bulky.

15 Stuff each arm and stitch into position on each shoulder to complete the bear. There are several ways of stitching the arms on to this kind of bear, but I suggest using a long needle and taking the thread through one arm and right through the body of the bear and out the other side. Pull the thread tight – but not so tight as to distort the shoulder – then go back the other way. Do this about three times and finish off the thread securely (this will not be visible on the finished bear as it will be covered by the T-shirt).

Accessories

T-shirt

1 Using the pattern on page 142, cut out the T-shirt in the white T-shirt material, making sure that both pieces are placed on the fold as indicated. With right sides together, sew front to back at the shoulder seams, then under one arm and down one side seam.

2 Fold the neck edge under. Once on the bear, this should stay in place, held by the pile. Fold the sleeve hem under as well and press (this should also stay in place without sewing).

3 Put the T-shirt on to the bear and sew up the remaining side seam and under the arm using ladder stitch, keeping the raw edges turned under.

Skirt

1 Using pinking shears if you have them (this will prevent fraying), cut out a rectangle of white cotton fabric 45 x 6cm (17¾ x 2⅜in). Fold over a 1cm (⅜in) hem and press. If you wish, you can also sew the hem, but this is not necessary.

2 The skirt must now be pleated and pressed. The tennis skirt shown on my bear has a flat piece of material overlapping in the front and the back and sides are pleated. Lay the fabric out right side up, then, leaving 9cm (3½in) on the right and 7cm (2¾in) on the left, fold pleats in between so that the pleated part measures 11cm (4¼in) (see Fig 8.2).

3 Cut out a strip of white fabric 23 x 2cm (9 x ¾in) for the waistband. With right sides together, sew this strip on to the skirt as a waistband, as shown in Fig 8.3. Fold the waistband over the top of the skirt and press into place. There is no need to stitch it as it will stay put once the skirt is fixed round the bear's waist.

4 Fold over the end of the front flap of the skirt, so that no raw edges can be seen, and press.

5 Wrap the skirt around the bear and fix the front flap into place by stitching at the waistband.

Tennis racket

1 Bend the garden wire into the shape shown in Fig 8.4.

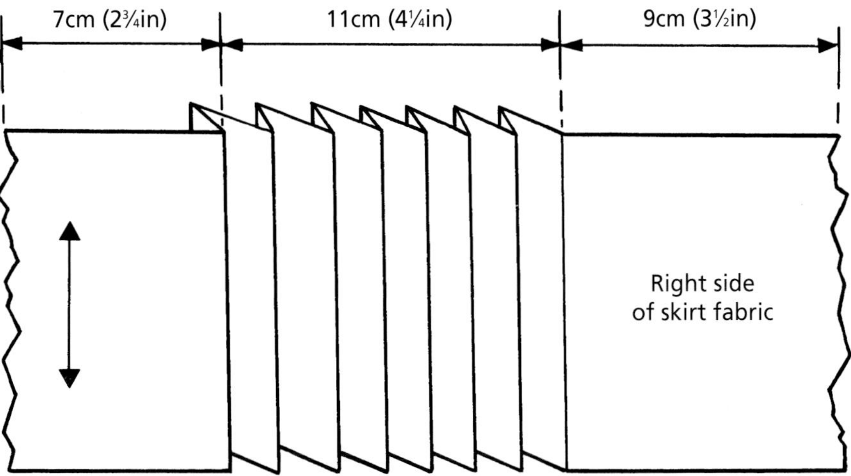

Fig 8.2 *The proportions of pleated and plain fabric on the tennis skirt.*

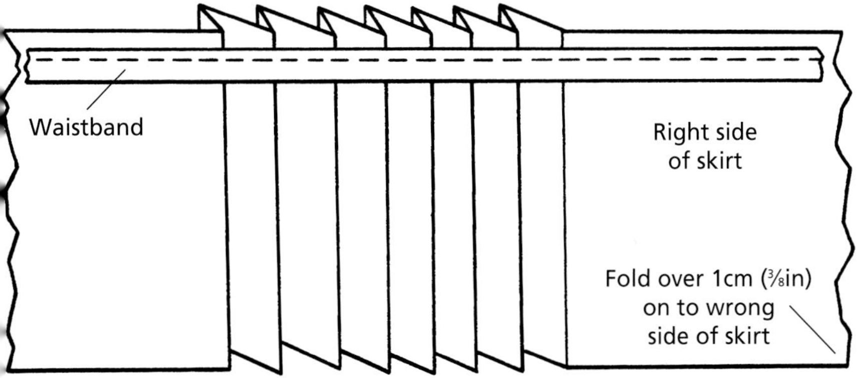

Fig 8.3 *Place the waistband just below the top of the skirt, with right sides together, and stitch along the top edge of the strip.*

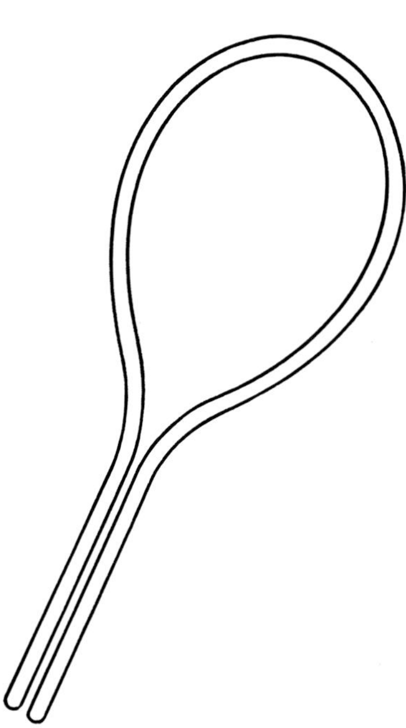

Fig 8.4 *The shape of the wire for the tennis racket frame.*

2 Wrap a length of dark blue ribbon round the wire for the shaft of the racket and light blue for the handle, fastening with a few stitches in matching cotton thread.

3 Stitch the racket on to the bear's hand with matching cotton thread.

THE RUGBY PLAYER

The Rugby Player is a compact 18cm (7in) high. He is a chunky, stocky bear with a furrowed brow and a determined look.

MATERIALS

BEAR

- Dark, medium staple, man-made fur fabric 35 x 25cm (13¾ x 9¾in)
- Suedette 6 x 8cm (2⅜ x 3⅛in)
- 1 pair of amber plastic safety eyes 7mm (¼in) in diameter
- Strong sewing thread
- Black wool (for the nose and mouth)
- 1 joint 3.5cm (1⅜in) in diameter
- 4 safety eyes 1.2cm (½in) in diameter (for arm and leg joints)
- Polyester stuffing 75g (3oz) approx.

ACCESSORIES

- White felt 10 x 8cm (4 x 3⅛in)
- Handful of polyester stuffing
- White sewing thread
- Brown embroidery thread

MAKING THE BEAR

TIP

Until you are familiar with the techniques of bear making you will need to refer regularly to the general instructions given in Chapter 4.

1 Using the pattern from page 143, cut out all the pieces.

2 Take the head gusset and sew the dart V to W on the wrong side.

3 Cut the ear slits on the head gusset from B to C, and on the head from B to A. With the right sides together, pin and stitch the head pieces on either side of the head gusset from D to B.

4 Take two ear pieces and pin right sides together. Sew around the long curved edge from G to G and turn right sides out. Repeat for the second ear. Insert the ears into slot A to C and pin. Overstitch each ear in place very securely.

5 Pin and stitch with right sides together on one side of the head only from B to E (leaving the other side open for stuffing). Sew from D to F and turn the head right sides out.

6 Sew the nose and mouth with the black wool. The Rugby Player should look a little stern, so do not make the mouth smiling.

7 Position the eyes approximately 2cm (¾in) from the tip of the nose.

8 Fold over one of the leg pieces with right sides together and pin and sew from N to O and from P round the top of the leg to Y. The section P to O will be left open for stuffing. Repeat for the second leg. Do not turn right sides out.

9 Take the sole of one paw cut from suedette. With the right sides facing inwards, pin on to the bottom of the leg, matching N to N and Q to Q. Sew around the whole paw and turn right sides out. Repeat for the second leg.

10 Snip the fabric of the arm pieces at H as shown on the pattern. Take each suedette paw pad and match H to H and J to J on the arm piece with right sides together. Sew from H to J.

11 Fold each arm over right sides together and sew from K to L and from M to H. Turn right sides out.

12 Pin together the two body pieces with right sides together and sew from S to T. Now sew from Z to U, leaving T to Z open for stuffing. Turn right sides out.

13 Assemble the bear as described in the general instructions (see pages 16–18).

ACCESSORIES

Rugby ball

1 Using the pattern on page 143, cut out the four pieces of the ball in white felt. Join the pieces with right sides together from I to R using a very neat and tight overstitch. Join all the pieces together, leaving the last side open in the middle for stuffing.

2 Turn the ball right sides out, stuff and oversew the opening.

3 Using the brown embroidery thread, start the needle from the side of the ball with the sewn-up opening, and make four stitches over the seam line on the opposite side of the ball (look at the photograph for exact positioning).

4 Finish off by taking the thread back to the opening side and use it to sew the ball on to the bear's paw.

THE FOOTBALL FAN

Like the Rugby Player, the Football Fan is just 18cm (7in) tall.
You can dress him in colours appropriate to your team.

MATERIALS

BEAR

- Short staple mohair 35 x 25cm (13¾ x 9¾in)
- Suedette 6 x 8cm (2⅜ x 3⅛in)
- 1 pair of amber plastic safety eyes 7mm (¼in) in diameter
- Strong sewing thread
- Black wool (for the nose and mouth)
- 1 joint 3.5cm (1⅜in) in diameter
- 4 safety eyes 1.2cm (½in) in diameter (for arm and leg joints)
- Polyester stuffing 75g (3oz) approx.

ACCESSORIES

- Odds and ends of double knitting wool in two contrasting colours
- 1 pair of size 3¼mm (No 10) knitting needles
- 15cm (6in) length of ribbon 1.5cm (⅝in) wide
- 5cm (2in) length of narrower ribbon in a contrasting colour

Making the Bear

TIP

Until you are familiar with the techniques of bear making you will need to refer regularly to the general instructions given in Chapter 4.

1. Using the pattern from page 144, cut out all the pieces.

2. Cut the ear slits on the head gusset from B to C, and on the head from B to A. With the right sides together, pin and stitch the head pieces on either side of the head gusset from D to B.

3. Take two ear pieces and pin right sides together. Sew around the long curved edge from G to G and turn right sides out. Repeat for the second ear. Insert the ears into slot A to C and pin. To give the ears shape, bend just the edges (G) towards the centre front of the ear. Bend in no more than 5mm (3⁄16in). Overstitch each ear in place very securely.

4. Pin and stitch with right sides together on one side of the head only from B to E (leaving the other side open for stuffing). Sew from D to F and turn the head right sides out.

5. Sew the nose and mouth with the black wool and position the eyes approximately 2cm (¾in) from the tip of the nose.

6. Fold over one of the leg pieces with right sides together and pin and sew from N round the top of the leg to Y. The section P to O will be left open for stuffing. Repeat for the second leg. Do not turn right sides out.

7. Take the sole of one paw cut from suedette and with the right sides facing inwards, pin on to the bottom of the leg, matching N to N and Q to Q. Stitch around the paw and turn the leg right sides out. Repeat for the second leg.

8. Take the suedette paw pads and match them H to H and J to J on the inner arms with right sides together. Pin and sew from H to J. Placing an inner arm with an outer arm, right sides together, pin and sew from K right around the arm to L. Leave K to L open for stuffing. Turn right sides out and repeat for the second arm.

9. Pin together the two body pieces, right sides together, and sew from S to T and from R to W, leaving T to R open for stuffing. Turn right sides out.

10. Assemble the bear as described in the general instructions (see pages 16–18).

ACCESSORIES

Scarf

1 Cast on 9 stitches with the darker of your two wools. The scarf is knitted entirely in rib (knit 1, purl 1).

2 Work 8 rows, change to the contrasting colour and work another 8 rows.

3 Continue repeating step 2 until the scarf is long enough to wrap around the Football Fan's neck and hang as long at the front and back as you wish. Finish with 8 rows of the original colour before casting off.

4 Using the darker colour, fringe the ends by looping a 5cm (2in) length of wool into the edge of the scarf, pulling the two ends through the loop and pulling tight (see page 36). Trim the fringe neatly when finished.

Rosette

1 Using the wider ribbon, gather 10cm (4in) along one side and draw up to make a circle. Finish the thread off securely.

2 Fold over the rest of the ribbon in half lengthways.

3 Fold over the narrower ribbon in a similar way and attach with a stitch to the middle of the circle. This makes the rosette.

THE GOLFERS

THE GOLFERS

These two entertaining characters will liven up a round of golf, fitting neatly over a club to add a touch of difference to an ordinary golfing bag. The fur-bodied bear is made in man-made fabric and can withstand a certain amount of rain. The bear with the knitted body should also be fairly resilient.

MATERIALS FOR GOLFER WITH FUR BODY

BEAR

- Medium staple, man-made fur fabric 30 x 68cm (12 x 27in)
- 1 pair of deep brown plastic safety eyes 1.2cm (½in) in diameter
- Strong sewing thread
- Black wool (for the nose and mouth)
- Handful of polyester stuffing
- 12cm (4¾in) length of black elastic 1cm (⅜in) wide
- Black Velcro 2cm (¾in)
- PVA glue

MAKING THE BEAR

TIP

Until you are familiar with the techniques of bear making you will need to refer regularly to the general instructions given in Chapter 4.

1 Using the pattern from page 145, cut out the head, head gusset, ears and a rectangle 24 x 32cm (9½ x 12½in), taking care that the pile lies down towards the shorter edge of the rectangle.

2 Cut the ear slits on the head gusset from B to C, and on the head from B to A. With the right sides together, pin and stitch the head pieces on either side of the head gusset from D to B.

3 Take two ear pieces and pin right sides together. Sew around the long curved edge from G to G and turn right sides out. Repeat for the second ear. Insert the ears into slot A to C and pin. To give the ears shape, bend just the edges (G) towards the centre front of the ear. Bend in no more than 1cm (⅜in). Overstitch each ear in place very securely.

4 Pin and stitch with right sides together on one side of the head only from B to E (leaving the other side open for access to the nose). Sew from D to F and turn the head right sides out.

5 Sew the nose and mouth with the black wool and position the eyes approximately 5cm (2in) from the tip of the nose.

6 Turn the head inside out again and liberally cover the snout on the wrong side with PVA glue. Push a handful of stuffing into the snout as you turn the head right sides out. Manipulate the nose and snout to get the shape you want and leave the glue to dry completely (see Tip opposite).

7 Sew up the gap from B to E with ladder stitch.

8 Now take the rectangle of fur fabric, which will form the body. With right sides together, backstitch along the short edge to make a cylinder. Make a 1cm (⅜in) hem at the bottom of the cylinder (remember that the pile should lie downwards).

TIP

The stuffing in the snout gives the head some shape, but the rest of the head is empty to take the golf club. Plenty of glue will ensure that the stuffing stays in place, but be careful not to use so much that it soaks through the fabric and mats the fur.

9 Gather the top of the cylinder and attach the head to the body using ladder stitch.

10 Oversew one end of the elastic 6cm (2⅜in) up the back seam of the body from the hem. At the other end of the elastic sew one part of the Velcro at right angles (to form a T-shape). Glue the other side of the Velcro to the golf bag, so that the bear can hang safely there while the club is in use.

MATERIALS FOR GOLFER WITH KNITTED BODY

BEAR

- Dark, medium staple, man-made fur fabric 35 x 30cm (14 x 12in)
- Dark brown felt 14 x 7cm (5½ x 2¾in)
- 1 pair of deep brown plastic safety eyes 1.2cm (½in) in diameter
- Strong sewing thread
- Black wool (for the nose and mouth)
- Handful of polyester stuffing
- PVA glue
- 12cm (4¾in) length of black elastic 1cm (⅜in) wide
- Black Velcro 2cm (¾in)
- Chunky knit wool 50g (2oz) (colour to tone with the fur fabric)
- 1 pair of 6.5mm (No 3) knitting needles

MAKING THE BEAR

TIP

Until you are familiar with the techniques of bear making you will need to refer regularly to the general instructions given in Chapter 4.

1 Use the pattern from page 146, cut out the head, head gusset, ears and two paw pads. Two further paw pads should be cut from the felt.

2 Cut the ear slits on the head gusset from B to C, and on the head from B to A. With the right sides together, pin and stitch the head pieces on either side of the head gusset from D to B.

3 Take two ear pieces and pin right sides together. Sew around the long curved edge from G to G and turn right sides out. Repeat for the second ear. Insert the ears into slot A to C and pin. To give the ears shape, bend just the edges (G) towards the centre front of the ear. Bend in no more than 1cm (⅜in). Overstitch each ear in place very securely.

4 Pin and stitch with right sides together on one side of the head only from B to E (leaving the other side open for access to the nose). Sew from D to F and turn the head right sides out.

5 Sew the nose and mouth with the black wool and position the eyes approximately 5cm (2in) from the tip of the nose.

6 Turn the head inside out again and liberally cover the snout on the wrong side in PVA glue. Push the stuffing into the snout as you turn the head right sides out. Manipulate the nose and snout to get the shape you want and leave the glue to dry completely.

7 Sew up the gap from B to E with ladder stitch.

8 To make the body, cast on 44 stitches with the wool. Then for row 1: (knit 2, purl 2) 11 times. For row 2: (purl 2, knit 2) 11 times. Continue repeating these rows until the work measures 22cm (8¾in). Cast off and oversew the seam to make a cylinder.

9 To make the arms, cast on 17 stitches. Then for row 1: Rib (knit 1, purl 1) to the end of the row. Repeat until the work measures 14cm (5½in). Cast off and oversew the side seam to make a cylinder. Repeat for the second arm.

Take one paw pad cut from fur fabric and one from felt. With right sides together, sew around the long edge from H to J and turn right sides out. Sew the paw on to the end of the arm and repeat for the other one.

10 Sew both arms to the body at either side of the neck edge.

11 Attach the head to the neck edge of the body with ladder stitch, having first gathered the neck edge.

12 Attach one end of the elastic at the back of the body, about 6cm (2⅜in) up from the bottom. At the other end of the elastic sew at right angles one part of the Velcro (to form a T-shape). Glue the other side of the Velcro to the golf bag in the same way as for the first Golfer.

9 Professional Bears

Teacher

Farmer

Doctor

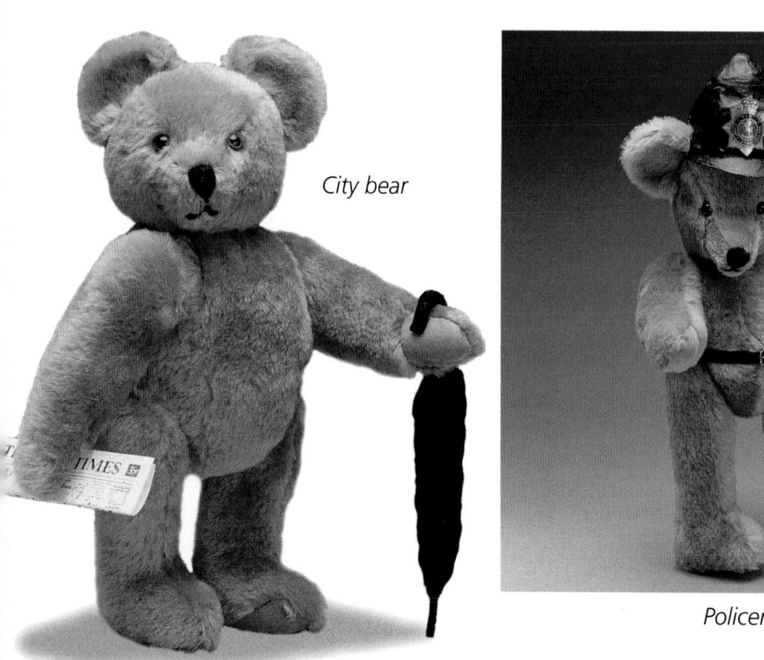

City bear

Policeman

Chef

THE TEACHER

THE TEACHER

The Teacher is an old-fashioned, gentle schoolmaster, 38cm (15in) tall. I have used crushed mohair to make him look old, but have also kept to minimal trimming round the snout to soften his expression. His waistcoat is the same style as those my great-grandfather used to wear, together with the watch chain. The books shown in the photograph used to belong to my grandmother.

MATERIALS

BEAR

- Crushed mohair 50 x 68cm (20 x 27in)
- Suedette 25 x 15cm (9¾ x 6in)
- 1 pair of soft brown, plastic safety eyes 1.6cm (⅝in) in diameter
- Strong sewing thread
- Black wool (for the nose and mouth)
- 5 joints 4.5cm (1¾in) in diameter
- Polyester stuffing 550g (20oz) approx.

ACCESSORIES

- Dark coloured, lightweight tweed 40 x 40cm (16 x 16in)
- Matching cotton thread
- Gold coloured necklace chain 8cm (3in) long
- 3 or 4 small black buttons (optional)
- Pair of glasses (available from most stockists of fur fabrics for bears)
- Old books

MAKING THE BEAR

TIP

Until you are familiar with the techniques of bear making you will need to refer regularly to the general instructions given in Chapter 4.

1. Using the pattern from pages 147–50, cut out all the pieces.

2. Cut the ear slits on the head gusset from B to E, and on the head from B to F. With right sides together, pin and then stitch the head pieces on either side of the head gusset from A to B.

3. Take two ear pieces and pin right sides together. Sew around the long curved edge from Z to Z and turn right sides out. Repeat for the second ear. Insert the ears into slot F to E. To give the ear shape, bend the edges (Z) towards the front middle of the ear by about 1cm (⅜in). Pin and overstitch the ears in place very securely.

4. Pin and stitch with right sides together on one side of the head only, from B to C (the other side must be left open for stuffing). Sew from A to D and turn the head right sides out.

5. Sew the nose and mouth with the black wool and position the eyes approximately 5cm (2in) from the tip of the nose.

6. Pin two leg pieces right sides together and sew from G over the top of the leg to H. Sew from K to J, leaving H to K open for stuffing. Repeat for the second leg.

7. Take the two soles of the paws cut from suedette and with right sides facing inwards, pin to the bottom of the legs, matching G to G and J to J. Sew securely all the way round. Turn both legs right sides out.

8. Snip the arm pieces at L as indicated on the pattern, then pin on the suedette paw pads, matching

at L and M and with right sides facing. Stitch from L to M. Open out the paw pads and fold over the arms, matching Q to Q and P to P with right sides facing. Pin and sew from L to Q and from P to W, leaving Q to P open for stuffing. Turn both arms right sides out.

9 With the right sides of the body pieces facing, pin and stitch together from V to T and from S to R, leaving T to S open for stuffing.

10 Assemble the bear as described in the general instructions (see pages 16–18).

Accessories

Waistcoat

> **TIP**
>
> The waistcoat is made of tweed and I have therefore cut down on the facings and linings as much as possible to reduce bulk. It is important to press with a damp cloth rather than straight on to the fabric, because this also helps reduce the bulk. Fit the waistcoat on the bear regularly while you are making it. The 'pockets' are very fiddly and could be left out if you wish, as could the buttons.

1 Fold the tweed fabric in half lengthways and with right sides together. Pin the waistcoat pattern pieces (see page 151) to the double material, taking care to ensure that the back is laid on the fold where indicated and that the front is cut out with special attention to the arrow indicating the straight of grain. Cut out the tweed facings in a similar way. It is a good idea to use pinking shears if you have them, as this will help to prevent fraying.

2 With right sides together, pin the facing on to the front pieces, matching points O, X and N. Sew from O, through X to N using backstitch or a sewing machine. Trim off the excess material at the corner X. Turn right sides out and press.

3 Take the front pieces and sew the dart on the wrong side as marked on the pattern. Turn right sides out and press downwards.

4 Sew the back and front together along the side seams with right sides together from # to U. (Do not sew from * to $ yet.) Press.

5 Turn up and pin a 3mm (⅛in) hem along the front and back on the wrong side, from N to N, and sew up using herringbone stitch (see Fig 9.1). Press flat.

6 Hem the back of the neck in the same way and press flat.

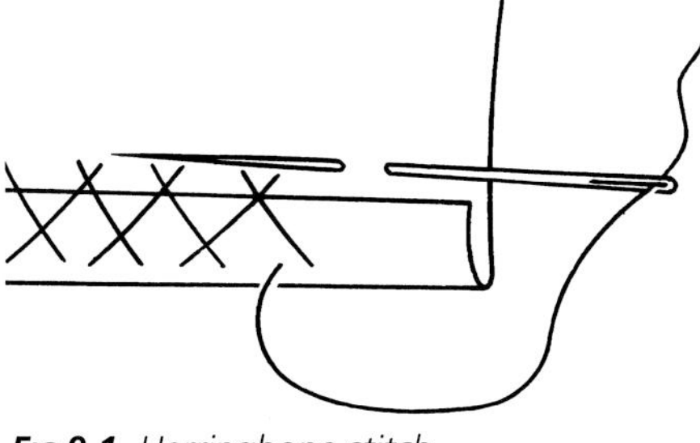

Fig 9.1 *Herringbone stitch.*

7 Fold back the lapel on to the right side so that O meets Y. With right sides together, pin the shoulder seam, so that the front and back of the waistcoat are joined from * to $. Sew and press, repeating for the other side.

8 Now hem the armhole using herringbone stitch and press flat.

9 Take the pocket pieces and, with right sides facing outwards, turn over the long raw edges and stitch them down. Turn the short ends under and stitch the pockets into place on the right side of the waistcoat. Press flat.

10 Press the lapels flat to the size and shape you prefer.

11 Put the waistcoat on the Teacher and stitch together at the front, then add the buttons, carefully covering any stitching which may show down the front.

12 Stitch on the gold coloured chain so that it stretches from pocket to pocket.

THE FARMER

The Farmer is the bulkiest bear in this book (although Ballet bear is taller, she is rather more dainty). He is 46cm (18in) tall and made from luxuriously long staple mohair. This size of bear is the largest which can be made with the joints available.

MATERIALS

BEAR

- Dark, long staple mohair 68 x 68cm (27 x 27in)
- Suedette 24 x 12cm (9½ x 4¾in)
- 1 pair of deep brown plastic safety eyes 1.2cm (½in) in diameter
- Strong sewing thread
- Black wool (for the nose and mouth)
- 5 joints 4.5cm (1¾in) in diameter
- Polyester stuffing 750g (26½oz) approx.

ACCESSORIES

- Strong garden wire 160cm (63in)
- Strips of newspaper
- Wallpaper paste
- Brown and black poster paint
- Spray-on clear acrylic lacquer
- 1 pair of green shop-bought wellington boots UK child size 3 (US size 4)

Making the Bear

TIP

Until you are familiar with the techniques of bear making you will need to refer regularly to the general instructions given in Chapter 4.

1. Using the pattern from pages 152–5, cut out all the pieces.

2. Cut the ear slits on the head gusset from B to C, and on the head from B to A. With the right sides together, pin and stitch the head pieces on either side of the head gusset from D to B.

3. Take two ear pieces and pin right sides together. Sew around the long curved edge from G to G and turn right sides out. Repeat for the second ear. To give the ears shape, bend just the edges (G) towards the centre front of the ear, no more than 1cm (⅜in). Insert the ears into slot A to C and pin. Overstitch each ear in place very securely.

4. Pin and stitch with right sides together on one side of the head only from B to E (leaving the other side open for stuffing). Sew from D to F and turn the head right sides out.

5. Sew the nose and mouth with the black wool and position the eyes approximately 5cm (2in) from the tip of the nose.

6. Pin two leg pieces right sides together and sew from N to O and from P round the top of the leg and down to Q. The section P to O will be left open for stuffing. Repeat for the second leg. Do not turn right sides out.

7. Take the sole of one paw cut from suedette and with the right sides facing inwards, pin on to the bottom of the leg, matching N to N and Q to Q. Sew around the paw and turn the leg right sides out. Repeat for the second leg.

8. Take a suedette paw pad and match H to H and J to J (right sides together) on one inner arm. Pin and sew from H to J. Flatten out the arm and, with right sides together, pin the inner arm to the outer arm and sew from K right around the arm to L. Leave L to K open for stuffing. Turn right sides out. Repeat for the second arm.

9. Pin together the two body pieces with right sides together and sew from S to T and from R round to V, leaving T to R open for stuffing. Turn right sides out.

10. Assemble the bear as described in the general instructions (see pages 16–18).

Accessories

Shepherd's crook

1. Bend the wire equally into three and twist all three strands together, then bend this into the traditional shepherd's crook shape.

2. Cover the wire with the wallpaper paste and strips of newspaper. Three layers of papier-mâché will be enough to make a crook of sufficient width. Leave to dry, then paint brown and leave to dry again. Use the black paint to make the crook look old and worn.

3. Cover the crook with two coats of spray-on acrylic lacquer, leaving to dry between the coats.

4. Finally stitch the crook on to one of the bear's paws so that its tip rests on the ground, and place the boots on his feet.

TIP

If the boots are too long, then turn them over at the top.

THE DOCTOR

The Doctor, standing 36cm (14in) tall, is unusual because he is made from loom state mohair. It is not easy to find, however, and normal medium length mohair can be used instead. The trick with the Doctor is to arrange his facial features in order to create an expression of kindly innocence.

MATERIALS

BEAR

- Loom state or medium staple mohair 50 x 68cm (20 x 27in)
- Suedette 20 x 12cm (8 x 4¾in)
- 1 pair of deep brown plastic safety eyes 1.2cm (½in) in diameter
- Strong sewing thread
- Black wool (for the nose and mouth)
- 5 joints 4.5cm (1¾in) in diameter
- Polyester stuffing 450g (1lb) approx.

ACCESSORIES

- Coaxial (electric) cable 30cm (12in)
- 2 wired paper ties (often supplied with bin liners)
- 1 small rubber suction pad (e.g. from the end of a toy arrow)
- Silver and black model paint
- Spray-on clear acrylic lacquer

Making the Bear

TIP

Until you are familiar with the techniques of bear making you will need to refer regularly to the general instructions given in Chapter 4.

1. Using the pattern from pages 156–8, cut out all the pieces.
2. Cut the ear slits on the head gusset from B to C, and on the head from B to A. With the right sides together, pin and stitch the head pieces on either side of the head gusset from D to B.
3. Take two ear pieces and pin right sides together. Sew around the long curved edge from G to G and turn right sides out. Repeat for the second ear. Insert the ears into slot A to C and pin. To give the ears shape, bend just the edges (G) towards the centre front of the ear, no more than 1cm (⅜in). Overstitch each ear in place very securely.
4. Pin and stitch with right sides together on one side of the head only from B to E (leaving the other side open for stuffing). Sew from D to F and turn the head right sides out.
5. Sew the nose and mouth with the black wool and position the eyes approximately 4.5cm (1¾in) from the tip of the nose.
6. Pin two leg pieces right sides together and sew from N to O and from P round the top of the leg and down to Q. The section P to O will be left open for stuffing. Repeat for the second leg. Do not turn right sides out.
7. Take the sole of one paw cut from suedette and with the right sides facing inwards, pin on to the bottom of the leg, matching N to N and Q to Q. Sew around the paw pad and turn the leg right sides out. Repeat for the second leg.

8 Snip the fabric on the arm pieces as shown at H on the pattern. Take the suedette paw pads and pin them to the arm pieces, matching H to H and J to J (right sides together). Sew from H to J. Fold the arms over right sides together and sew from K to L and from M to H. Leave K to M open for stuffing. Turn each arm right sides out.

9 Take the two side body pieces and pin with right sides together. Sew from U to T and catch the fabric together at S. Take the front body piece and match R to R and T to T on the side pieces. Pin and sew down both sides of the front from R to T. Leave S to U open for stuffing. Turn right sides out.

10 Assemble the bear as described in the general instructions (see pages 16–18).

Accessories

Stethoscope

1 Take the coaxial cable and remove the inner part. The outer section can be put to one side as it will not be used for the stethoscope.

2 Cut the inner part of the cable into three equal lengths of 10cm (4in). Remove 1cm (3⁄8in) of the outer covering from one end of two of the lengths. This exposes the wire. Twist the wire on the two lengths together, then push the twisted wire down into the end of the third length. Secure this joint by wrapping it around tightly with the wire ties.

3 Push the rubber suction pad into the other end of the third length (this can be secured with some PVA glue if necessary).

TIP

If you can, try to make sure that the other end of each of these two lengths has a matching bend from the way the cable was stored – to help the stethoscope sit comfortably round the Doctor's neck.

4 Paint the cable black and allow to dry.

5 Paint the rubber sucker, the joint and the two remaining ends (which are the ear pieces) silver. Allow to dry.

6 Spray with the acrylic clear lacquer, allow to dry and then put on a second coat. Allow to dry once again before hanging the stethoscope around the Doctor's neck.

TIP

This stethoscope is only designed to hang around the bear's neck. If you wish to put the ear pieces in his ears, different proportions for the stethoscope need to be used. You will have to measure your own bear for this, but roughly 2 to 3cm (approx 1in) will need to be added to two of the lengths of cable.

THE POLICEMAN

THE POLICEMAN

The Policeman is a particularly distinctive bear with a fine, long snout and elegantly long limbs. He is made of short staple mohair and measures 38cm (15in) or 43cm (17in) with his helmet on.

MATERIALS

BEAR

- Short staple mohair 60 x 68cm (24 x 27in)
- Suedette 22 x 18cm (8¾ x 7in)
- 1 pair of deep brown plastic safety eyes 1.2cm (½in) in diameter
- Strong sewing thread
- Black wool (for the nose and mouth)
- 5 joints 4.5cm (1¾in) in diameter
- Polyester stuffing 500g (17oz) approx.

ACCESSORIES

- Bowl (to fit the bear's head)
- Plasticine
- Vaseline
- Strips of newspaper
- Wallpaper paste
- PVA glue
- Strips of white paper
- Card 15 x 15cm (6 x 6in) (a cereal packet works well)
- Silver, navy blue and black model or poster paints
- Spray-on clear acrylic lacquer
- 15cm (6in) length of black ribbon 5mm (3/16in) wide
- Black embroidery thread
- 40cm (16in) length of leather or plastic 1cm (⅜in) wide (for the belt)
- Buckle to fit the belt (I used a buckle from a discarded watch strap)

MAKING THE BEAR

TIP

Until you are familiar with the techniques of bear making you will need to refer regularly to the general instructions given in Chapter 4.

❶ Using the pattern from pages 159–61, cut out all the pieces.

❷ Cut the ear slits on the head gusset from B to C, and on the head from B to A. With the right sides together, pin and stitch the head pieces on either side of the head gusset from D to B.

❸ Take two ear pieces and pin right sides together. Sew around the long curved edge from G to G and turn right sides out. Repeat for the second ear. Insert the ears into slot A to C and pin. To give the ears shape, bend just the edges (G) towards the centre front of the ear, no more than 1cm (⅜in). Overstitch each ear in place very securely.

❹ Pin and stitch with right sides together on one side of the head only from B to E (leaving the other side open for stuffing). Sew from D to F, and turn the head right sides out.

5 Sew the nose and mouth with the black wool and position the eyes approximately 5cm (2in) from the tip of the nose.

6 Pin two leg pieces right sides together and sew from N to O and from P round the top of the leg and down to Q. The section P to O will be left open for stuffing. Repeat for the second leg. Do not turn right sides out.

7 Take the sole of one paw cut from suedette and with the right sides facing inwards, pin on to the bottom of the leg, matching N to N and Q to Q. Sew around the paw and turn right sides out. Repeat for the second leg.

8 Take the suedette paw pads and pin to the inner arms, matching H to H and J to J (right sides together). Sew from H to J. Pin the inner arms to the outer arms, right sides together, and sew from K right around each arm to L. Leave K to L open for stuffing. Turn the arms right sides out.

9 Pin together the two body pieces, right sides together, and sew from S to T and from R to W, leaving T to R open for stuffing. Turn right sides out.

10 Assemble the bear as described in the general instructions (see pages 16–18).

ACCESSORIES

Helmet

1 Take the bowl as the base for a mould and add plasticine to the top to make the shape of a policeman's helmet.

2 Cover the mould liberally with Vaseline (to aid removal of the finished papier-mâché helmet) and then cover with strips of newspaper soaked in wallpaper paste. Three layers will be sufficient to make the helmet. Leave to dry (about 24 hours on a radiator, or 48 hours without extra heat).

3 Remove the helmet from its mould. This may be a little difficult and if the shape has to be torn slightly during the removal process, repairs can be made with more newspaper and glue. Leave to dry again if necessary.

4 Place on the head of the Policeman and mark where the ears are. Cut out a triangle shape from the helmet to accommodate each ear.

5 Using the pattern from page 161, cut out the brims of the helmet in cardboard and glue to the front and back of the helmet with PVA glue. The 'teeth' should be stuck on the inside of the helmet. Use clothes pegs to keep the brim in place while the glue is drying.

TIP

Depending on the size of your finished helmet, the size and/or shape of the brims may need altering to suit.

6 Cover the whole helmet with strips of the white paper and leave to dry. This will help the paint to 'take' evenly.

7 Paint with two coats of navy blue paint, making sure that each coat is left to dry before continuing.

8 Varnish with two coats of spray-on clear acrylic lacquer, leaving to dry between coats.

9 Cut out a badge from paper and paint it silver. I was fortunate enough to obtain a badge sticker from my local police station which turned out to be just the right size.

Truncheon

1 Roll up a 7cm ($2\frac{3}{4}$in) length of newspaper and then build up with paper strips and paste to create a truncheon shape. Leave to dry.

2 Paint the truncheon with two coats of black paint, allowing each coat to dry.

3 Varnish with spray-on clear lacquer as for the helmet, leaving to dry between the two coats.

4 Glue the ribbon in a loop on to the thin end of the truncheon.

5 Wrap the black embroidery thread around the thin end to mark out the handle and glue down the end of the thread. The truncheon can be hung over the Policeman's paw.

Belt

1 Place the buckle on one end of the strip of leather or plastic, make a hole with a large darning needle and insert the buckle spoke. Staple in position.

2 Put the belt around the bear's waist and find the right position for the hole. Make the hole with a darning needle.

TIP

If you wish to hang the truncheon on the Policeman's belt, halve the length of the ribbon.

THE CHEF

The Chef is a 40cm (16in) bear. His ears are positioned quite forward on his head and his chin is slightly raised as though he is gazing up for inspiration. Having ears slightly forward has the practical advantage of accommodating his chef's hat without hiding the ears.

MATERIALS

BEAR

- Long staple, man-made fur fabric 60 x 68cm (24 x 27in)
- Suedette 20 x 12cm (8 x 4¾in)
- 1 pair of deep brown plastic safety eyes 1.2cm (½in) in diameter
- Strong sewing thread
- Black wool (for the nose and mouth)
- 5 joints 4.5cm (1¾in) in diameter
- Polyester stuffing 500g (17oz) approx.

ACCESSORIES

- White cotton fabric 25 x 50cm (9¾ x 20in)
- White cotton thread
- Miniature rolling pin 15cm (6in) long (I bought mine from a souvenir shop, but toy shops also stock such items)

Making the Bear

TIP

Until you are familiar with the techniques of bear making you will need to refer regularly to the general instructions given in Chapter 4.

1. Using the pattern from pages 162–5, cut out all the pieces.

2. Cut the ear slits on the head gusset from B to C, and on the head from B to A. With the right sides together, pin and stitch the head pieces on either side of the head gusset from D to B.

3. Take two ear pieces and pin right sides together. Sew around the long curved edge from G to G and turn right sides out. Repeat for the second ear. Insert the ears into slot A to C and pin. To give the ears shape, bend just the edges (G) towards the centre front of the ear, no more than 1cm (⅜in). Overstitch each ear in place very securely.

4. Pin and stitch with right sides together on one side of the head only from B to E (leaving the other side open for stuffing). Sew from D to F and turn the head right sides out.

5. Sew the nose and mouth with the black wool, flattening out the mouth so that it is smiling upwards. Position the eyes approximately 5cm (2in) from the tip of the nose.

6. Fold over one of the leg pieces with right sides together, matching Q to Q, and pin and sew from Q round the top of the leg to P. The section N to O will be left open for stuffing. Make sure the fabric is fastened together, with a stitch if necessary, at N. Repeat for the second leg. Do not turn right sides out.

7 Take the sole of one paw cut from suedette and with the right sides facing inwards, pin and sew on to the bottom of the leg, matching N to N and Q to Q. Turn right sides out and repeat for the second leg.

8 Snip the fabric on the arm pieces as shown at H on the pattern. Take the suedette paw pads and pin to the arms, matching H to H and J to J (right sides together). Sew from H to J.

9 Fold the arms over with right sides together and pin and sew from K to L and from M to H, leaving L to M open for stuffing. Turn right sides out.

10 Pin together the two body pieces, right sides together, and sew from S to T and from R to W, leaving T to R open for stuffing. Turn right sides out.

11 Assemble the bear as described in the general instructions (see pages 16–18).

Accessories

Chef's hat

1 Cut two rectangles from the white cotton fabric, one measuring 28 x 10cm (11 x 4in) for the headband and one measuring 50 x 15cm (19⅝ x 6in) for the crown of the hat.

2 Take the fabric for the headband and fold it in half so that the band measures 28 x 5cm (11 x 2in). Sew the two short edges together to make a ring. Turn the ring the other way out so that the seam ends up on the inside of the ring.

3 Now take the fabric for the crown of the hat and with right sides together sew up the short edge to make a cylinder.

4 Gather both the top and bottom of this cylinder, then fit the lower edge on to the raw edge of the headband and sew it into position with backstitch.

5 Pull the gathering at the crown's top edge tightly together so that all the raw edges are on the wrong side. Fasten the thread off securely.

6 If necessary, stuff the hat with a little white tissue paper to make it stand tall.

7 Place the hat on the bear's head and catch it in place with a few discreet stitches.

City Bear

City Bear

City Bear is made from sober, short staple mohair, and is ready for work with his rolled umbrella and a newspaper to read on the train. He stands 38cm (15in) tall.

MATERIALS

BEAR

- Short staple mohair 60 x 68cm (24 x 27in)
- Suedette 20 x 12cm (8 x 4¾in)
- 1 pair of deep brown plastic safety eyes 1.2cm (½in) in diameter
- Strong sewing thread
- Black wool (for the nose and mouth)
- 5 joints 4.5cm (1¾in) in diameter
- Polyester stuffing 550g (20oz) approx.

ACCESSORIES

- Strong garden wire 50cm (20in)
- Strips of newspaper
- Wallpaper paste
- Black embroidery thread
- Black felt 30 x 30cm (12 x 12in)
- Black model or poster paint
- Spray-on clear acrylic lacquer
- PVA glue
- Photocopy of a page from a newspaper (reduced in size)

Making the Bear

TIP

Until you are familiar with the techniques of bear making you will need to refer regularly to the general instructions given in Chapter 4.

1. Using the pattern from pages 166–9, cut out all the pieces.

2. Cut the ear slits on the head gusset from B to C, and on the head from B to A. With the right sides together, pin and stitch the head pieces on either side of the head gusset from D to B.

3. Take two ear pieces and pin right sides together. Sew around the long curved edge from G to G and turn right sides out. Repeat for the second ear. Insert the ears into slot A to C and pin. To give the ears shape, bend just the edges (G) towards the centre front of the ear, no more than 1cm (⅜in). Overstitch each ear in place very securely.

4. Pin and stitch with right sides together on one side of the head only from B to E (leaving the other side open for stuffing). Sew from D to F and turn the head right sides out.

5. Sew the nose and mouth with the black wool and position the eyes approximately 4.5cm (1¾in) from the tip of the nose.

6. Pin two leg pieces right sides together and sew from N to O and from P round the top of the leg and down to Q. The section P to O will be left open for stuffing. Repeat for the second leg. Do not turn right sides out.

7. Take the sole of one paw cut from suedette and with the right

sides facing inwards, pin on to the bottom of the leg, matching N to N and Q to Q. Sew around the paw and turn right sides out. Repeat for the second leg.

8 Snip the fabric on the arm pieces as shown at H in the pattern. Pin the suedette paw pads to the arms, matching H to H and J to J (right sides together). Sew from H to J. Fold the arms over right sides together and pin and sew from K to L and from M to H. Leave L to M open for stuffing. Turn the arms right sides out.

9 Pin together the two side body pieces, right sides together, and sew from S to U. Take the front body and match R to R and T to T on the side body pieces. Sew down both sides of the body front from R to T, leaving U to T open for stuffing. Turn right sides out.

10 Assemble the bear as described in the general instructions (see pages 16–18).

Accessories

Umbrella

1 Take the wire and bend it in half. Shape the top into the U shape of an umbrella handle.

2 Cover with strips of newspaper soaked in wallpaper paste, making about three layers. Leave the papier-mâché to dry.

3 Paint the umbrella black, leave to dry and add another coat.

4 Spray with two coats of clear lacquer, leaving to dry after each coat.

5 Cover the handle with PVA glue and wrap around the black embroidery thread.

6 Take the square of black felt and cut out a circle with a diameter of 30cm (12in). I used a suitably sized tray as a template.

7 Make a hole in the centre of the circle and insert the spoke of the umbrella. Use a dab of PVA glue to secure the felt 2.5cm (1in) from the top of the spoke.

8 Pleat the felt near the handle and then wrap it around like the folds of an umbrella. Wrap around some black embroidery thread and secure with a stitch.

9 Hang the umbrella over City Bear's paw.

Newspaper

For the newspaper you will need access to a photocopier (most newsagents now have one). I reduced down the front page of my newspaper again and again until I was happy with the size – about 14cm (5½in) across. Fold the paper and tuck under City Bear's arm.

TIP

The newspaper could be fixed to the bear's paw with a discreet stitch.

10 National Bear

American

Irish

Scottish

British

English

Welsh

Australian

National Bear

National bear is a friendly-looking character made of man-made fur fabric, 36cm (14in) tall. The same pattern is used for all the bears shown in the photographs, with different accessories being created to suit the nationality you wish to represent. Of course, the bear's expression can also be altered for different effects.

MATERIALS

BEAR

- Man-made fur fabric 55 x 68cm (22 x 27in)
- Suedette 20 x 12cm (8 x 4¾in)
- 1 pair of deep brown plastic safety eyes 1.2cm (½in) in diameter
- Strong sewing thread
- Black wool (for the nose and mouth)
- 5 joints 4.5cm (1¾in) in diameter
- Polyester stuffing 500g (17oz) approx.

ACCESSORIES

SCOTTISH PLAID

- Cotton check fabric in the style of tartan, or real tartan fabric if the pattern is small enough, 40 x 70cm (16 x 28in) – the pattern must be in proportion to the size of the bear
- 1 brass button (for 'Celtic' style brooch)

IRISH SHAMROCK

- Dark, medium and light green felt, 20 x 20cm (8 x 8in) of each
- Dark green cotton thread
- Safety pin 3cm (1⅛in) long

WELSH DAFFODIL

- 1 pipe cleaner
- Green felt 17 x 1.5cm (6¾ x ⅝in)
- Yellow felt 12 x 12cm (4¾ x 4¾in)
- Green and yellow cotton thread to match
- Orange felt 7 x 7cm (2¾ x 2¾in)
- 4 artificial, double-ended stamens (available from most art shops)

ENGLISH TABARD

- White felt 20 x 15cm (8 x 6in)
- 80cm (31½in) length of red ribbon 1.5cm (⅝in) wide
- White and red cotton thread to match
- 25cm (9¾in) length of white ribbon 1cm (⅜in) wide
- Velcro 8cm (3⅛in)

BRITISH COSTUME

- Blue felt 26 x 17cm (10¼ x 6¾in)
- 30cm (12in) length of red ribbon 1.5cm (⅝in) wide
- 45cm (18in) length red ribbon 5mm (3/16in) wide
- 30cm (12in) length of white ribbon 2.2cm (⅞in) wide
- 45cm (18in) length of white ribbon 1.2cm (½in) wide
- Red and white cotton thread to match
- Dark coloured Velcro 6cm (2⅜in)
- Dark cotton to match
- Navy or dark blue lining fabric 70 x 12cm (2¾ x 4¾in) or 30 x 24cm (12 x 9½in)
- Blue cotton thread to match

AMERICAN HAT

- Card (cereal packets are ideal) big enough to provide rectangles of 30 x 12cm (12 x 4¾in) 18 x 18cm (7 x 7in) and 10 x 10cm (4 x 4in)
- Blue cartridge paper of same dimensions as card
- Red shiny paper 10 x 12cm (4 x 4¾in)
- 1 packet of silver stars (I used two differently sized stars, but this is not essential)
- 30cm (12in) length of silver braid 1cm (⅜in) wide
- PVA glue
- Clothes pegs (for holding paper in place during gluing)

AUSTRALIAN HAT

- Brown felt 40 x 30cm (16 x 12in)
- Cotton thread to match
- Card 10 x 7cm (4 x 2¾in)
- Wine bottle cork
- Strong thread (as used for making the bears)

Making the Bear

TIP

Until you are familiar with the techniques of bear making you will need to refer regularly to the general instructions given in Chapter 4.

1. Using the pattern from pages 170–2, cut out all the pieces.

2. Cut the ear slits on the head gusset from B to C, and on the head from B to A. With the right sides together, pin and stitch the head pieces on either side of the head gusset from D to B.

3. Take two ear pieces and pin right sides together. Sew around the long curved edge from G to G and turn right sides out. Repeat for the second ear. Insert the ears into slot A to C and pin. To give the ears shape, bend just the edges (G) towards the centre front of the ear, no more than 1cm (⅜in). Overstitch each ear in place very securely.

4. Pin and stitch with right sides together on one side of the head only from B to E (leaving the other side open for stuffing). Sew from D to F and turn the head right sides out.

5. Sew the nose and mouth with the black wool and position the eyes approximately 4.5cm (1¾in) from the tip of the nose.

6. Pin two leg pieces right sides together and sew from N to O and from P round the top of the leg and down to Q. The section P to O will be left open for stuffing. Repeat for the second leg. Do not turn right sides out.

7. Take the sole of one paw cut from suedette and with the right sides facing inwards, pin on to the bottom of the leg, matching N to N and Q to Q. Sew around the sole and turn the leg right sides out. Repeat for the second leg.

8. Take an inner arm and a suedette paw pad and match H to H and J to J (right sides together). Pin and sew from H to J. Now pin an inner and outer arm right sides together and sew from K right around the arm to L. Leave K to L open for stuffing. Turn right sides out. Repeat for the second arm.

9. Pin together the two body pieces, right sides together, and sew from S to T and from V to W, leaving T to V open for stuffing. Turn right sides out.

10. Assemble the bear as described in the general instructions (see pages 16–18).

Accessories

Scottish plaid

1. Fray one of the short ends of the tartan fabric.

2. Now drape the fabric round the bear. (It should go over the left shoulder and under the right arm,

meeting at the back.) Pleat the fabric on the shoulder and hold it in place with a pin. Bring the material under the right arm and round the back to join up with the main part of the plaid which is hanging down from the left shoulder. Hold temporarily in place with another pin.

3 When you are satisfied with the arrangement of the fabric, slip stitch the plaid in place.

4 Sew the button on to the shoulder as decoration after stitching the pleats in place and removing the pin.

Irish shamrock

1 Using the pattern on page 173, cut out eight to ten shamrock shapes in each shade of green felt (making about 30 in all).

2 Sew a 5cm (2in) length of green cotton thread to the middle of each shape.

3 Tie all the threads together and fasten the bunch on to the safety pin. Pin this on to the bear's chest.

Welsh daffodil

1 Using the pattern on page 173, cut out the daffodil flower shape in yellow felt. Fold over along the solid lines indicated in Fig 10.1 (lines a, b and c) and make a running stitch on the edge of these folds. Turn the felt over and do the same on the other side for the dotted lines d, e and f. The running stitch will hold the folds in place.

2 Cut out the trumpet in orange felt and fold in half to match g to g. Oversew from g to h to make a flat seam.

3 Cover the pipe cleaner in the green felt, oversewing down the long edge and at the ends.

4 Fold the stamens in half and sew to one end of the pipe cleaner.

5 Insert the point of the trumpet (h) into the middle of the daffodil flower.

6 Push the end of the stem without the stamens through the trumpet and the flower and pull through until the stamens are placed inside the trumpet. When in place, stitch securely to hold all the parts of the flower together.

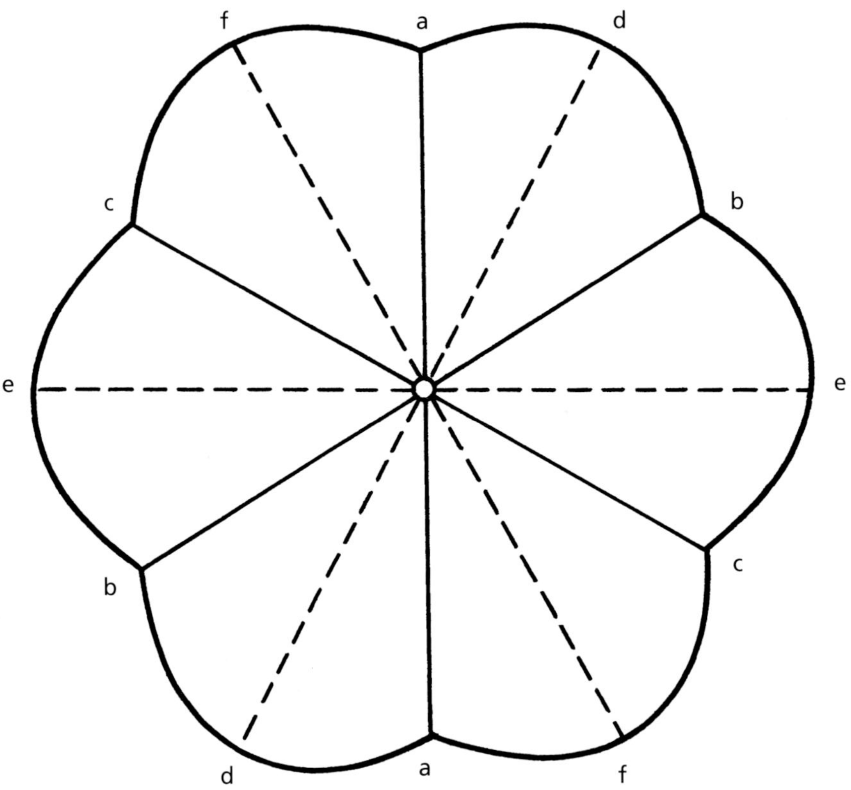

FIG 10.1 The fold lines for the Welsh daffodil flower.

English tabard

1 Using the pattern on page 173, cut out two tabard shapes in white felt.

2 Cut the lengths of red ribbon for the crosses to go on the front and back of the tabard. The vertical pieces should be cut 1cm (3/8in) longer than the tabard. The horizontal stripes should be cut 16cm (6¼in) longer than the width of the tabard, to allow 8cm (3⅛in) free on either side to fasten the tabard round the bear's body.

3 Pin the ribbon in place on each tabard piece and slip stitch with red thread, turning over 1cm (3/8in) of the vertical stripes on to the wrong side of the felt at top and bottom.

4 Neaten the ends of the ribbon on the horizontal stripes with a small hem, then stitch on the Velcro so that when the side ribbons are overlapped and fastened the tabard will fit closely to the bear's body.

5 Now cut two lengths of white ribbon for the shoulder straps and sew in place on the wrong side of the front shoulder edges. Sew the other end of one of the ribbons to the wrong side of the back shoulder edge. On the other end of the second ribbon sew one half of a small piece of Velcro and sew the other half of the Velcro to the wrong side of the second back shoulder edge. The tabard will then be easy to put on and take off the bear.

British costume

1 Using the pattern on page 174, cut out two waistcoat fronts (one in reverse) in blue felt and two (one in reverse) in blue lining material. Also cut two backs from the lining material.

2 Lay the felt waistcoat fronts down on a work surface and arrange the various ribbons on them as shown in Fig 10.2. Pin and sew each ribbon in place with slip stitch in thread to match the ribbon.

3 To put the waistcoat together, take one of the lining backs and the two felt fronts and with right sides together match j to j and k to k. Backstitch at the shoulders from j to k and under the arms from m to n.

4 Make up the lining by joining the shoulders and under the arms in the same way as in step 3.

Fig 10.2 *The arrangement of the ribbons for the British costume waistcoat.*

5 Pin the waistcoat to the lining with right sides together and backstitch from n to o up to p and along to j, across the back to q, up the other side to j, down the front and through p and o and on to n.

6 Turn right sides out and press. Tuck the raw edges along the bottom on to the wrong side (i.e. between the lining and the waistcoat), pin and slip stitch from n through r and across to n on the other side. Do the same around the armholes and press before putting the waistcoat on the bear.

American hat

TIP

However carefully you have followed the pattern, your bear will not be exactly the same size and shape as mine. Consequently you may have to make minor adjustments to the hat in order to achieve a perfect fit. The clothes pegs are used to hold the pieces of card and paper in place while they are drying. It frees your hands to be doing other things. PVA glue is used throughout for the American hat.

1 Cut out a rectangle from the card measuring 28 x 11cm (11 x 4¼in). Glue the short edges together to form a cylinder.

2 Cut out the front and back brims of the hat from card, using the pattern on page 175. Carefully cut around the 'teeth' of the brims. Glue the brims to the cylinder, folding the 'teeth' over on to the inside.

3 Cut out the crown of the hat from card and snip out the 'teeth'. Stick the crown on to the hat, folding up the 'teeth' so that they stick to the inside of the cylinder.

4 At this stage, try the hat on the bear's head and cut out two triangles to make room for the ears. You may need to trim the brims of the hat as well.

5 Now the hat must be covered with the blue paper. Cut out the crown of the hat first and this time stick the 'teeth' on the outside of the hat. Next cover the upper side of the brims with blue paper, using the pattern on page 176. The 'teeth' on the inside edge of the brim should be stuck to the outside of the cylinder; those on the outside edge should be folded under to the underside of the card brim. Cover the underside of the brim with blue paper that fits exactly and has no 'teeth' at all. You must cut this to fit your own hat. Now cover the main cylinder of the hat with the blue paper. The 'teeth' from the brim and crown of the hat will be hidden by this.

6 Decorate the hat by gluing on strips of red shiny paper and silver stars.

7 Glue on the silver braid last of all, taking care to hide the ends neatly on the inside of the hat.

Australian hat

1 Cut the felt into two rectangles of 20 x 30cm (8 x 12in). These pieces of felt need to be glued together with PVA glue. Spread the glue over one piece of felt as if you are spreading butter. Place the other piece on top and press down with a large book for five minutes.

TIP

As with the American hat, it may be necessary to make slight alterations to the size and shape in order for it to fit your bear perfectly.

TIP

The hat must be made while the PVA glue is still wet. This will enable you to mould the finished hat to the desired shape.

2 Using the pattern from page 177, cut one main piece from the double layer of felt. Place the ends together, matching s to s and t to t. Oversew from s to t to form a flat seam.

3 Cut out the felt crown, and oversew in place, matching t to t. Cut out the card crown and slip this inside the hat to help the felt crown keep its shape.

4 Cut out and sew on the front and back brims.

5 Mould the hat to fit the bear's head and leave to dry completely.

6 Cut the cork into nine sections to be sewn around the brim. Stitch on with strong sewing thread so that they dangle from the brim. Take care to ensure that they are evenly spaced, with five at the front and four at the back.

Part Three
Full-Size Patterns

indicates space to leave open for stuffing

indicates ear slits

indicates a dart

indicates fold lines

indicates position of facing

indicates direction of pile

indicates position of joint

NOTE: all patterns include a 3mm (1/8in) seam allowance.

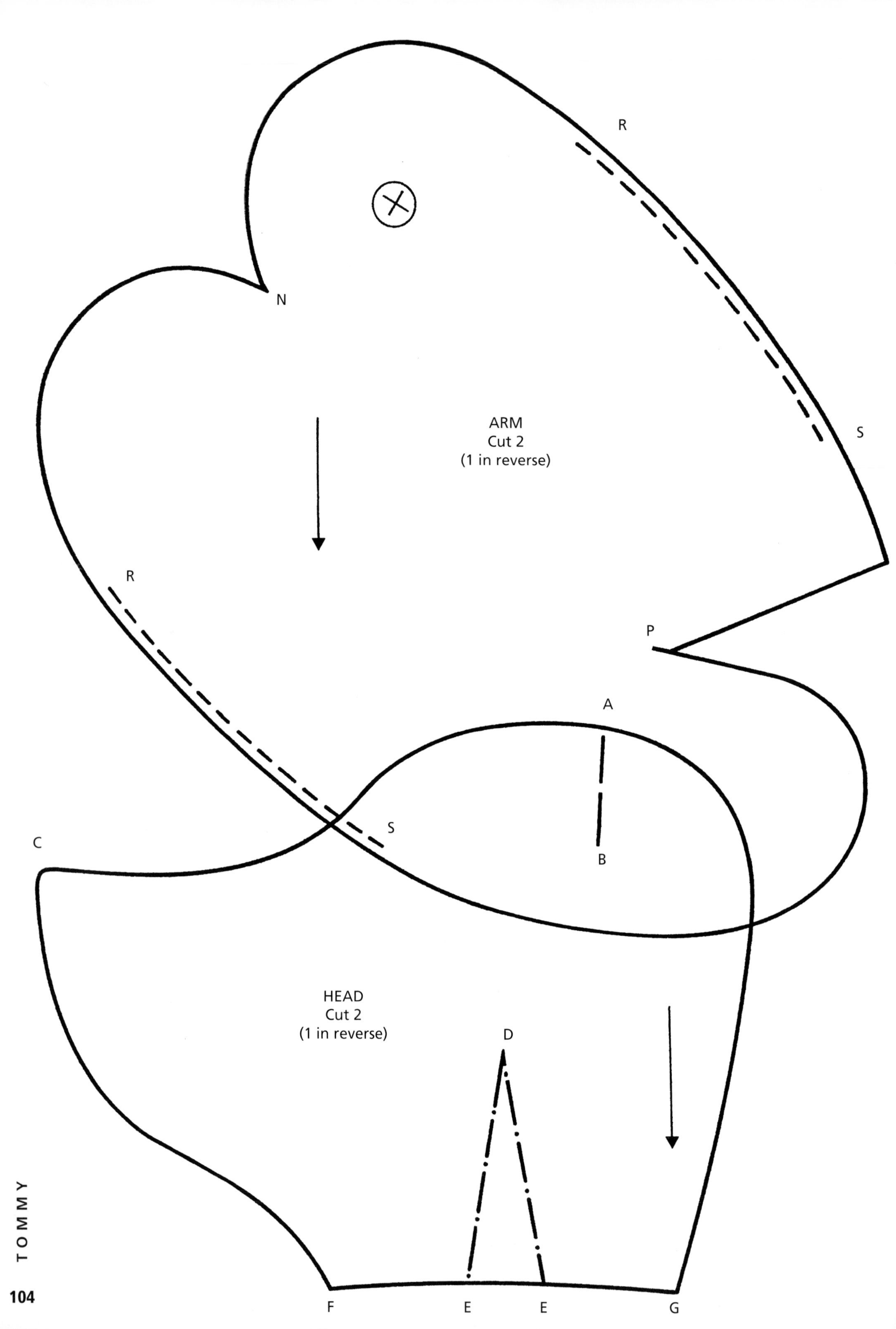
R
N
ARM
Cut 2
(1 in reverse)
S
R
P
A
S
C
B
HEAD
Cut 2
(1 in reverse)
D
F
E
E
G

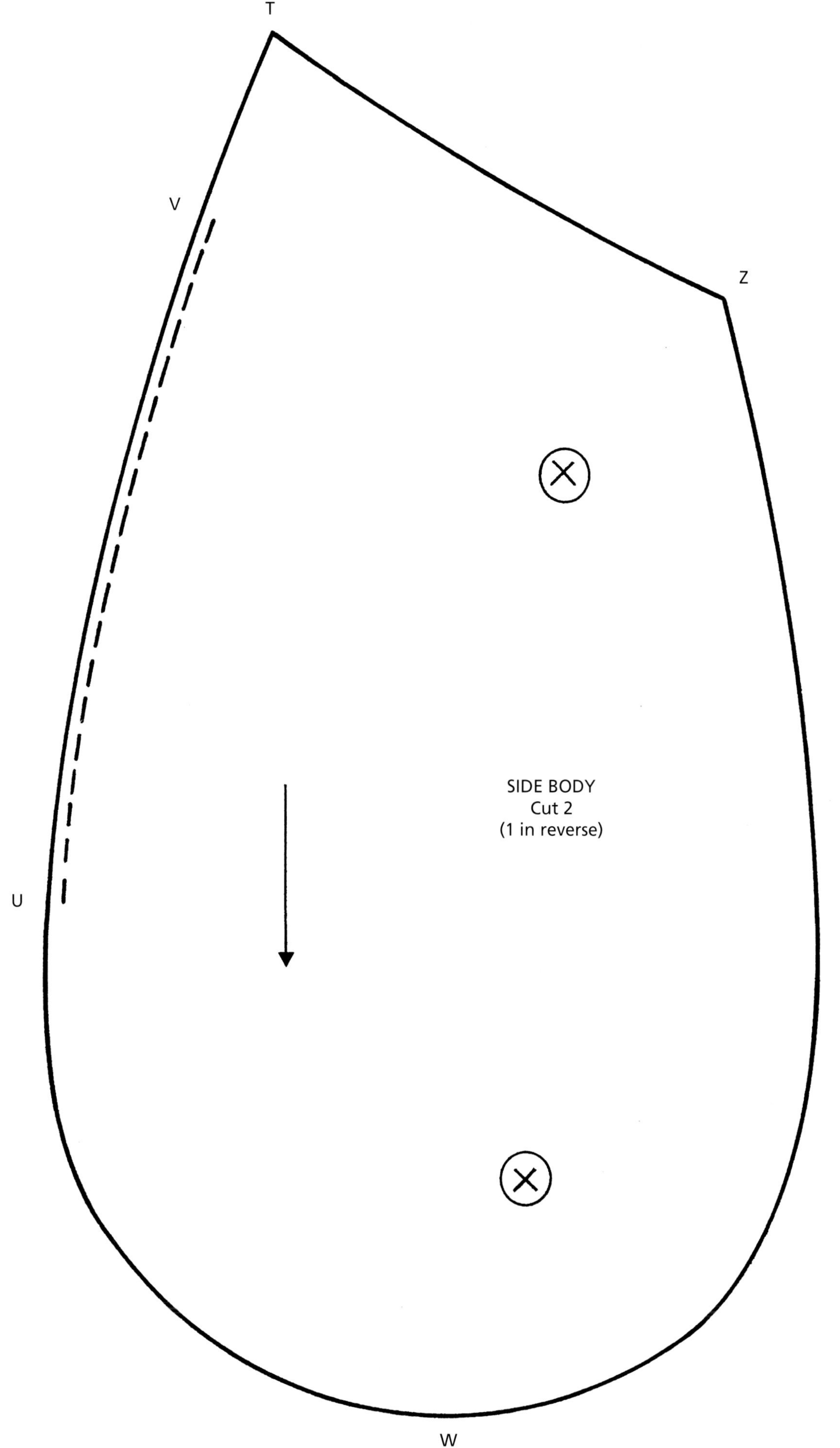
T
V
Z
SIDE BODY
Cut 2
(1 in reverse)
U
W

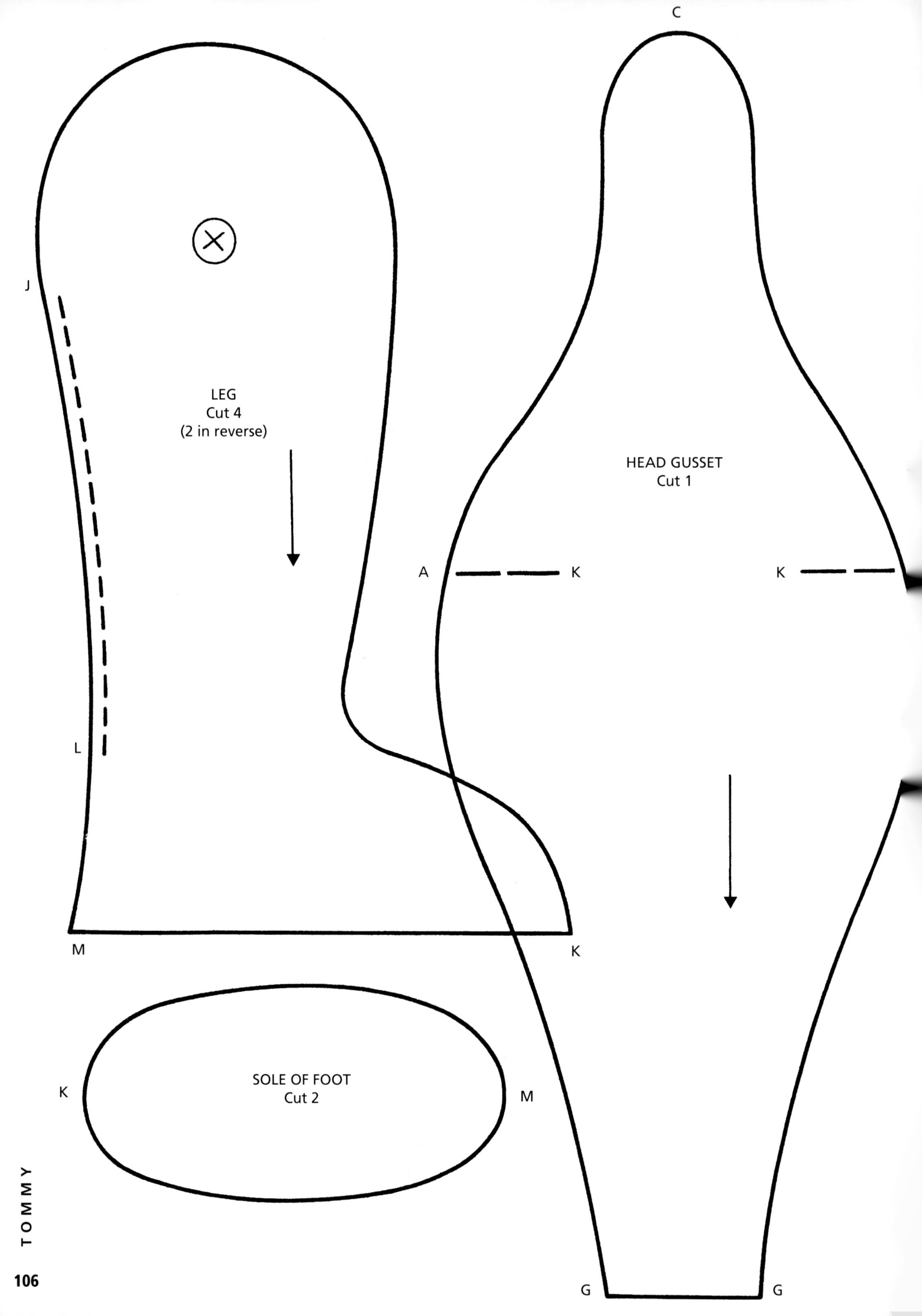
C
J
LEG
Cut 4
(2 in reverse)
L
M
K
HEAD GUSSET
Cut 1
A
K
K
K
SOLE OF FOOT
Cut 2
M
G
G

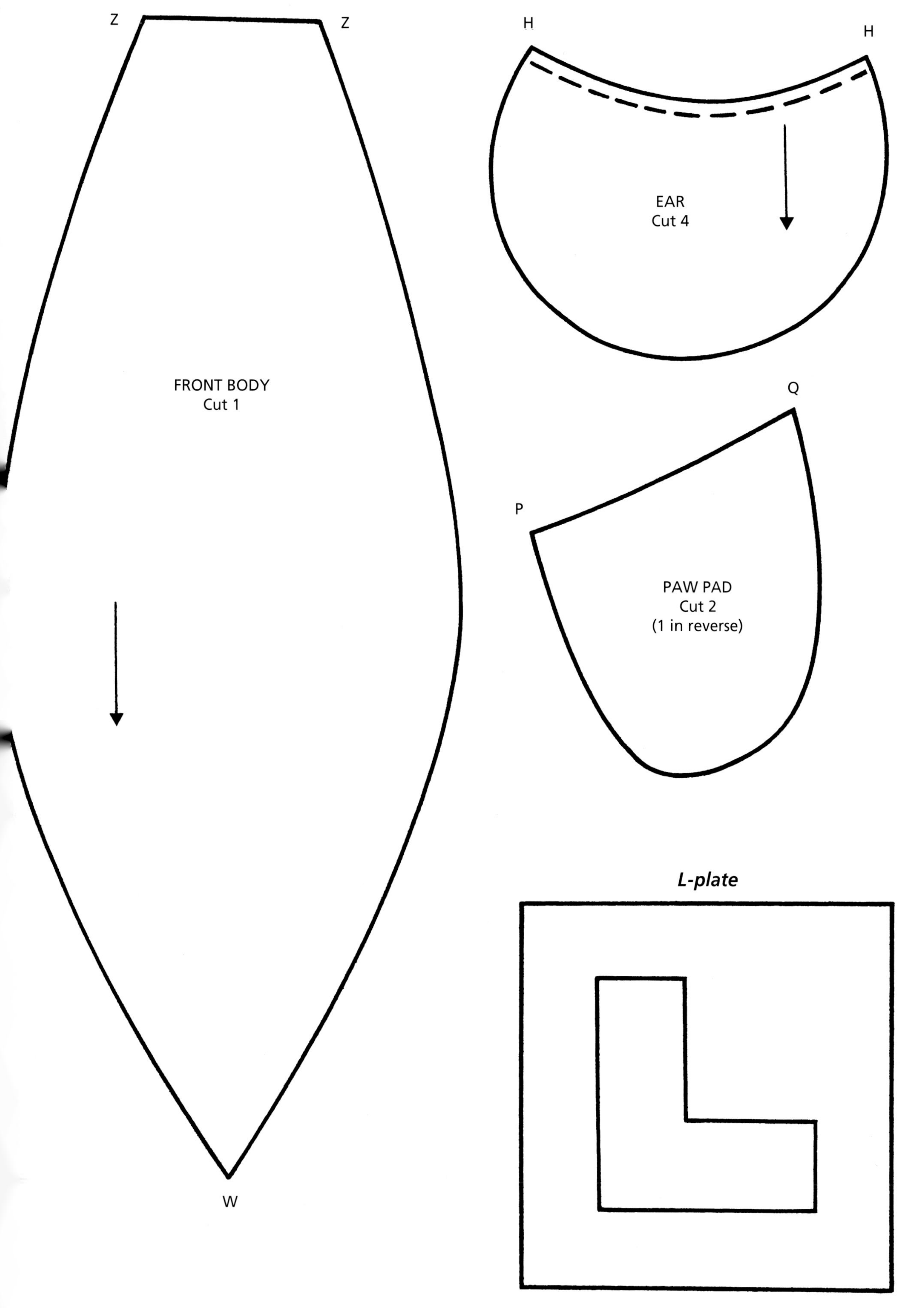
Z
Z
FRONT BODY
Cut 1
W
H
H
EAR
Cut 4
Q
P
PAW PAD
Cut 2
(1 in reverse)
L-plate

Anniversary cushion designs

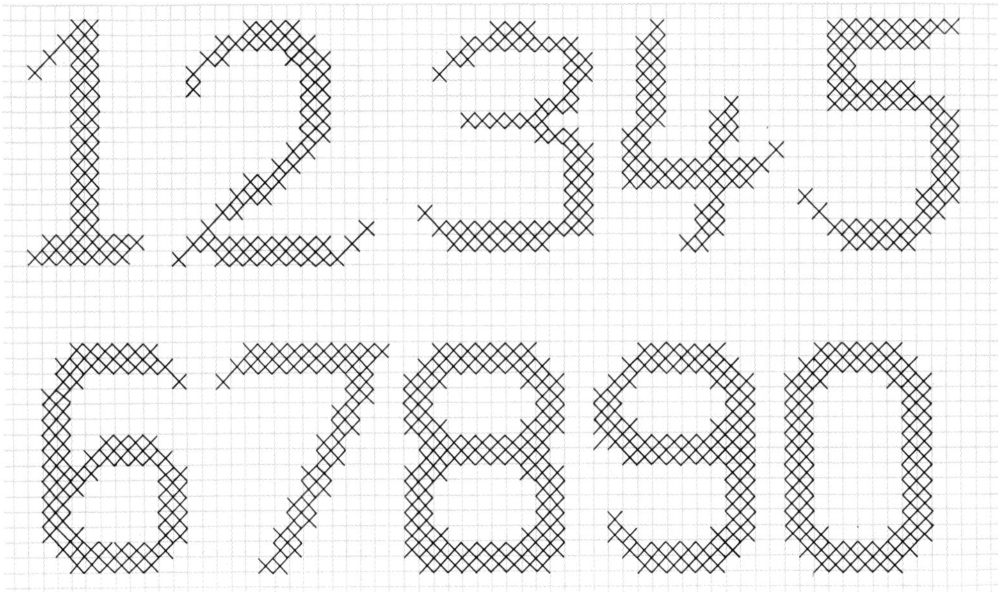

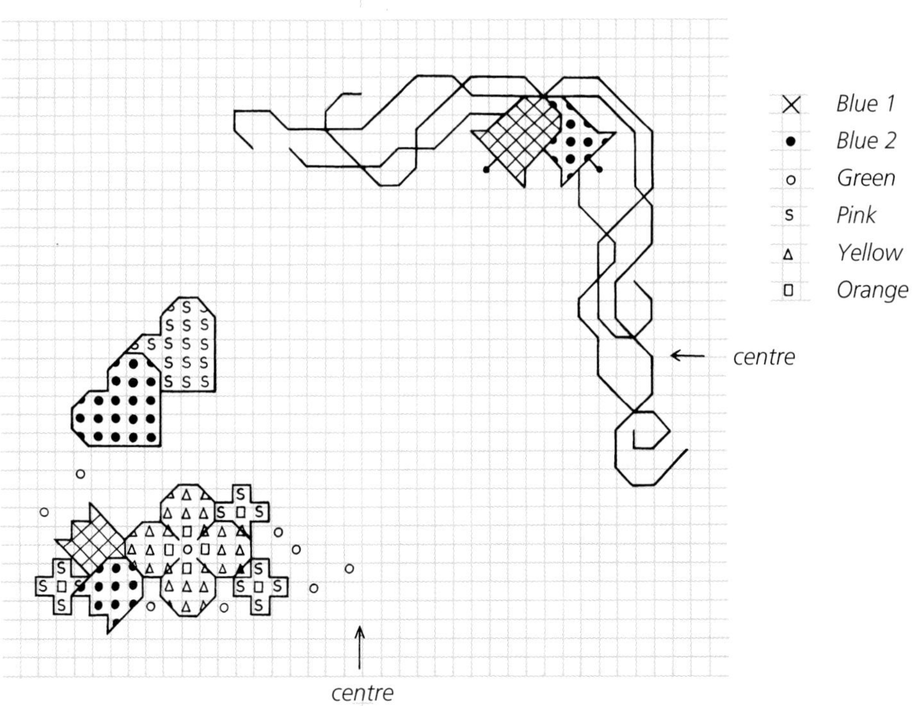

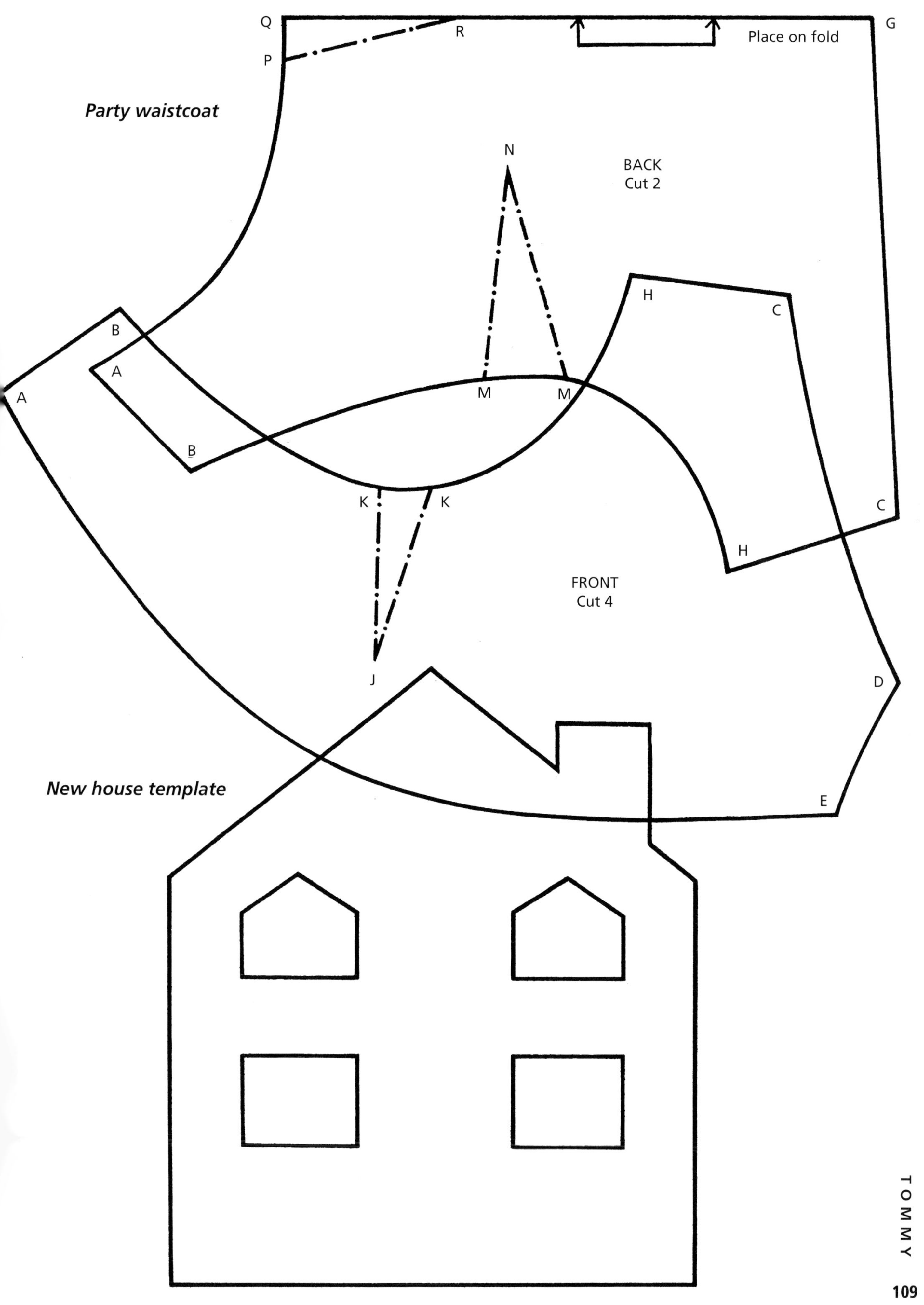
Q
R
G
Place on fold
P
Party waistcoat
N
BACK
Cut 2
H
C
B
A
A
M
M
B
K
K
C
H
FRONT
Cut 4
J
D
New house template
E

LEG
Cut 2
(1 in reverse)
F
Y
H
G
Z
G
HEAD
Cut 2
(1 in reverse)
Eye
D
B
A
W
E
HEAD GUSSET
Cut 1
D
B
C
C
B
E
E
BODY
Cut 2
(1 in reverse)
P
S
R
Q
PAW PAD
Cut 2
(1 in reverse)
L
M
SOLE OF FOOT
Cut 2
Z
G
EAR
Cut 4
V
V
ARM
Cut 2
(1 in reverse)
N
O
M
L
N
M

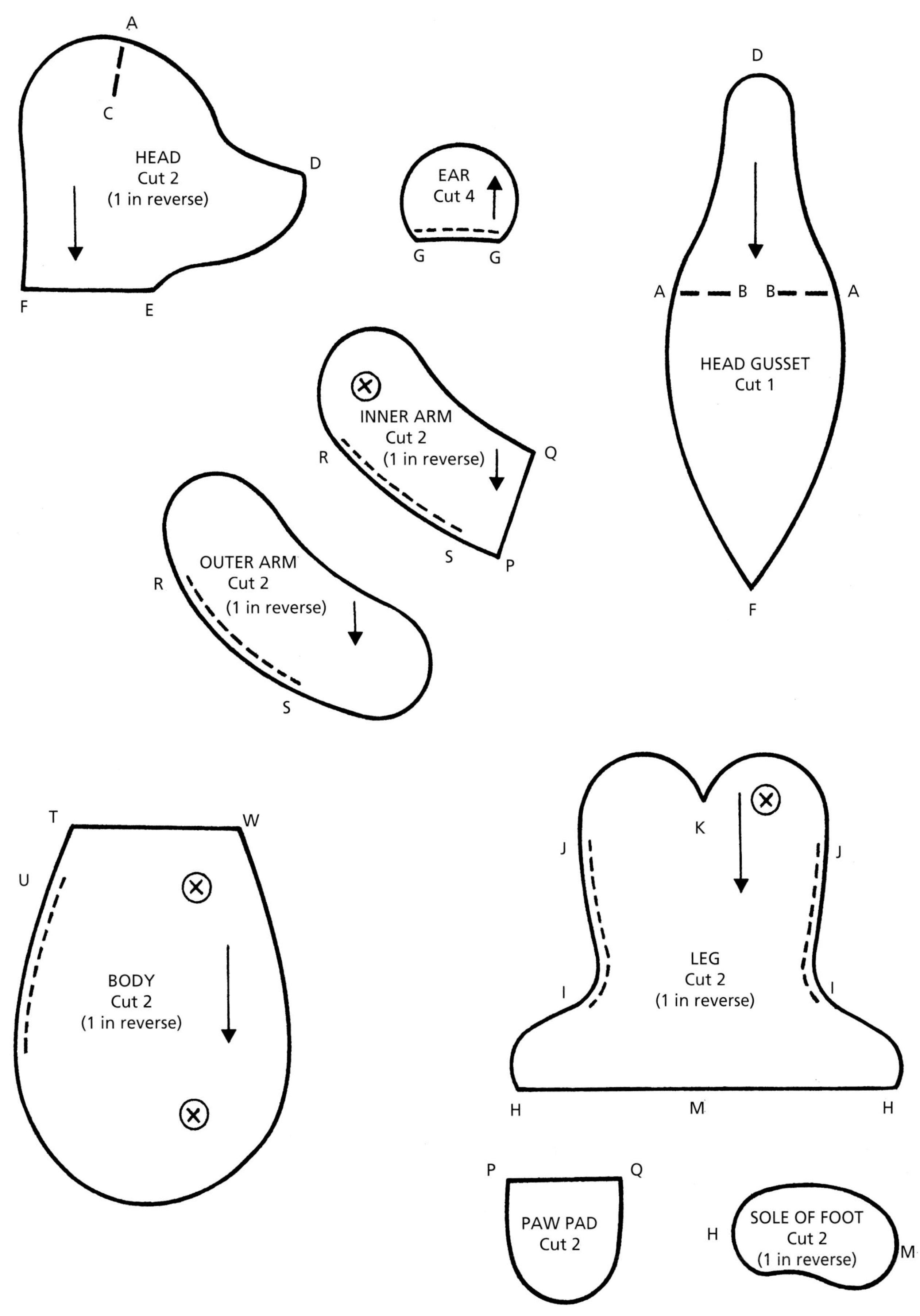
A
C
HEAD
Cut 2
(1 in reverse)
D
F
E
EAR
Cut 4
G
G
D
A
B
B
A
HEAD GUSSET
Cut 1
F
INNER ARM
Cut 2
(1 in reverse)
R
Q
S
P
OUTER ARM
Cut 2
(1 in reverse)
R
S
T
W
U
BODY
Cut 2
(1 in reverse)
V
K
J
J
LEG
Cut 2
(1 in reverse)
I
I
H
M
H
P
Q
PAW PAD
Cut 2
H
SOLE OF FOOT
Cut 2
(1 in reverse)
M

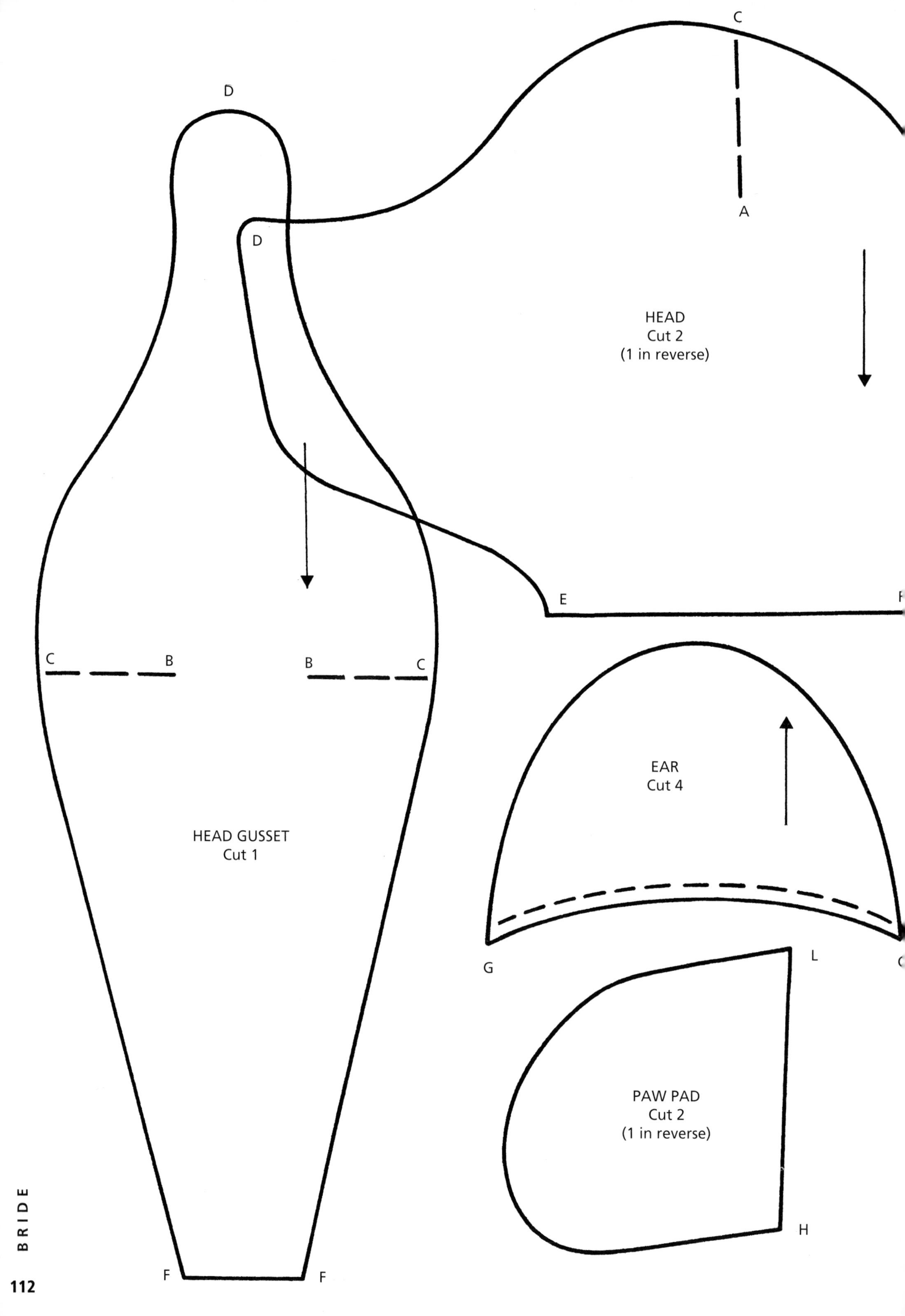
C
D
A
D
HEAD
Cut 2
(1 in reverse)
E
C
B
B
C
EAR
Cut 4
G
L
HEAD GUSSET
Cut 1
PAW PAD
Cut 2
(1 in reverse)
H
F
F

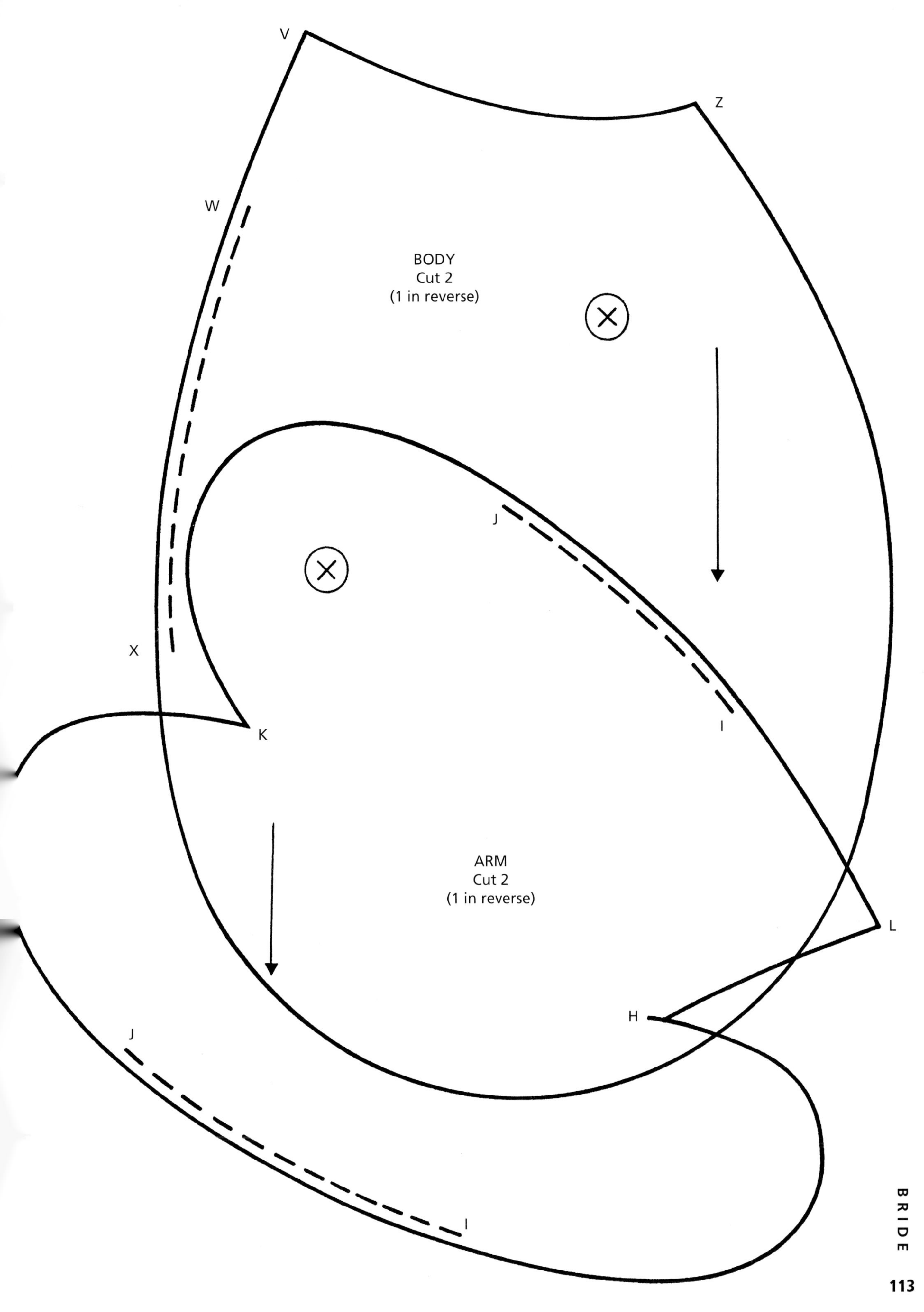
V
Z
W
BODY
Cut 2
(1 in reverse)
J
X
K
I
ARM
Cut 2
(1 in reverse)
L
H
J
I

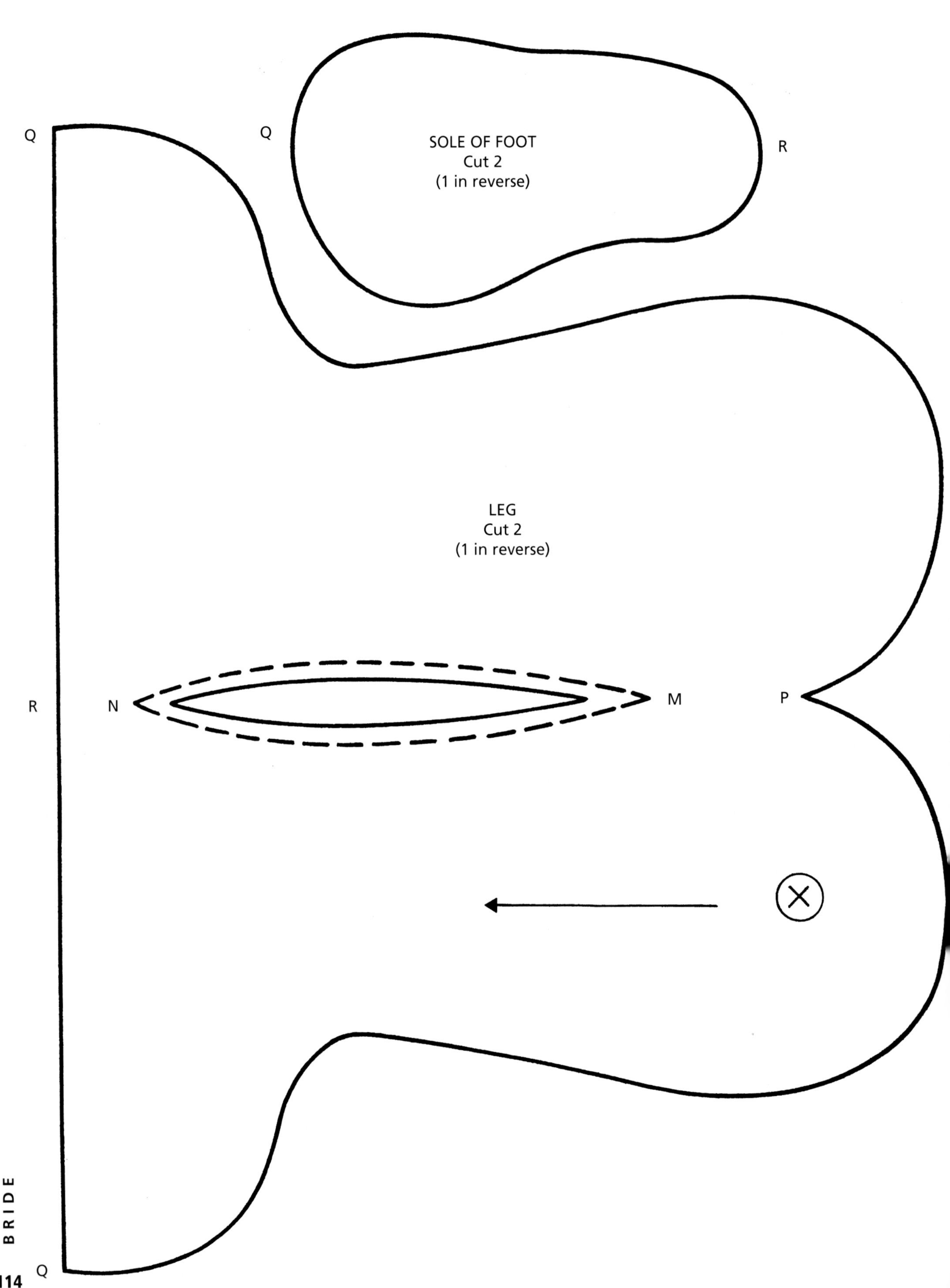
SOLE OF FOOT
Cut 2
(1 in reverse)
Q
R
Q
LEG
Cut 2
(1 in reverse)
R
N
M
P
Q

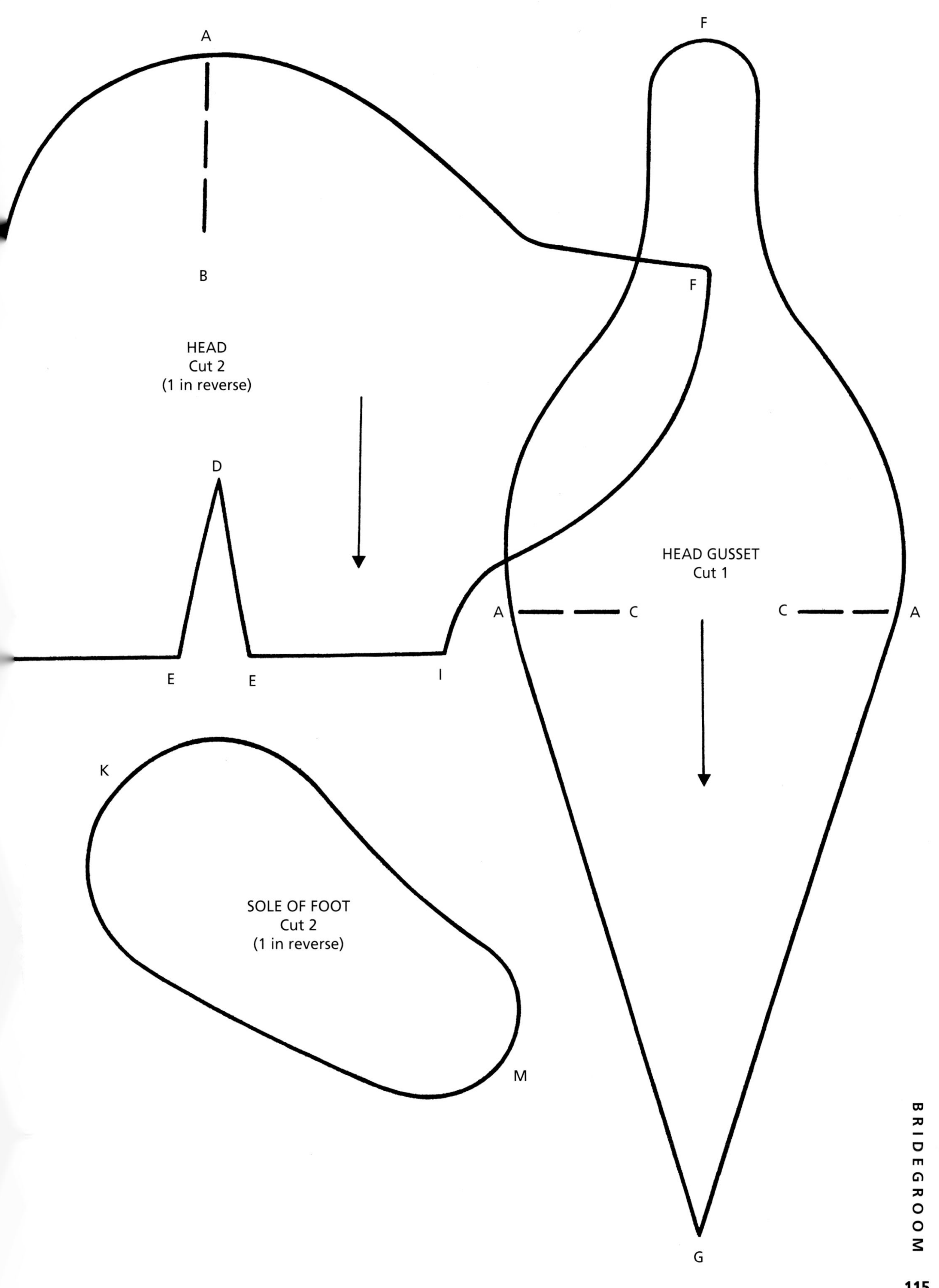
A
B
HEAD
Cut 2
(1 in reverse)
D
E
E
I
F
F
HEAD GUSSET
Cut 1
A
C
C
A
G
K
SOLE OF FOOT
Cut 2
(1 in reverse)
M

T

Z

V

BODY
Cut 2
(1 in reverse)

J

W

L

LEG
Cut 4
(2 in reverse)

M

K

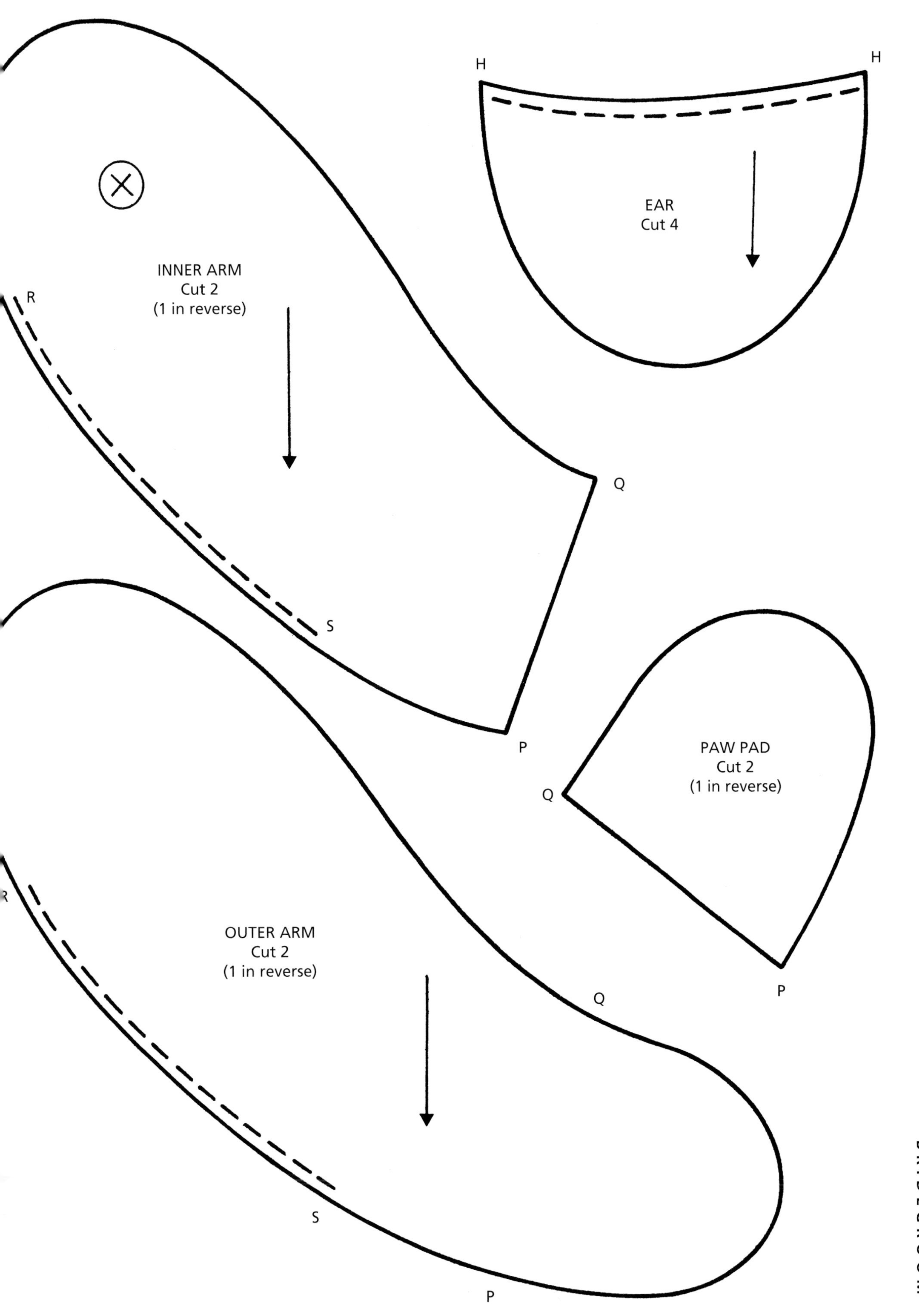
H
H
EAR
Cut 4
INNER ARM
Cut 2
(1 in reverse)
R
Q
S
P
PAW PAD
Cut 2
(1 in reverse)
Q
P
OUTER ARM
Cut 2
(1 in reverse)
R
Q
S
P

Bridegroom's collar

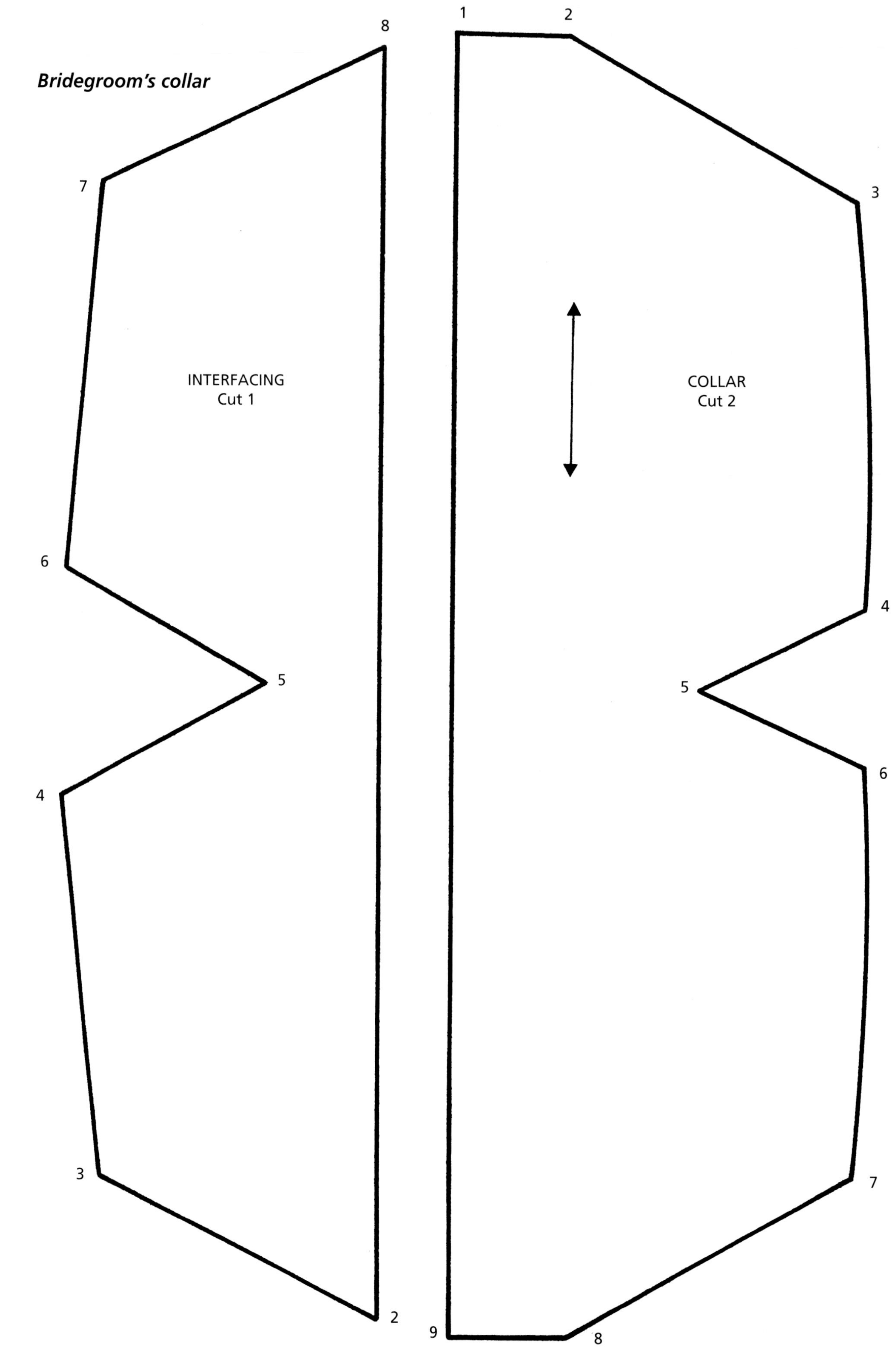

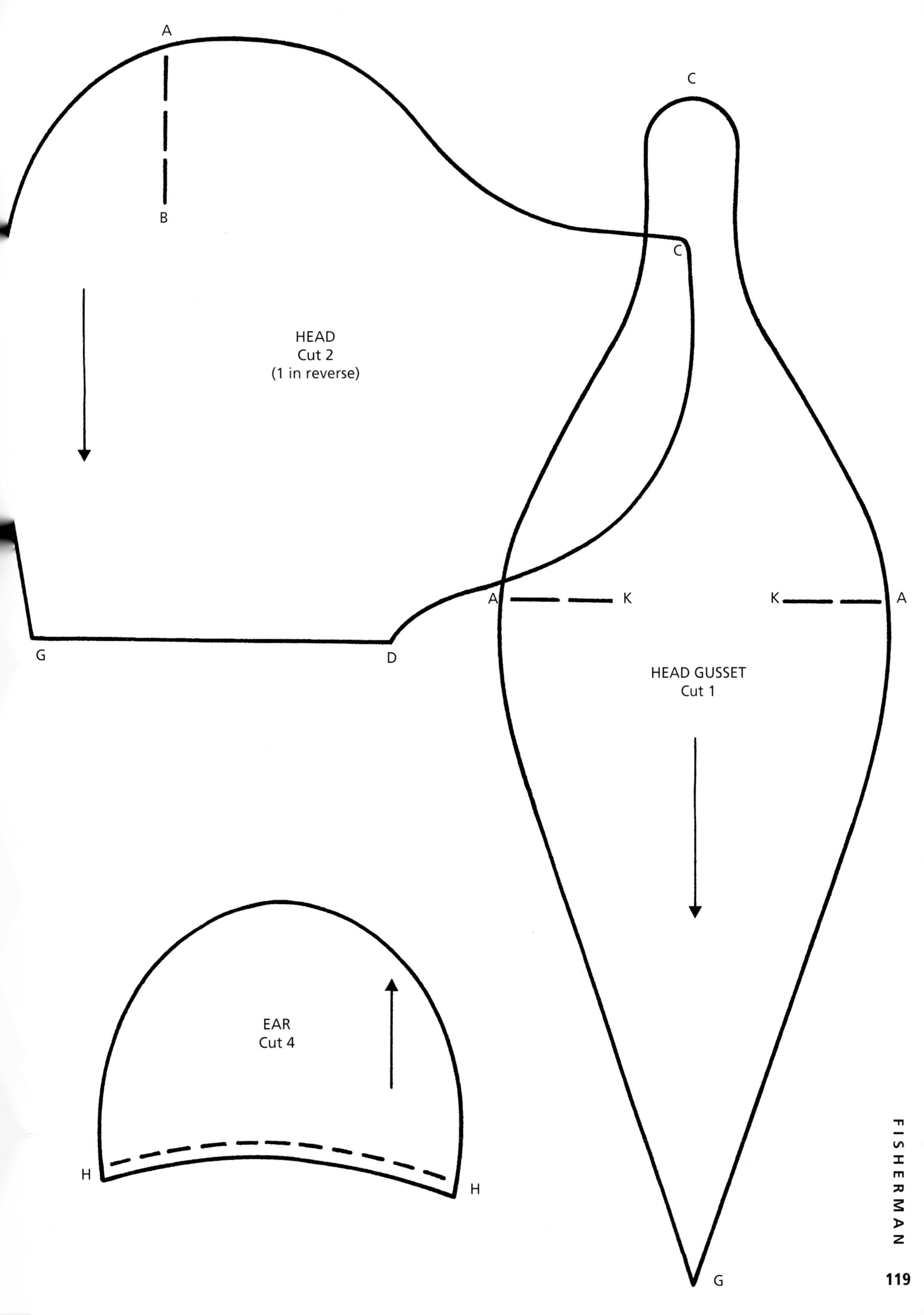
A
B
C
HEAD
Cut 2
(1 in reverse)
C
A
K
K
A
G
D
HEAD GUSSET
Cut 1
EAR
Cut 4
H
H
G

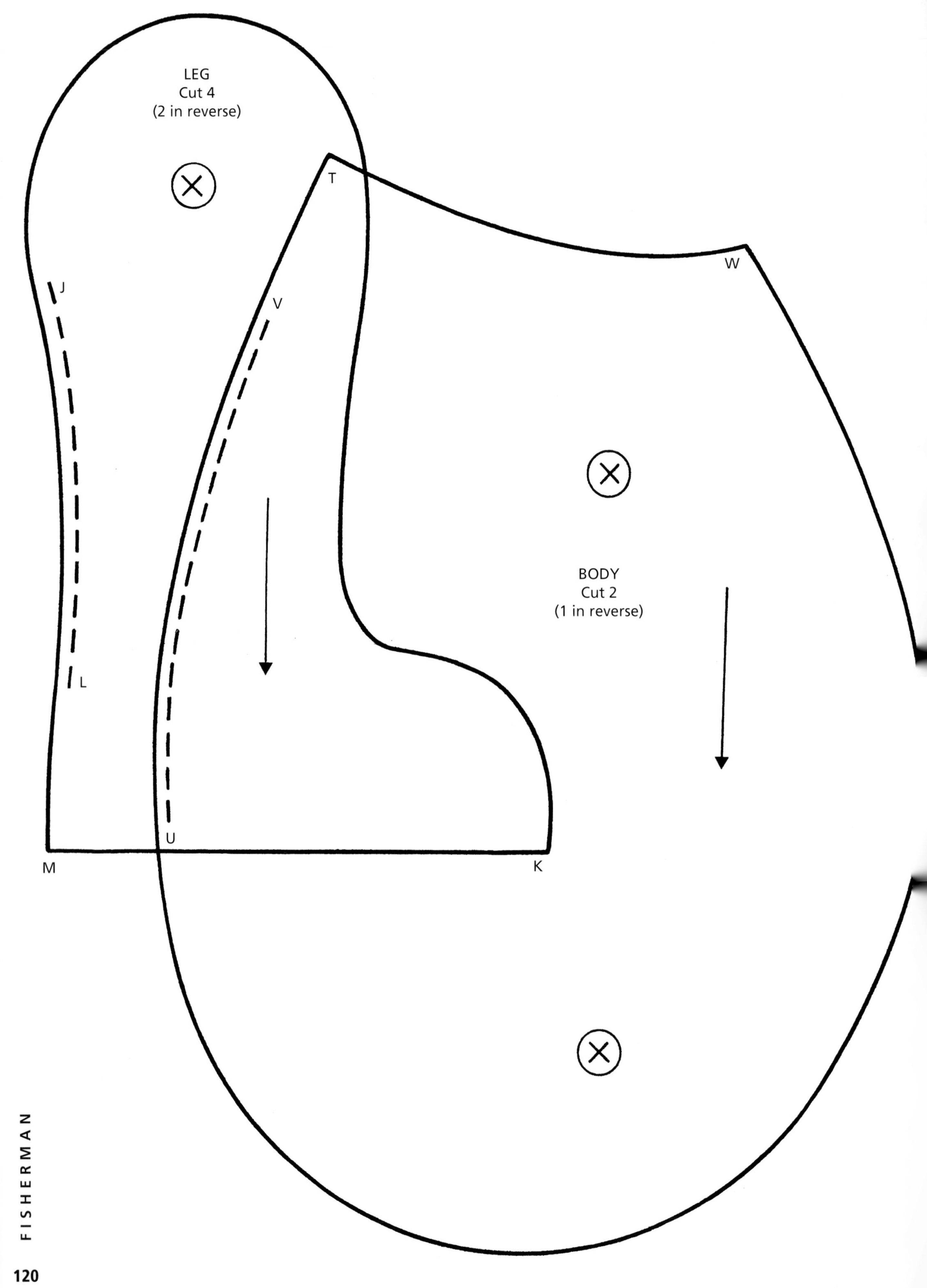
LEG
Cut 4
(2 in reverse)
T
W
J
V
L
U
M
K
BODY
Cut 2
(1 in reverse)

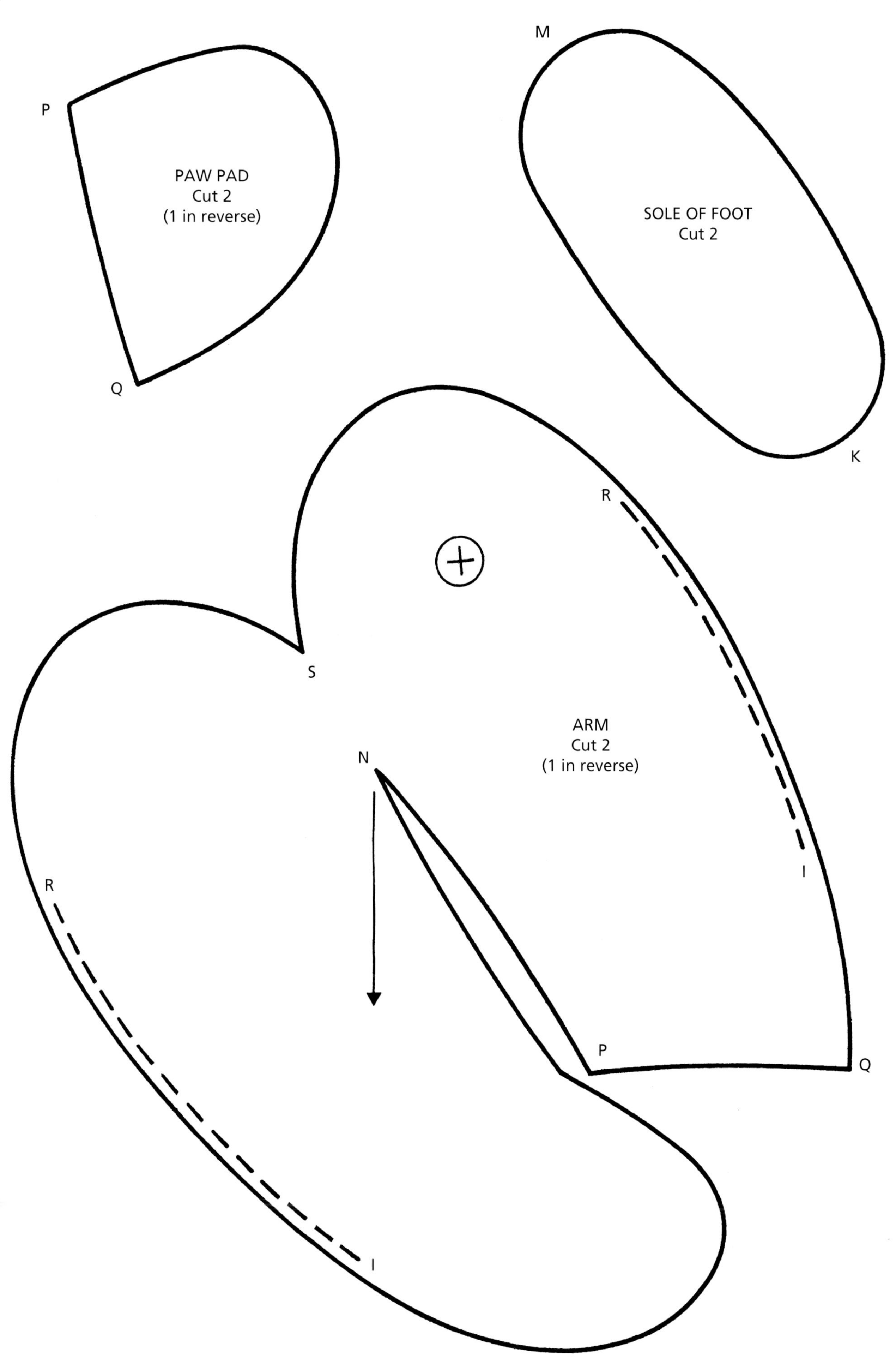
M
P
PAW PAD
Cut 2
(1 in reverse)
SOLE OF FOOT
Cut 2
Q
K
R
S
ARM
Cut 2
(1 in reverse)
N
I
R
P
Q
I

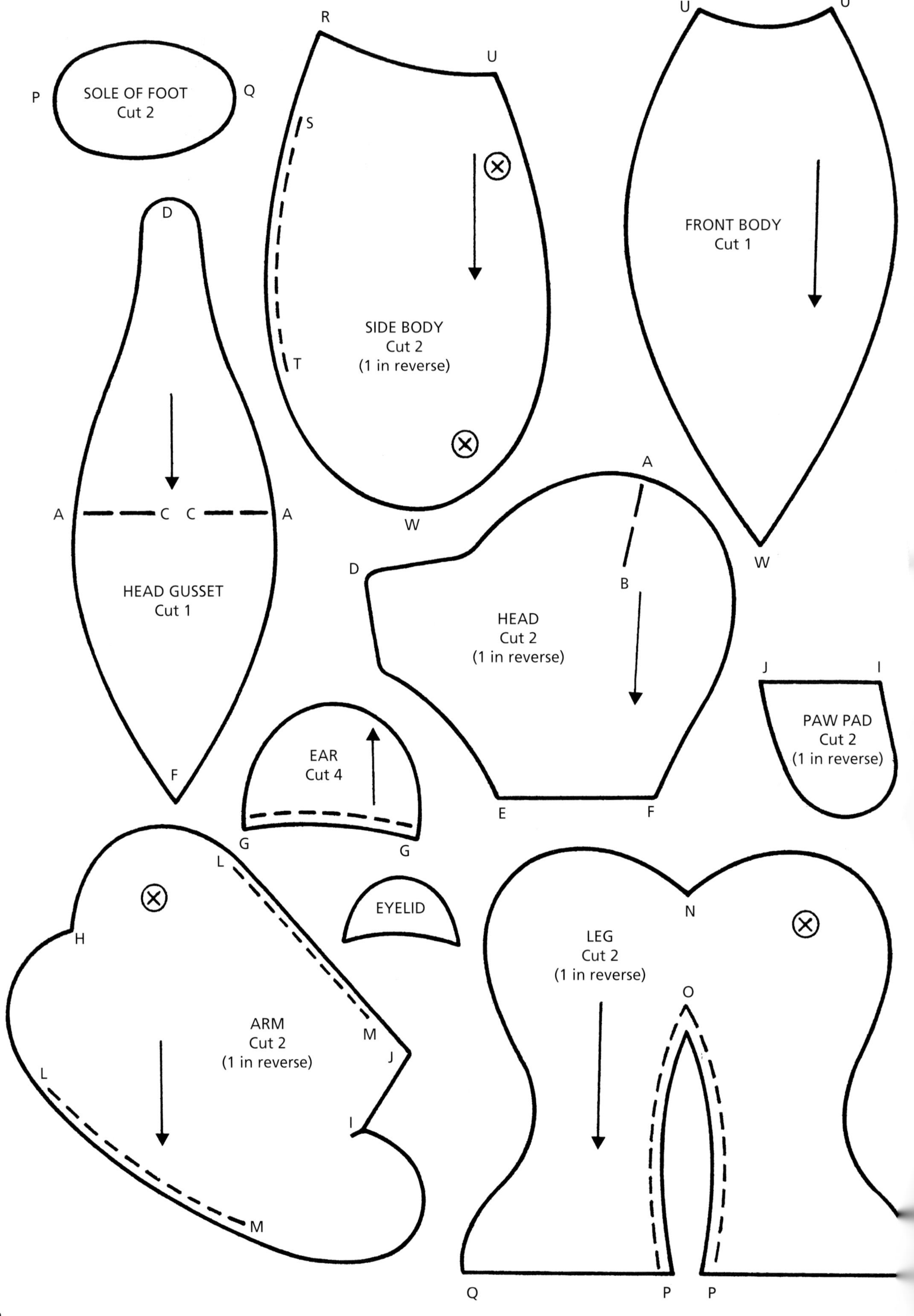
SOLE OF FOOT
Cut 2
P
Q
R
U
S
T
SIDE BODY
Cut 2
(1 in reverse)
W
U
U
FRONT BODY
Cut 1
W
D
A
C
C
A
HEAD GUSSET
Cut 1
F
A
B
D
HEAD
Cut 2
(1 in reverse)
E
F
J
I
PAW PAD
Cut 2
(1 in reverse)
EAR
Cut 4
G
G
L
H
EYELID
ARM
Cut 2
(1 in reverse)
M
J
L
I
M
N
LEG
Cut 2
(1 in reverse)
O
Q
P
P

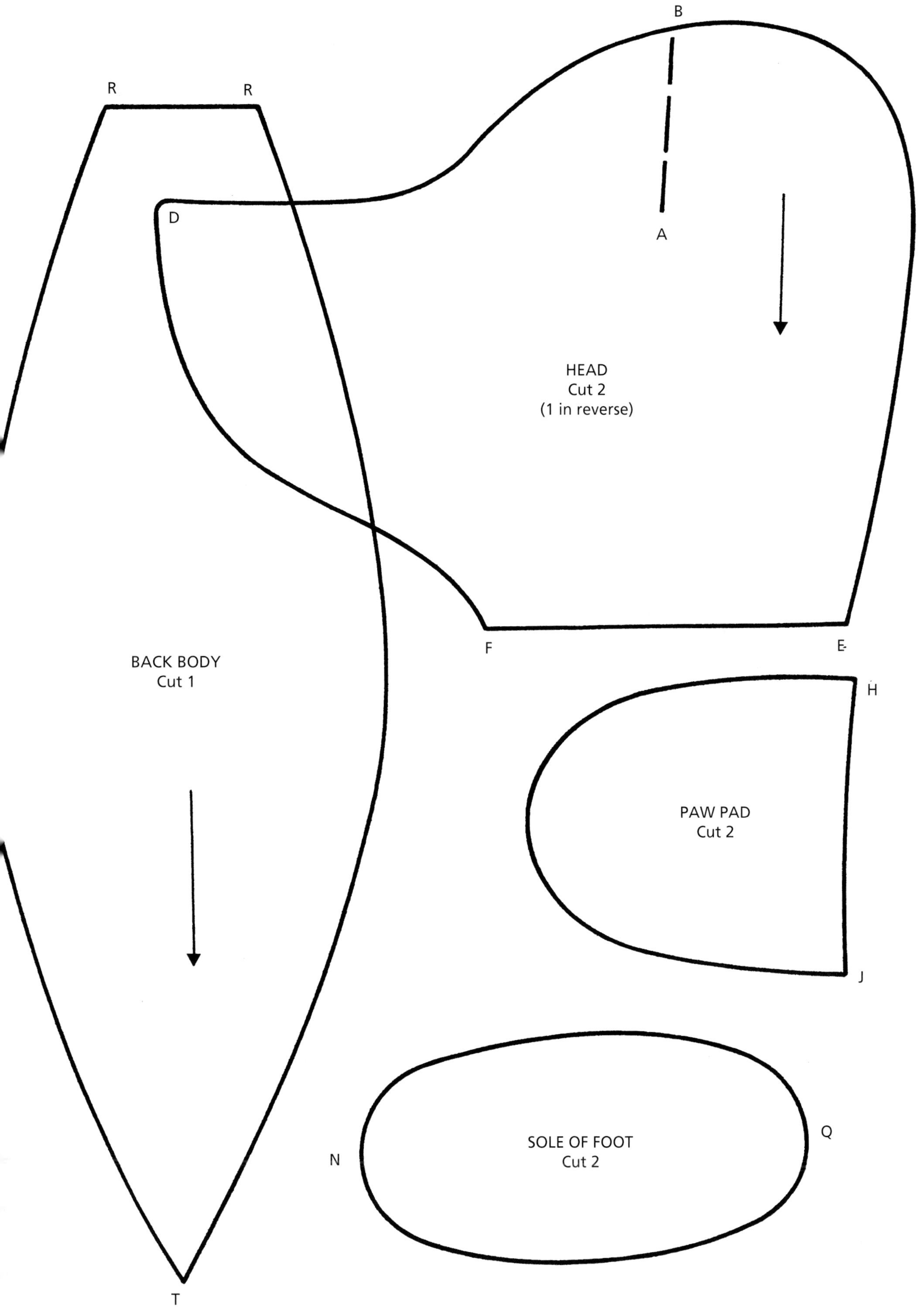
B
R
R
D
A
HEAD
Cut 2
(1 in reverse)
F
E
BACK BODY
Cut 1
H
PAW PAD
Cut 2
J
Q
N
SOLE OF FOOT
Cut 2
T

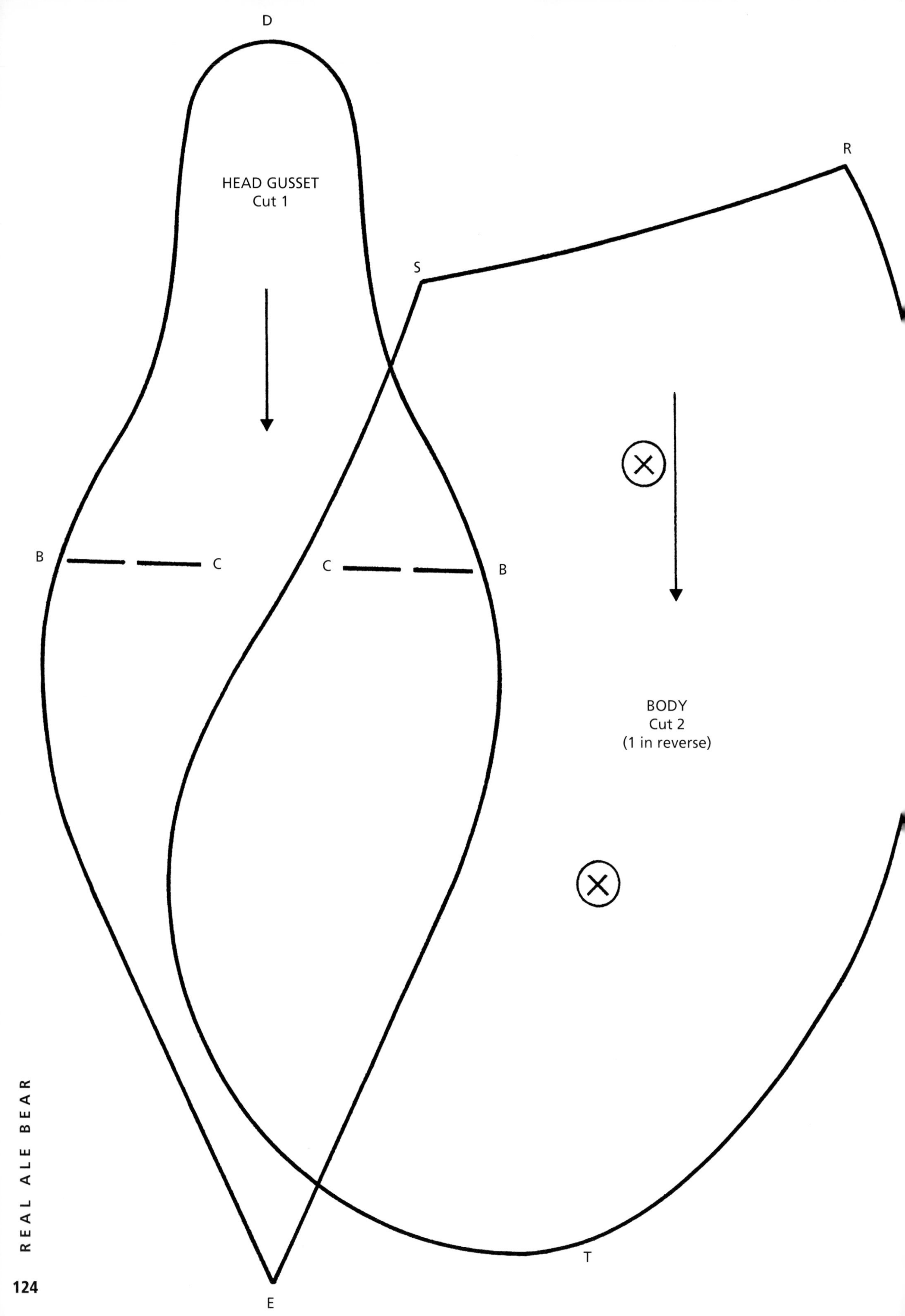
D
HEAD GUSSET
Cut 1
R
S
B
C
C
B
BODY
Cut 2
(1 in reverse)
T
E

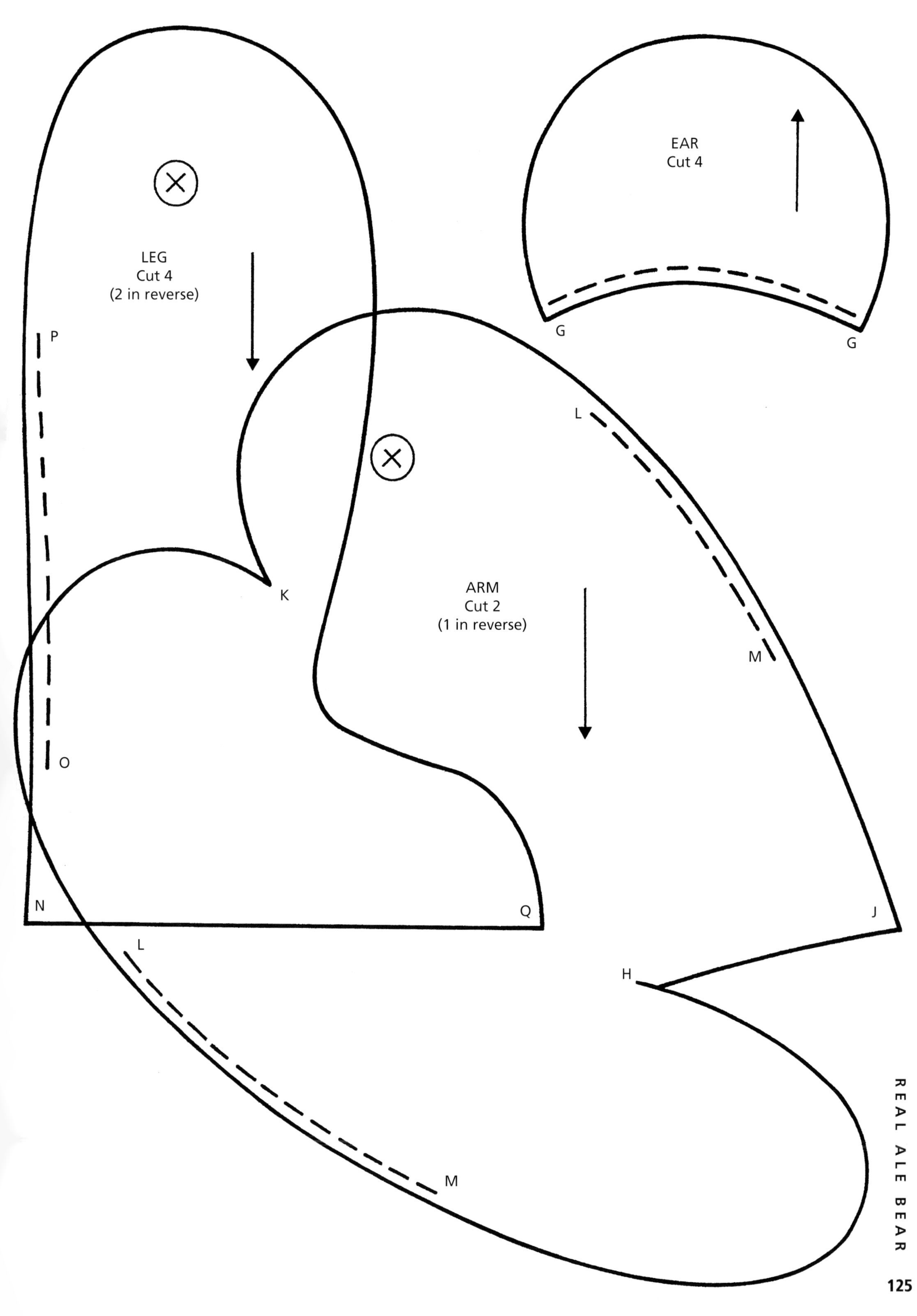

LEG
Cut 4
(2 in reverse)
P
O
K
N
Q
EAR
Cut 4
G
G
L
M
ARM
Cut 2
(1 in reverse)
J
H
L
M

K

INNER ARM
Cut 2
(1 in reverse)

H

B

L

J

A

D

HEAD
Cut 2
(1 in reverse)

E

F

E

E

Q

SOLE OF FOOT
Cut 2
(1 in reverse)

N

K

C

C

B

L

HEAD GUSSET
Cut 1

OUTER ARM
Cut 2
(1 in reverse)

D

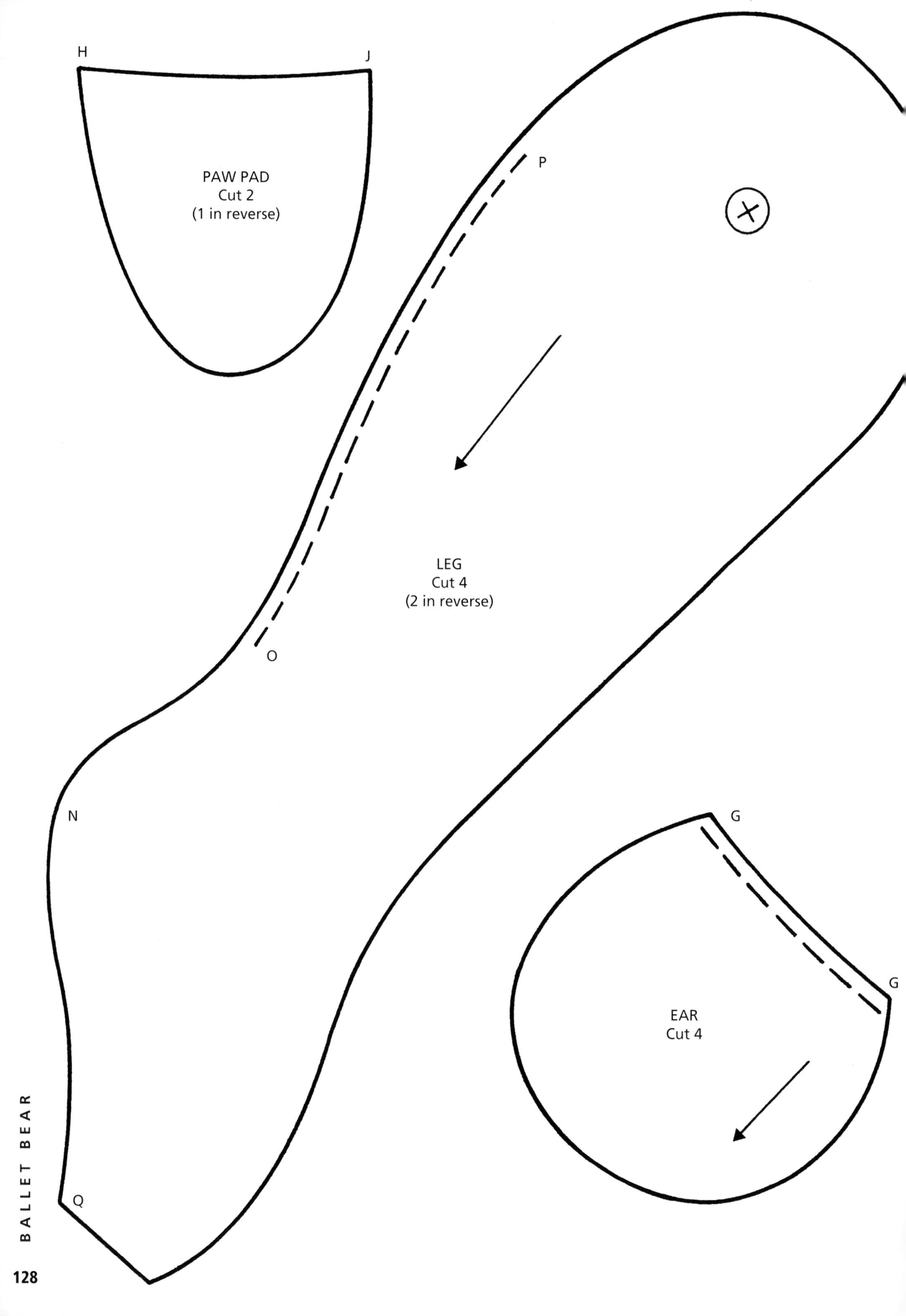
H
J
PAW PAD
Cut 2
(1 in reverse)
P
LEG
Cut 4
(2 in reverse)
O
N
Q
G
G
EAR
Cut 4

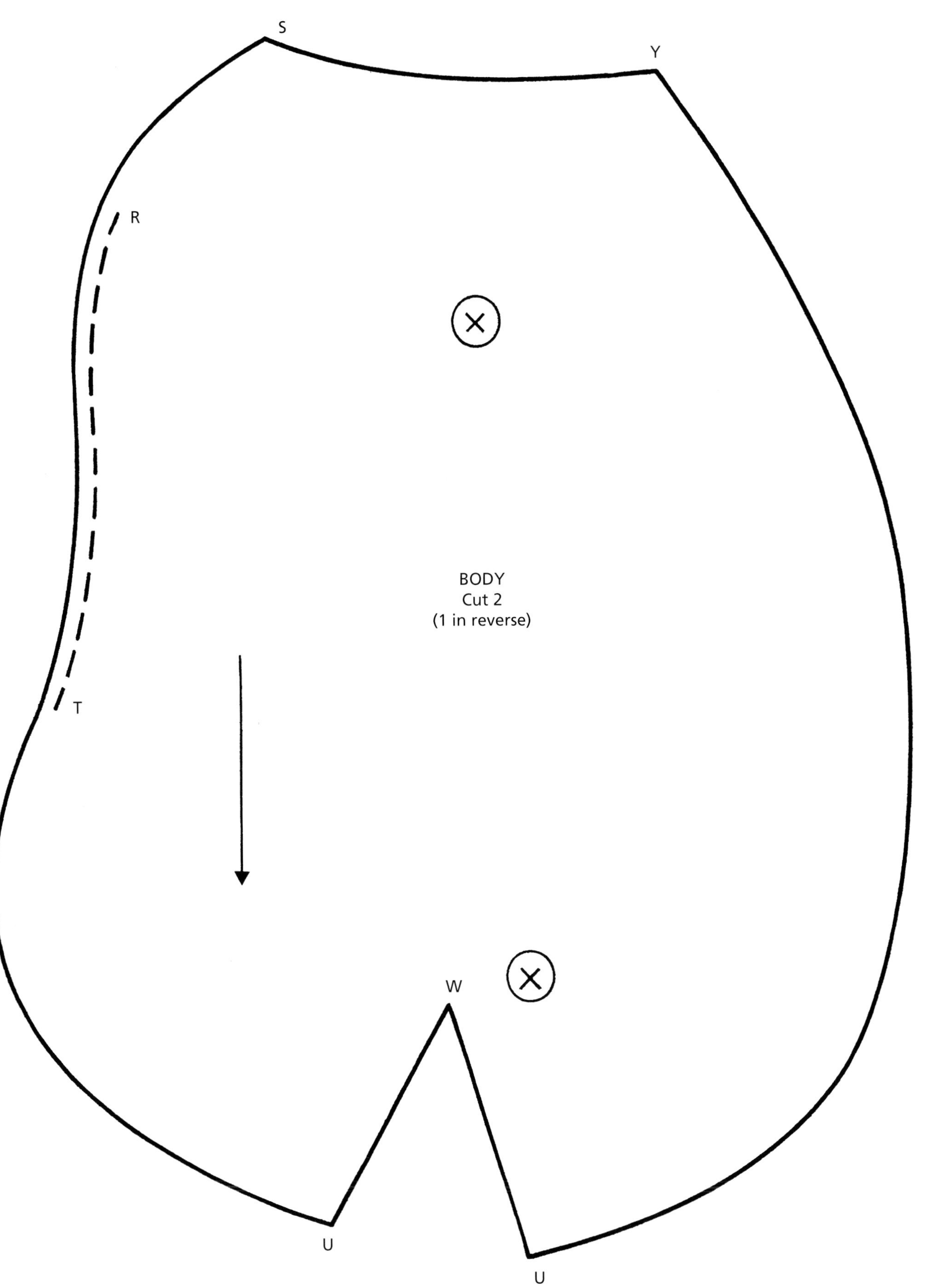
S
Y
R
T
BODY
Cut 2
(1 in reverse)
W
U
U

B

A

D

HEAD
Cut 2
(1 in reverse)

F

E

V

S

FRONT BODY
Cut 2
(1 in reverse)

T

INNER ARM
Cut 2
(1 in reverse)

K

L

J

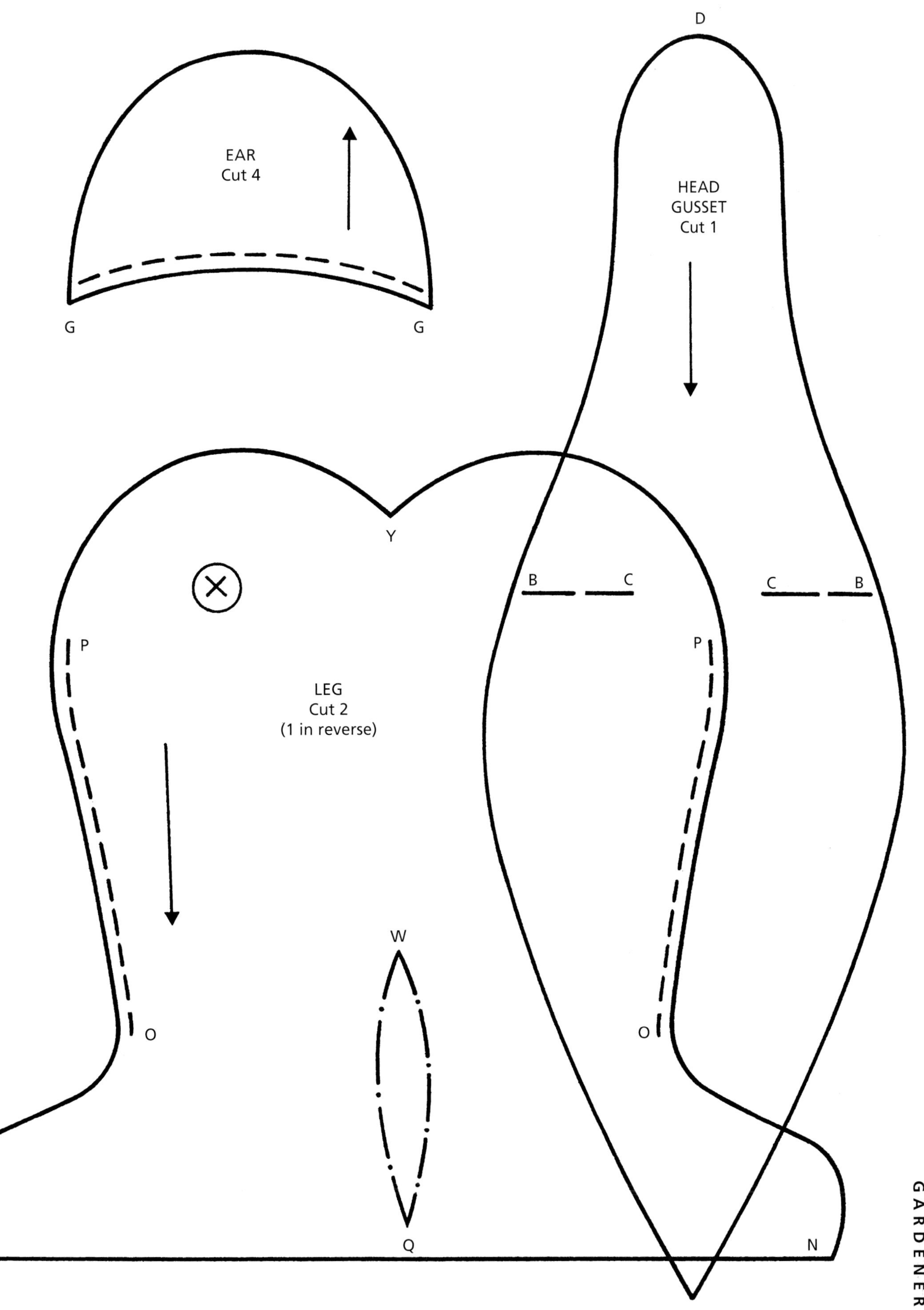
D
EAR
Cut 4
G
G
HEAD
GUSSET
Cut 1
Y
B
C
C
B
P
P
LEG
Cut 2
(1 in reverse)
W
O
O
Q
N
E

N

SOLE OF FOOT
Cut 2

V V

BACK BODY
Cut 1

Q

Z

T T

K

OUTER ARM
Cut 2
(1 in reverse)

L

H J

PAW PAD
Cut 2

Flower pot
a
a
POT
Brown felt
Cut 1
b
b
BASE
Brown felt
Cut 1
a
a
POT
Card
Cut 1
b
b
Daffodils and yucca plant
TRUMPET
Orange
card
FLOWER
Yellow card
YUCCA
STEM
Brown
felt
Cut 1
LEAVES
Green card

Seed tray and trowel

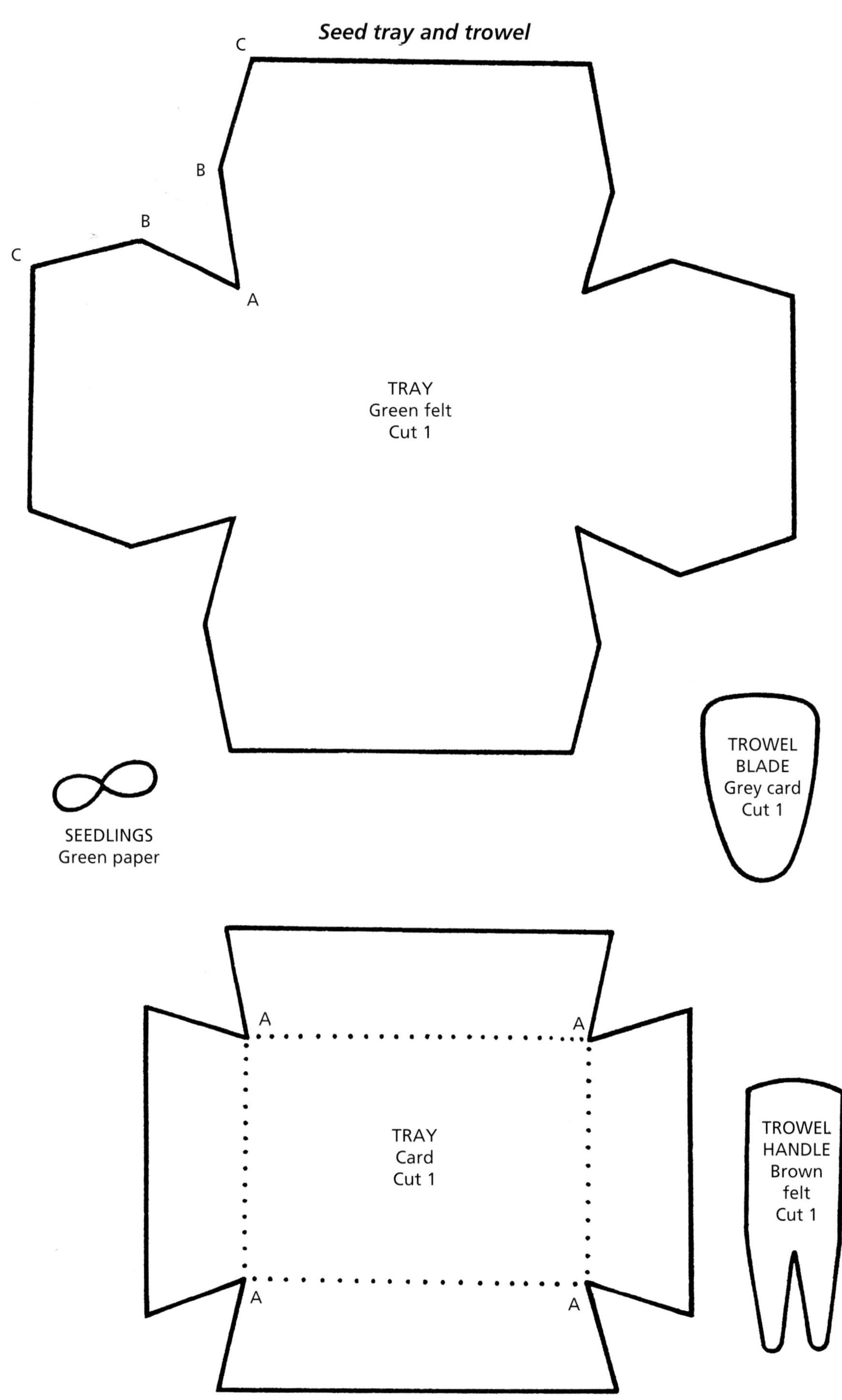

D

B

C

C

B

HEAD GUSSET
Cut 1

E

B

A

D

HEAD
Cut 2
(1 in reverse)

F

E

N

SOLE OF FOOT
Cut 2
(1 in reverse)

Q

O

LEG
Cut 2
(1 in reverse)

P

EAR
Cut 4

G

G

N

Q

N

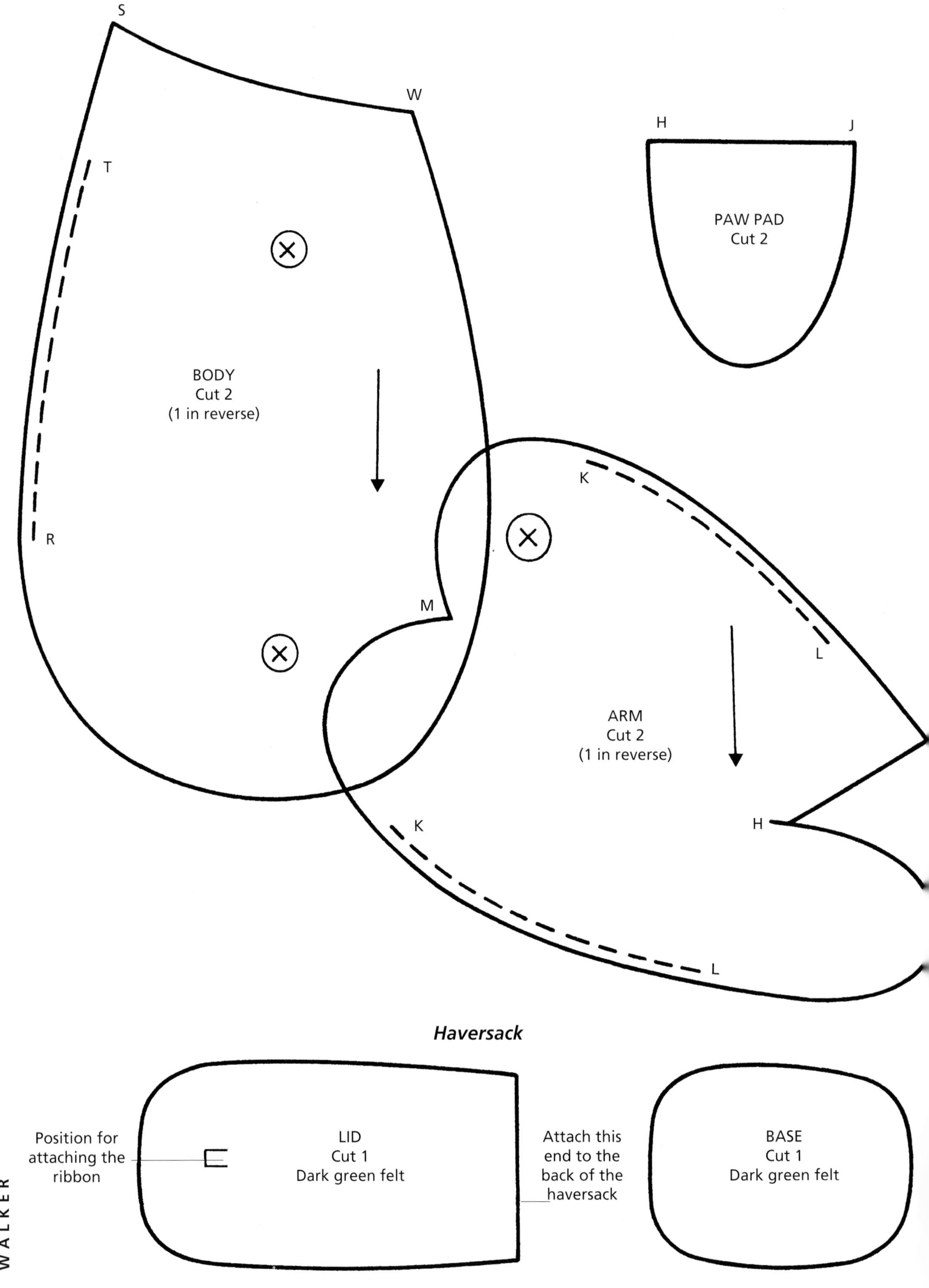
S
W
T
R
BODY
Cut 2
(1 in reverse)
M
H
J
PAW PAD
Cut 2
K
L
ARM
Cut 2
(1 in reverse)
K
H
L
Haversack
Position for attaching the ribbon
LID
Cut 1
Dark green felt
Attach this end to the back of the haversack
BASE
Cut 1
Dark green felt

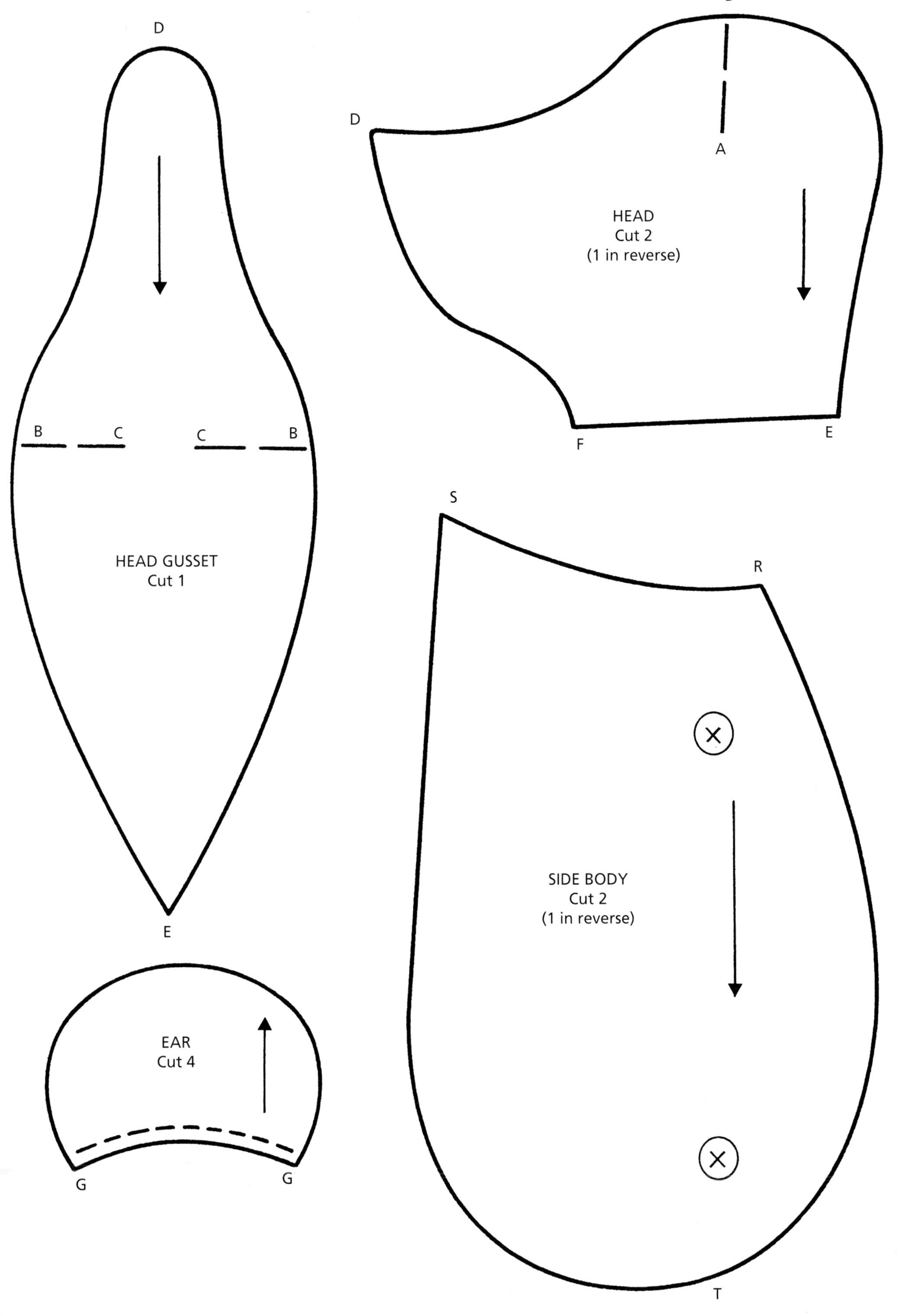
D
D
B
A
HEAD
Cut 2
(1 in reverse)
F
E
B
C
C
B
HEAD GUSSET
Cut 1
E
S
R
SIDE BODY
Cut 2
(1 in reverse)
T
EAR
Cut 4
G
G

J

H

PAW PAD
Cut 2
(1 in reverse)

N

SOLE OF
FOOT
Cut 2

W

L

K

M

ARM
Cut 2
(1 in reverse)

L

J

H

M

R R

Q

P P

LEG
Cut 2
(1 in reverse)

FRONT BODY
Cut 1

O

O

N W N

T

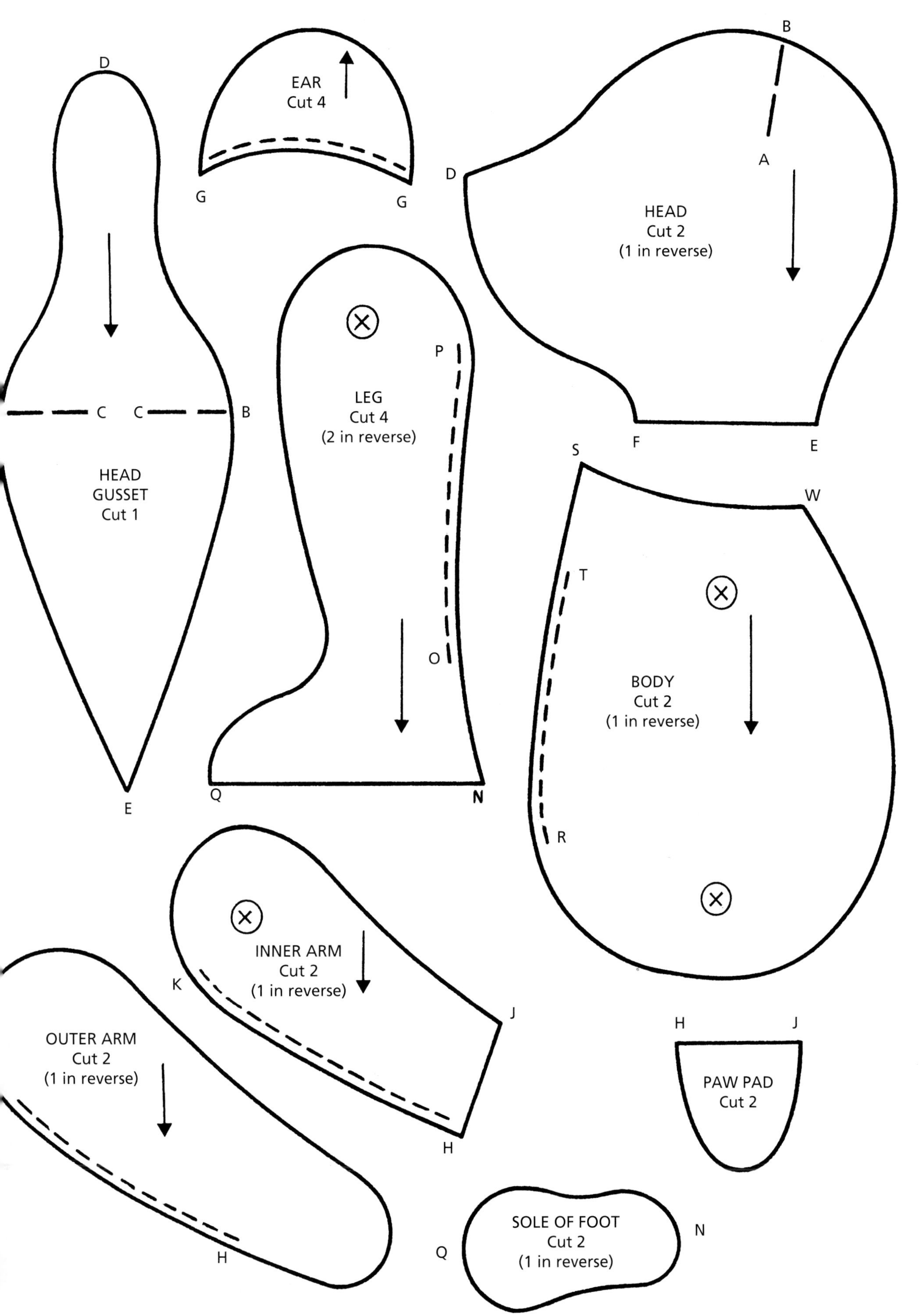
EAR
Cut 4
G
G
D
HEAD
GUSSET
Cut 1
C
C
B
E
HEAD
Cut 2
(1 in reverse)
B
A
D
F
E
LEG
Cut 4
(2 in reverse)
P
O
Q
N
BODY
Cut 2
(1 in reverse)
S
W
T
R
INNER ARM
Cut 2
(1 in reverse)
K
J
H
OUTER ARM
Cut 2
(1 in reverse)
H
PAW PAD
Cut 2
H
J
SOLE OF FOOT
Cut 2
(1 in reverse)
Q
N

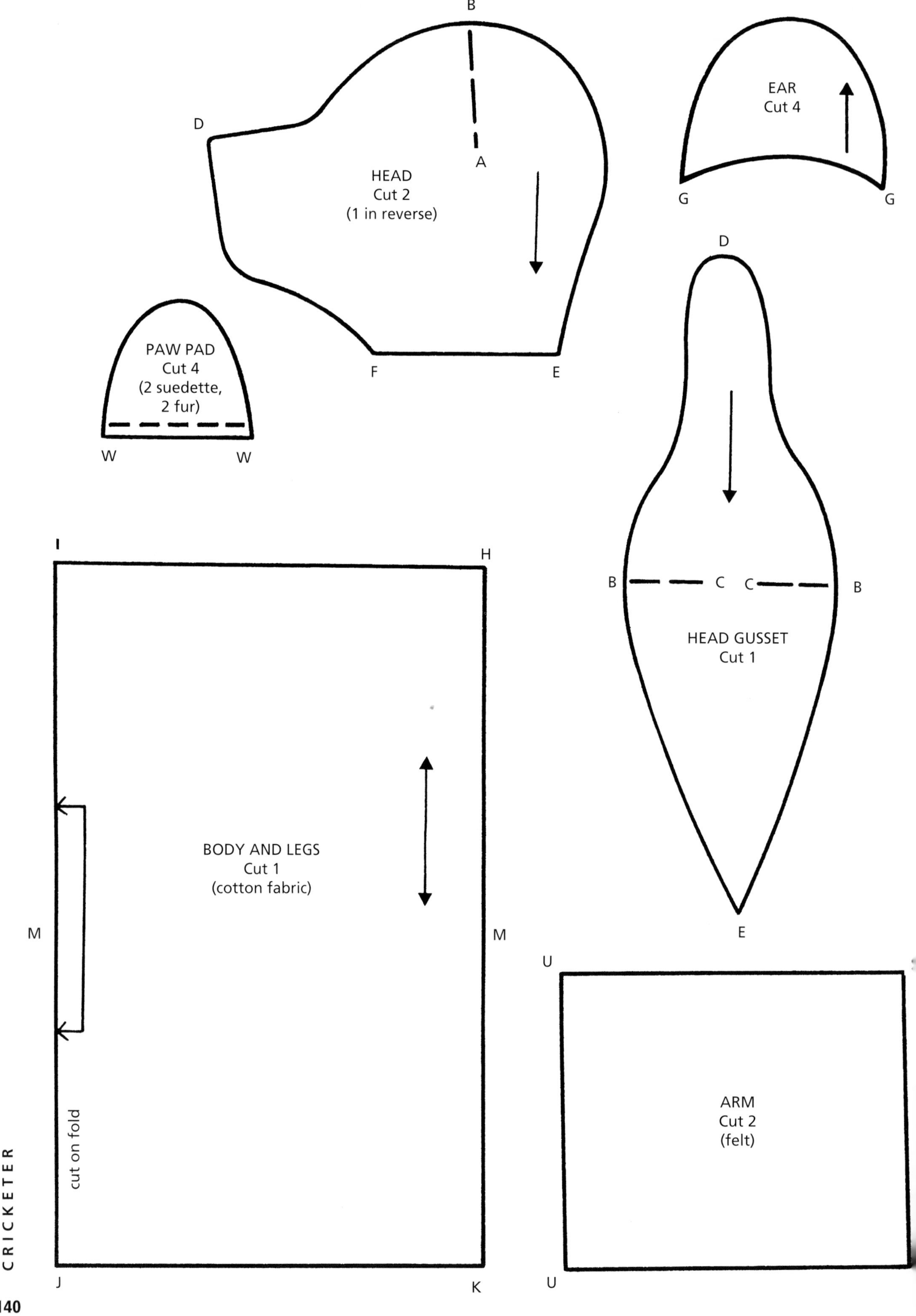
B
D
A
HEAD
Cut 2
(1 in reverse)
F
E
EAR
Cut 4
G
G
PAW PAD
Cut 4
(2 suedette,
2 fur)
W
W
D
I
H
B
C
C
B
HEAD GUSSET
Cut 1
E
BODY AND LEGS
Cut 1
(cotton fabric)
M
M
cut on fold
J
K
U
ARM
Cut 2
(felt)
U

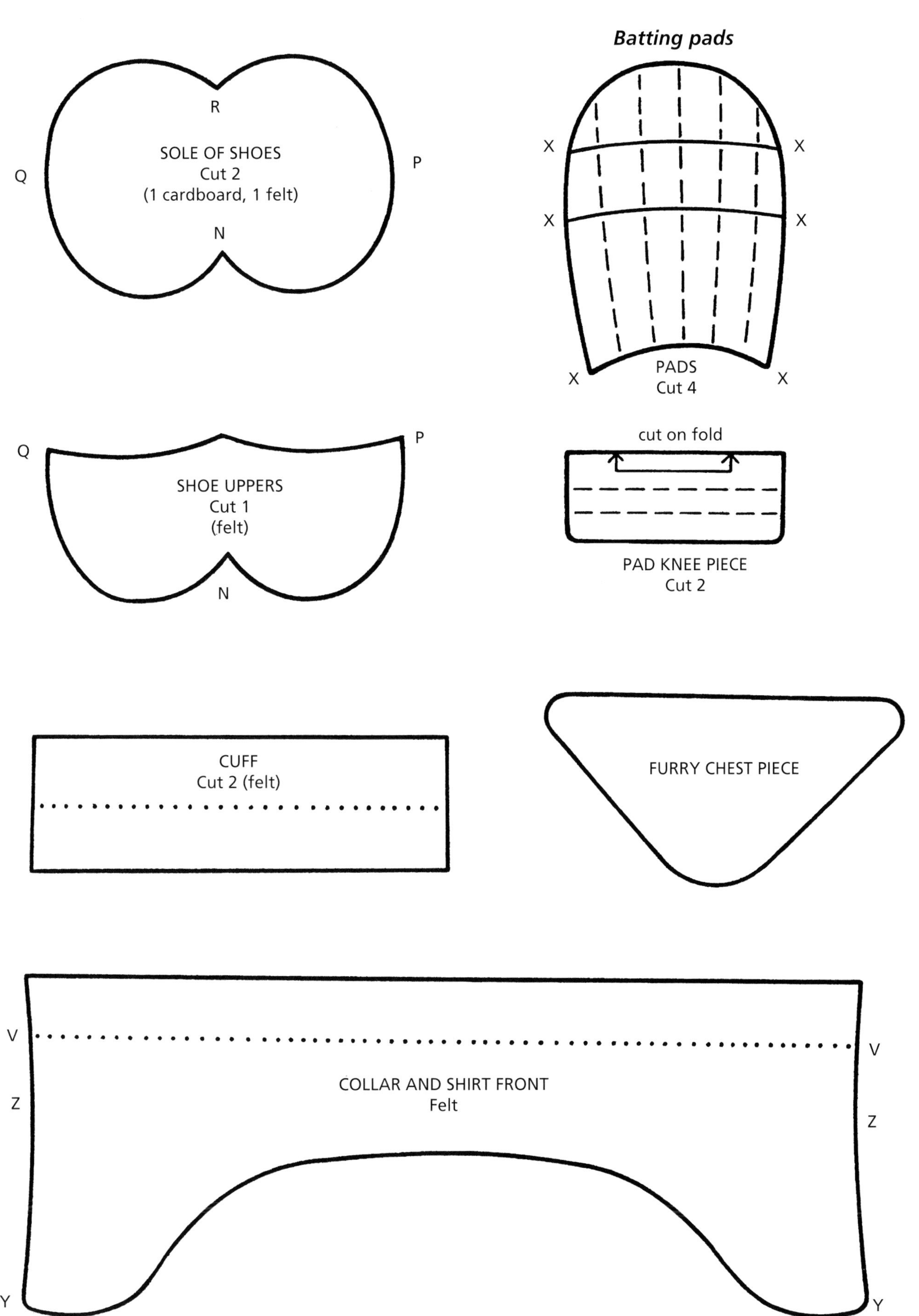

Batting pads
R
SOLE OF SHOES
Cut 2
(1 cardboard, 1 felt)
Q
P
N
X
X
X
X
X
X
PADS
Cut 4
Q
P
SHOE UPPERS
Cut 1
(felt)
N
cut on fold
PAD KNEE PIECE
Cut 2
CUFF
Cut 2 (felt)
FURRY CHEST PIECE
V
V
COLLAR AND SHIRT FRONT
Felt
Z
Z
Y
Y

B
D
A
HEAD
Cut 2
(1 in reverse)
F
E

D
B C C B
HEAD GUSSET
Cut 1
E

EAR
Cut 4
G G

Q P
SHOE UPPERS
Cut 1
(white felt)
N

R
Q P
SOLE OF SHOES
Cut 2
(1 cardboard,
1 white felt)
N

INNER ARM
Cut 2
(1 in reverse)
M
H
K
J

OUTER ARM
Cut 2
(1 in reverse)
M
K

H
PAW PAD
Cut 2
J

T-shirt

T-SHIRT
Cut 2
(both on fold)

Rugby ball

BALL
Cut 4
(white felt)
R
I

K
L
M
J
ARM
Cut 2
(1 in reverse)
K
H
M
J

EAR
Cut 4
G
G

J
H
PAW PAD
Cut 2
(1 in reverse)

D
V
W
B
C
C
B
HEAD GUSSET
Cut 1
E
E

B
D
A
HEAD
Cut 2
(1 in reverse)
F
E

N
SOLE OF FOOT
Cut 2
Q

Y
P
P
LEG
Cut 2
(1 in reverse)
O
O
Q
N

S
U
T
BODY
Cut 2
(1 in reverse)
Z

B
A
D
HEAD
Cut 2
(1 in reverse)
E
F

EAR
Cut 4
G
G

N
SOLE OF FOOT
Cut 2
(1 in reverse)
Q

D
B
C
C
HEAD GUSSET
Cut 1
E
E

J
H
PAW PAD
Cut 2
(1 in reverse)

K
INNER ARM
Cut 2
(1 in reverse)
H
L
J

K
OUTER ARM
Cut 2
(1 in reverse)
L

W
S
T
BODY
Cut 2
(1 in reverse)
R

Y
LEG
Cut 2
(1 in reverse)
O
P
N
Q
N

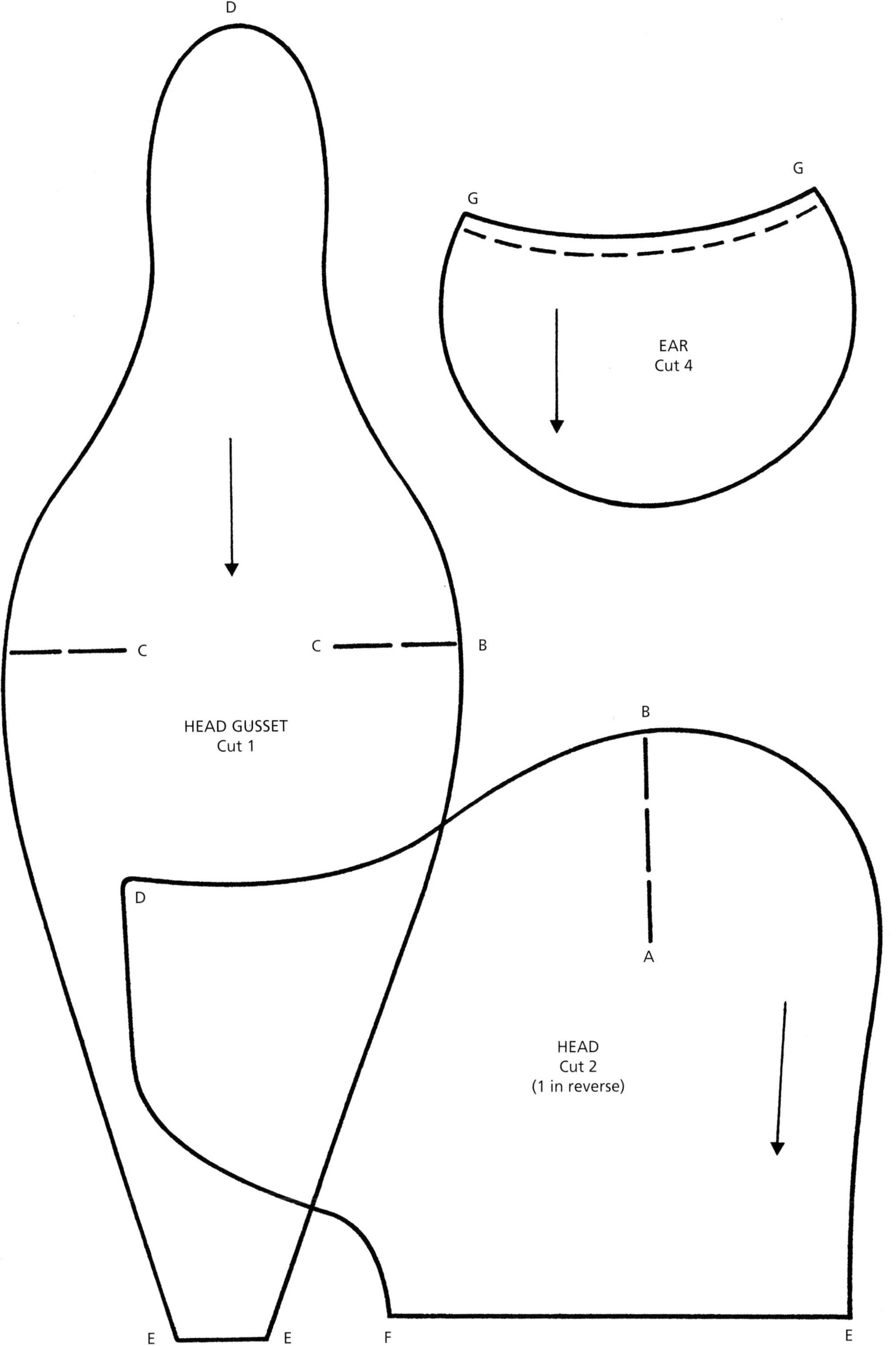
D
G
G
EAR
Cut 4
C
C
B
HEAD GUSSET
Cut 1
B
D
A
HEAD
Cut 2
(1 in reverse)
E
E
F
E

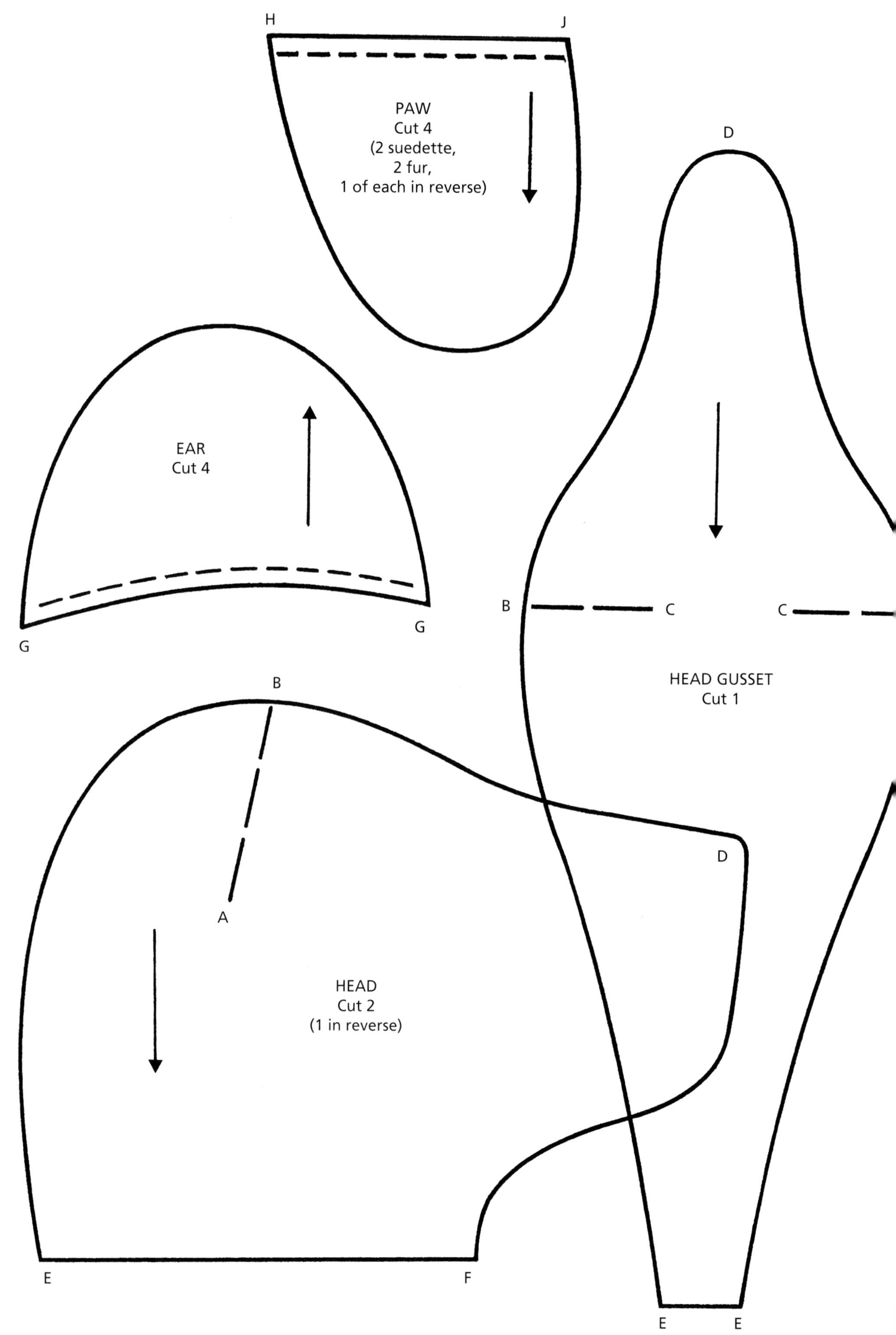
H
J
PAW
Cut 4
(2 suedette,
2 fur,
1 of each in reverse)
D
EAR
Cut 4
G
G
B
C
C
HEAD GUSSET
Cut 1
B
D
A
HEAD
Cut 2
(1 in reverse)
E
F
E
E

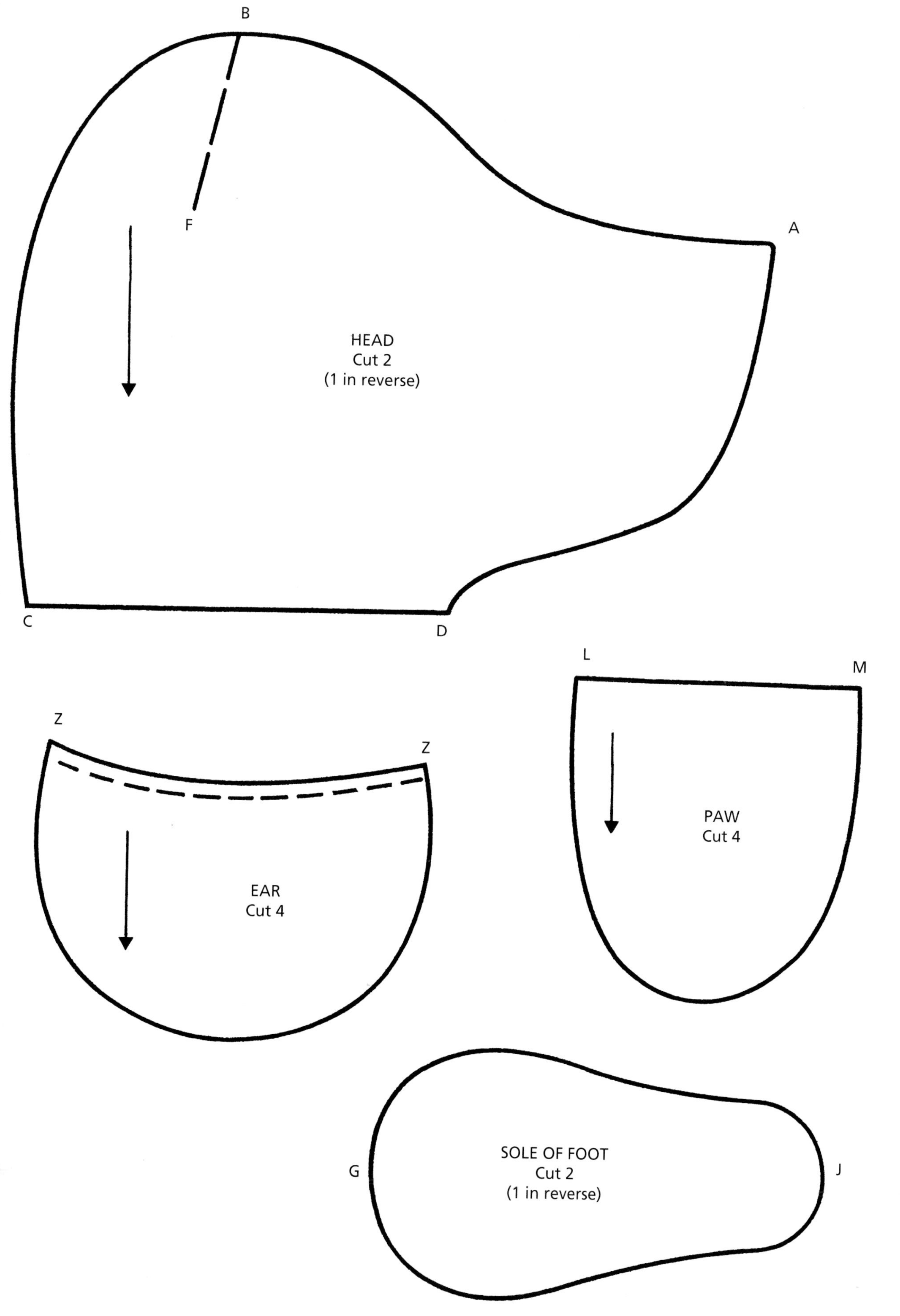
B
F
A
HEAD
Cut 2
(1 in reverse)
C
D
L
M
Z
Z
PAW
Cut 4
EAR
Cut 4
SOLE OF FOOT
Cut 2
(1 in reverse)
G
J

A

B E E B

HEAD GUSSET
Cut 1

C C

H

LEG
Cut 4
(2 in reverse)

K

G J

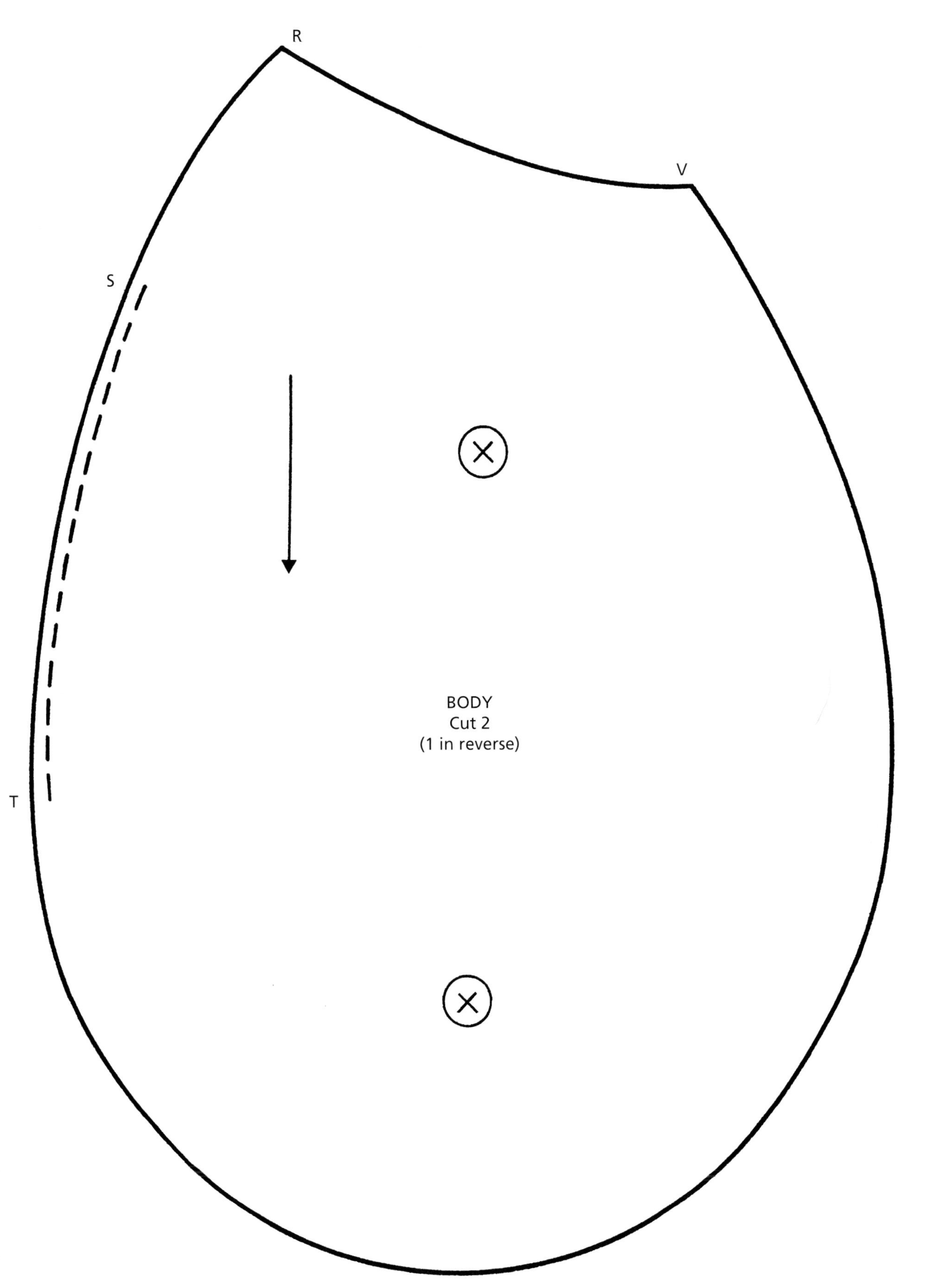
R
V
S
T
BODY
Cut 2
(1 in reverse)

P

W

Q

ARM
Cut 2
(1 in reverse)

P

M

L

Q

Teacher's waistcoat

O

$

Y

*

$

*

WAISTCOAT
BACK
Cut 1 on fold

Dart

WAISTCOAT
FRONT
Cut 2
(1 in reverse)

$

#

O

cut on fold

U

Pocket

#

N

X

U

WAISTCOAT
LAPEL
Cut 2
(1 in reverse)

N

POCKET
Cut 2

X

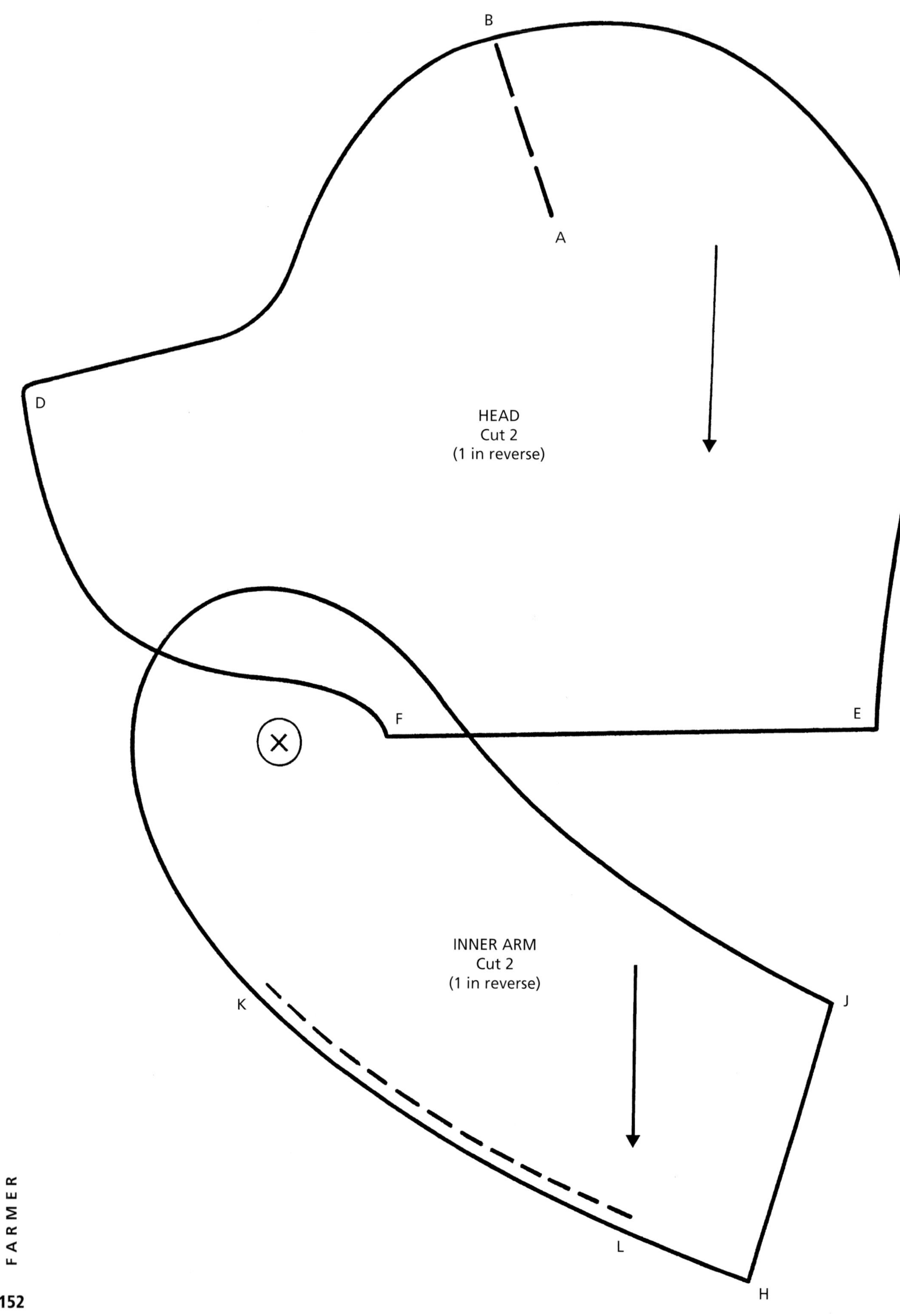
B
A
D
HEAD
Cut 2
(1 in reverse)
F
E
INNER ARM
Cut 2
(1 in reverse)
K
J
L
H

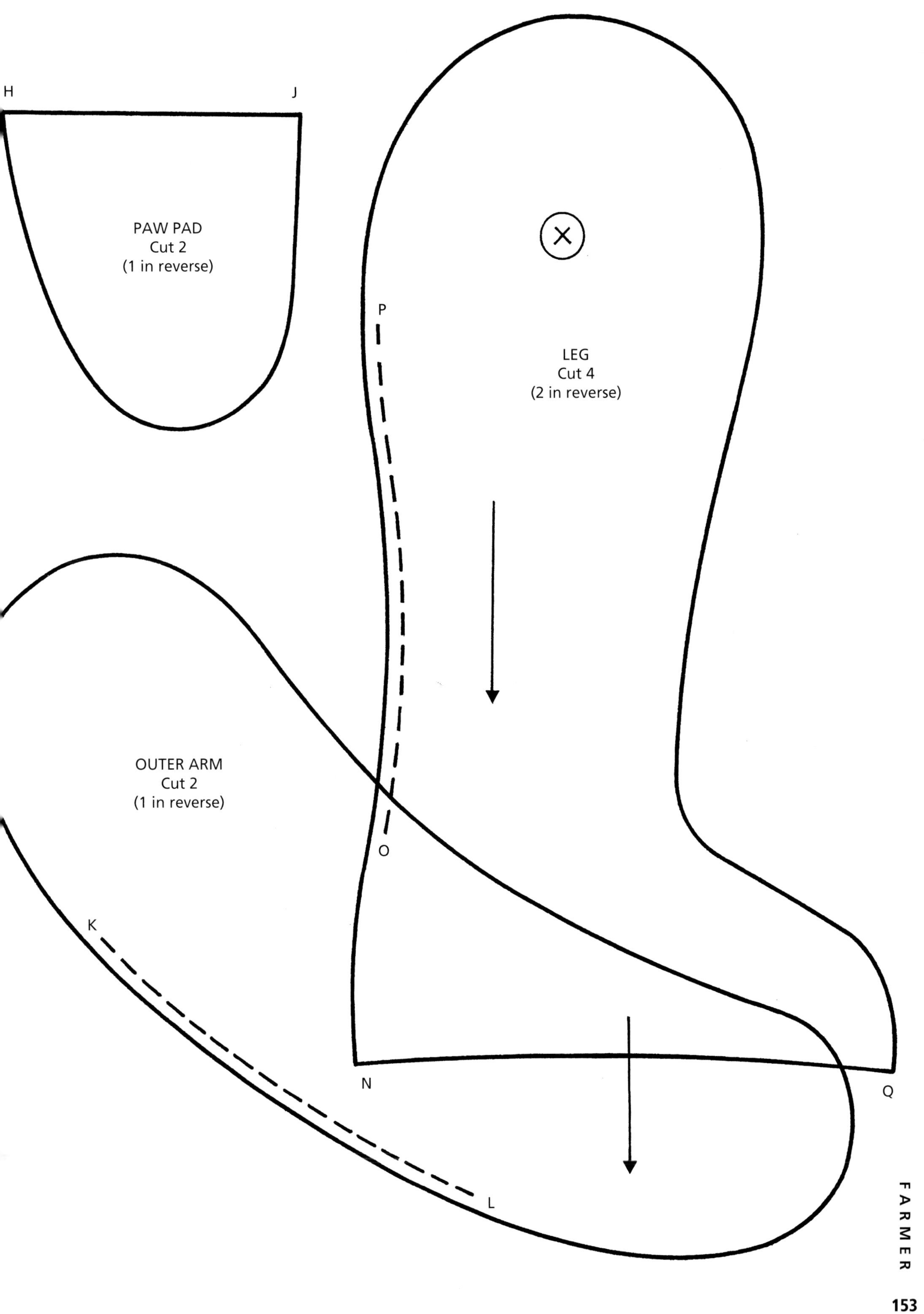
H
J
PAW PAD
Cut 2
(1 in reverse)
P
LEG
Cut 4
(2 in reverse)
OUTER ARM
Cut 2
(1 in reverse)
O
K
N
Q
L

E

EAR
Cut 4

G

G

HEAD GUSSET
Cut 1

N

B

C

C

B

SOLE OF FOOT
Cut 2
(1 in reverse)

Q

D

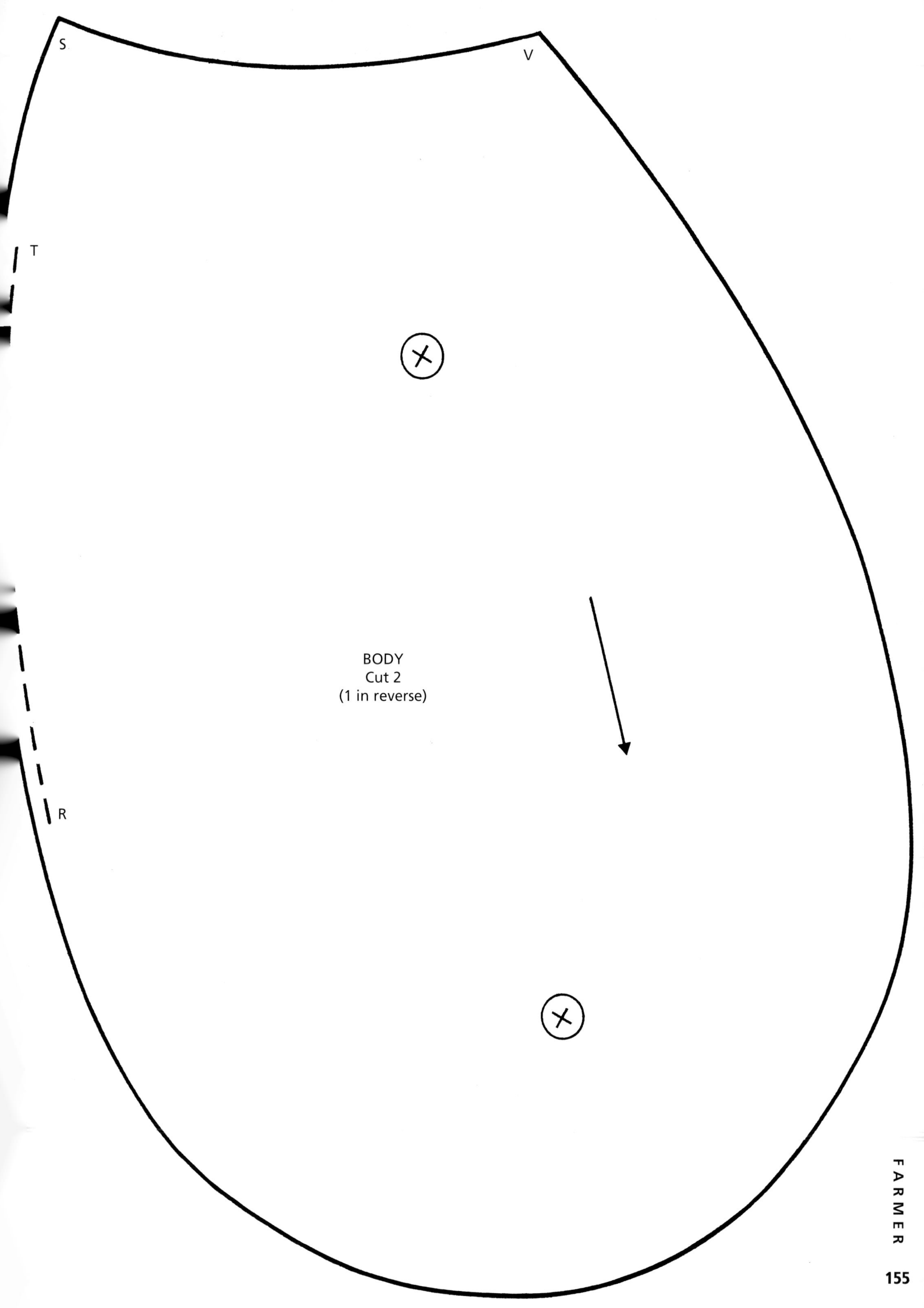
S
V
T
BODY
Cut 2
(1 in reverse)
R

B

A

HEAD
Cut 2
(1 in reverse)

D

E

F

K

V

ARM
Cut 2
(1 in reverse)

M

K

J

H

M

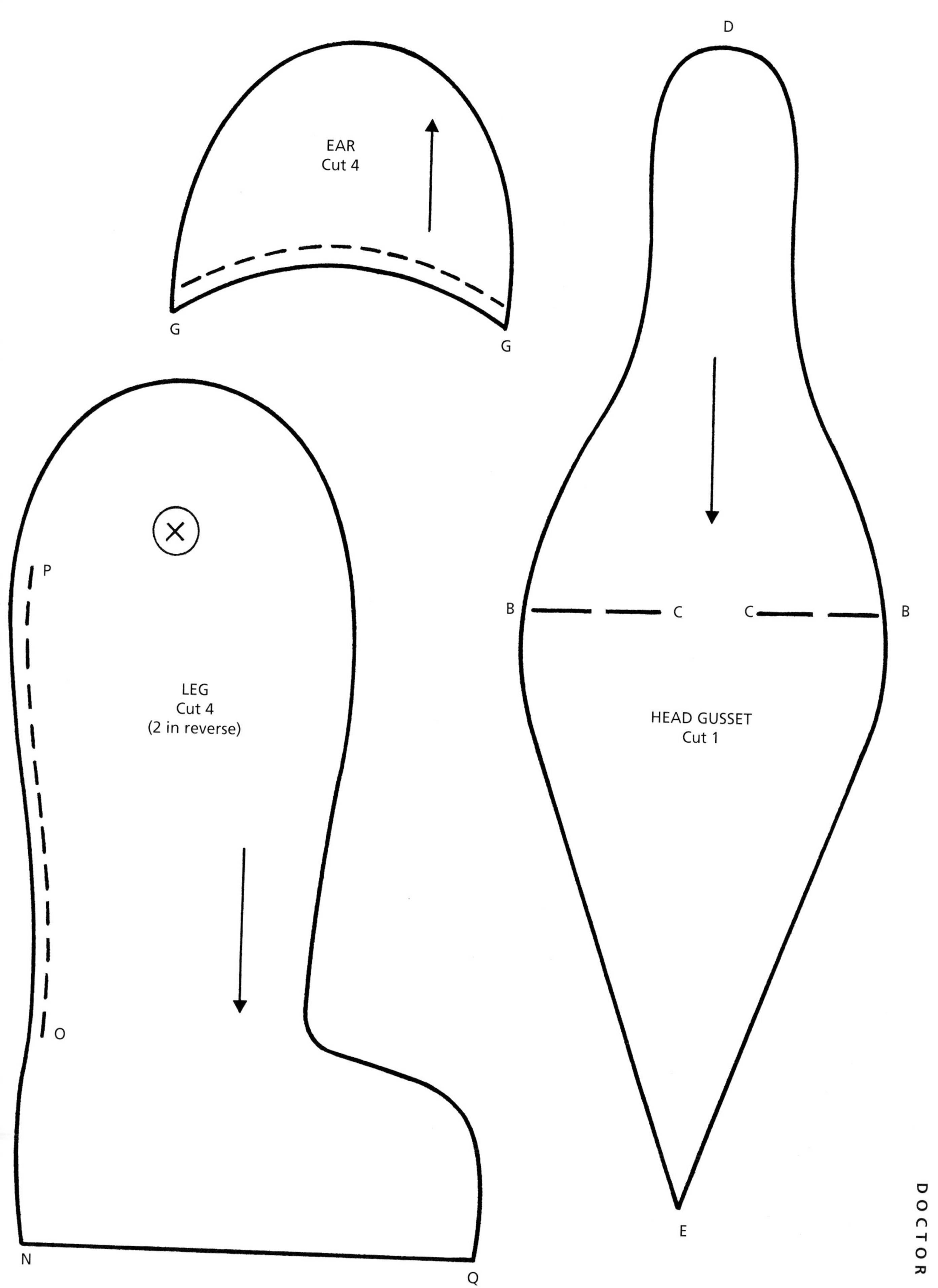
D
EAR
Cut 4
G
G
B
C
C
B
P
LEG
Cut 4
(2 in reverse)
HEAD GUSSET
Cut 1
O
E
N
Q

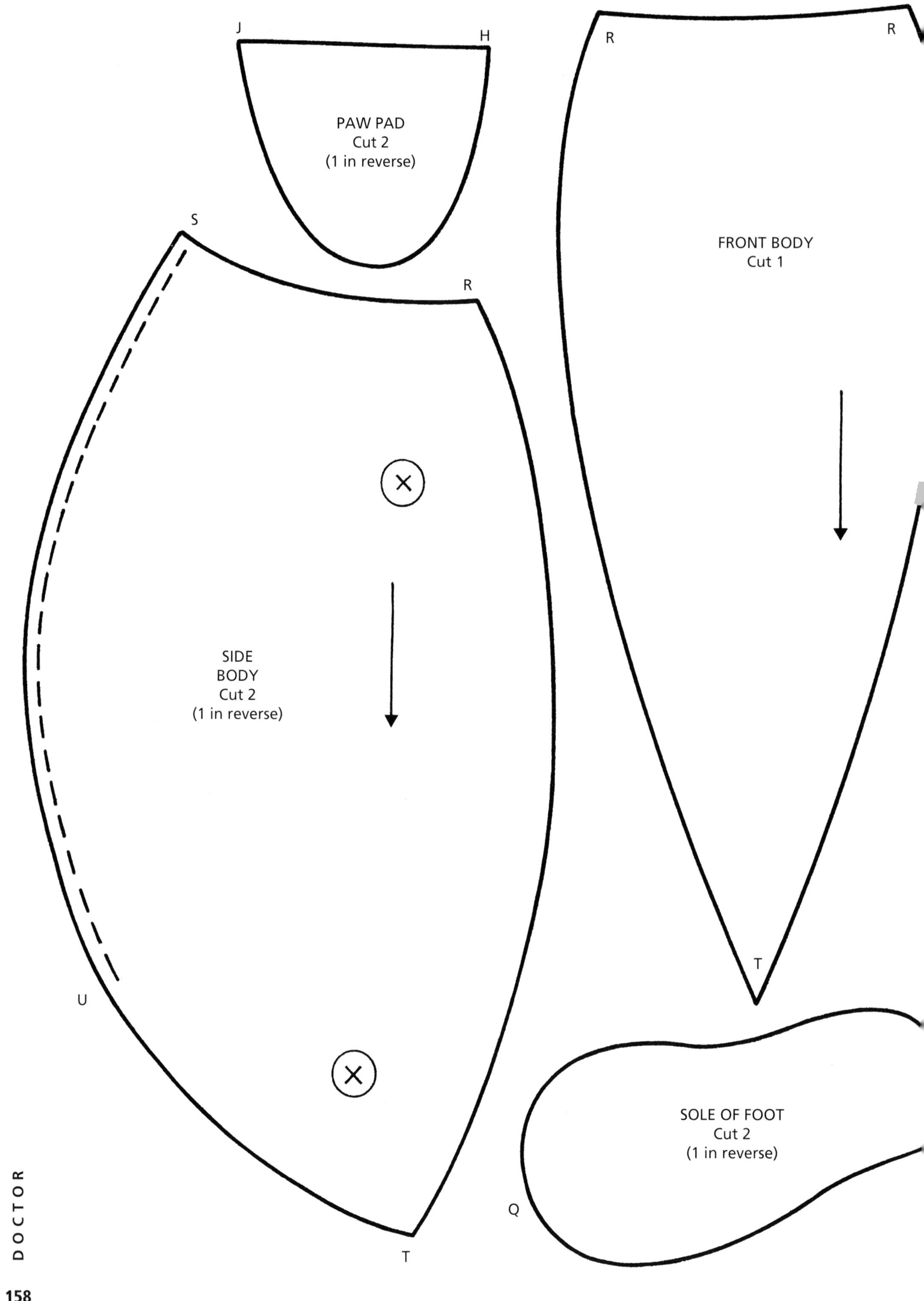
J
H
PAW PAD
Cut 2
(1 in reverse)
R
R
FRONT BODY
Cut 1
S
R
SIDE
BODY
Cut 2
(1 in reverse)
T
U
SOLE OF FOOT
Cut 2
(1 in reverse)
Q
T

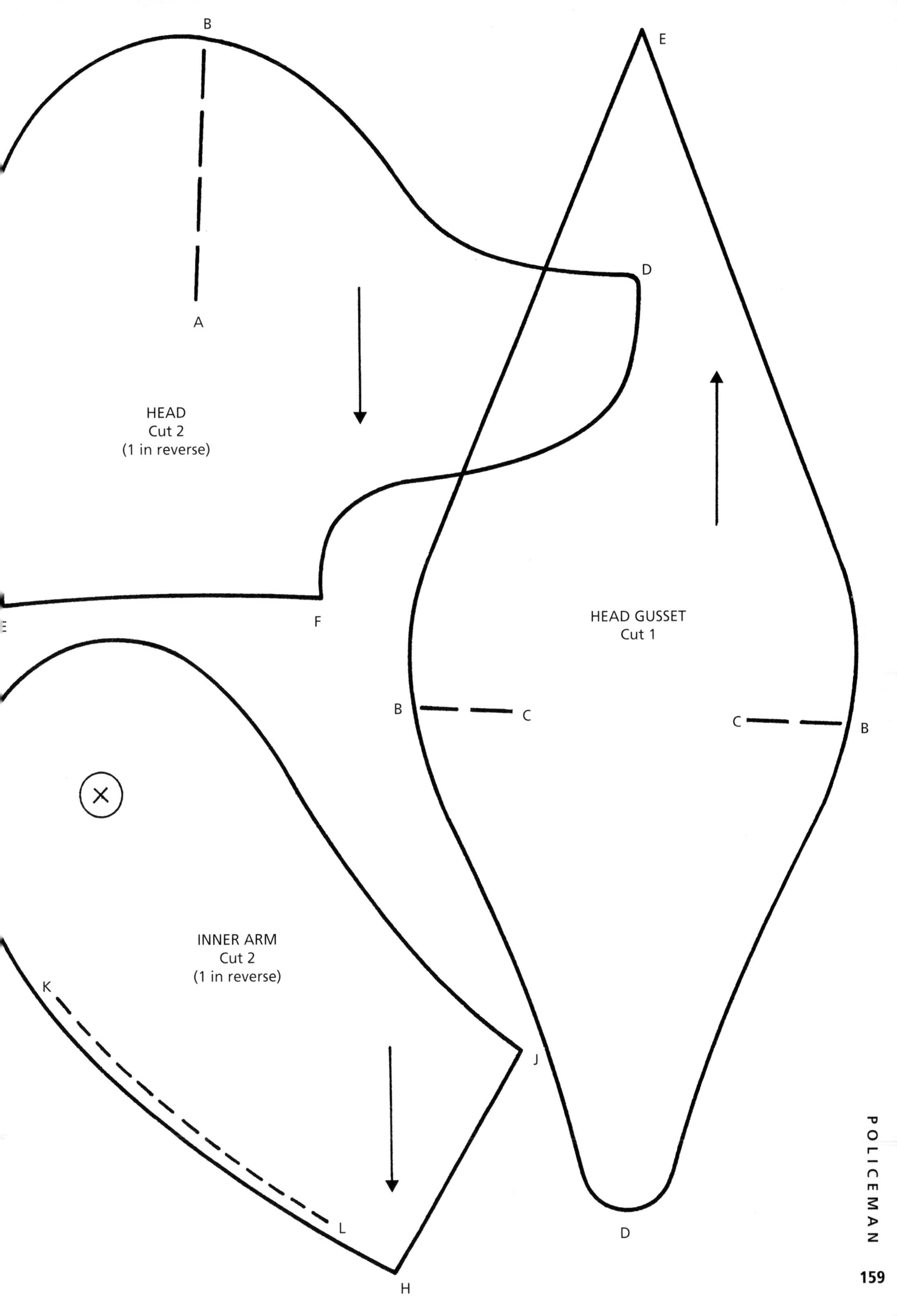
B
E
A
D
HEAD
Cut 2
(1 in reverse)
E
F
HEAD GUSSET
Cut 1
B
C
C
B
INNER ARM
Cut 2
(1 in reverse)
K
J
L
D
H

EAR
Cut 4

G

G

OUTER ARM
Cut 2
(1 in reverse)

K

L

LEG
Cut 4
(2 in reverse)

P

O

Q

N

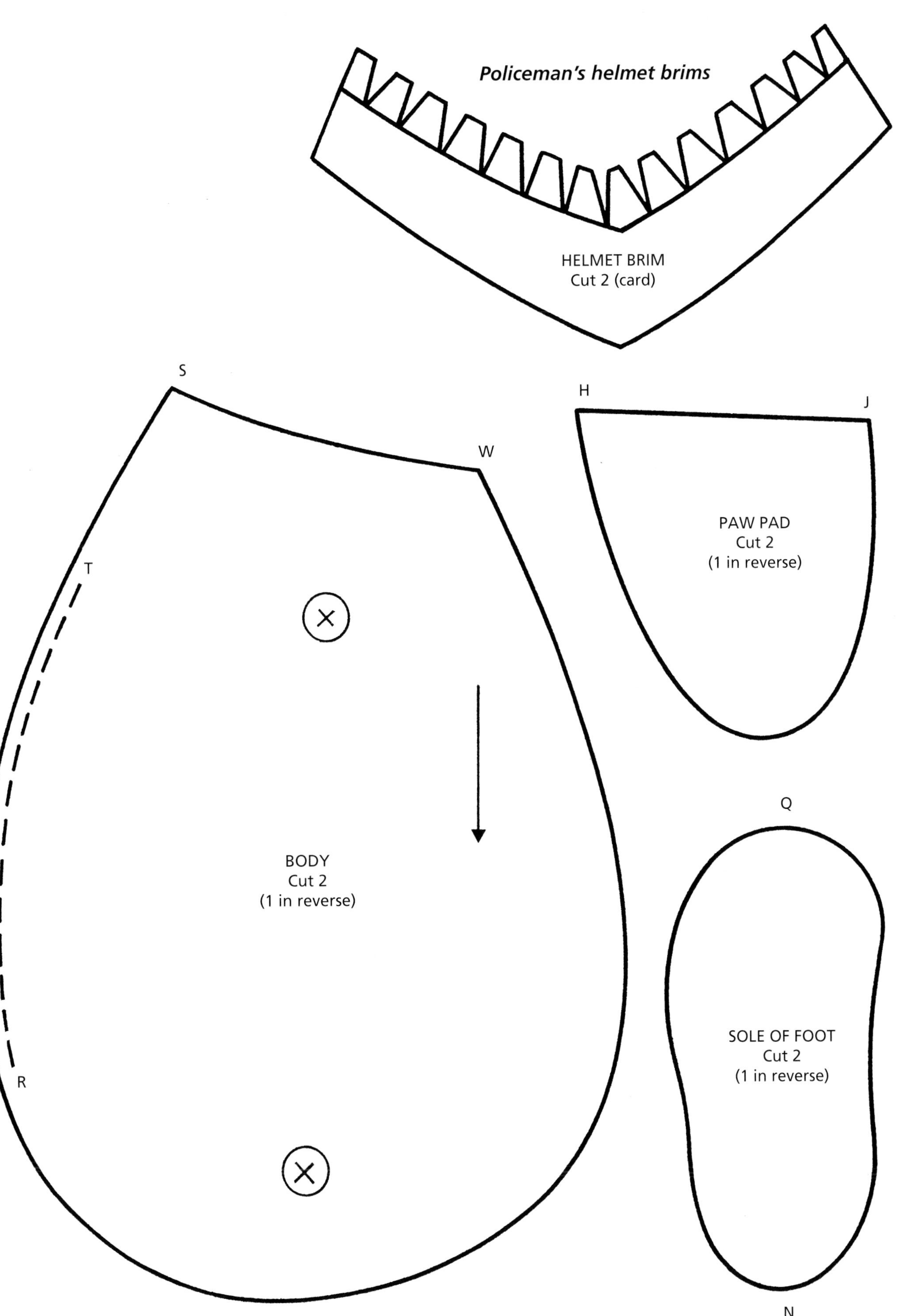
Policeman's helmet brims
HELMET BRIM
Cut 2 (card)
S
W
T
R
BODY
Cut 2
(1 in reverse)
H
J
PAW PAD
Cut 2
(1 in reverse)
Q
SOLE OF FOOT
Cut 2
(1 in reverse)
N

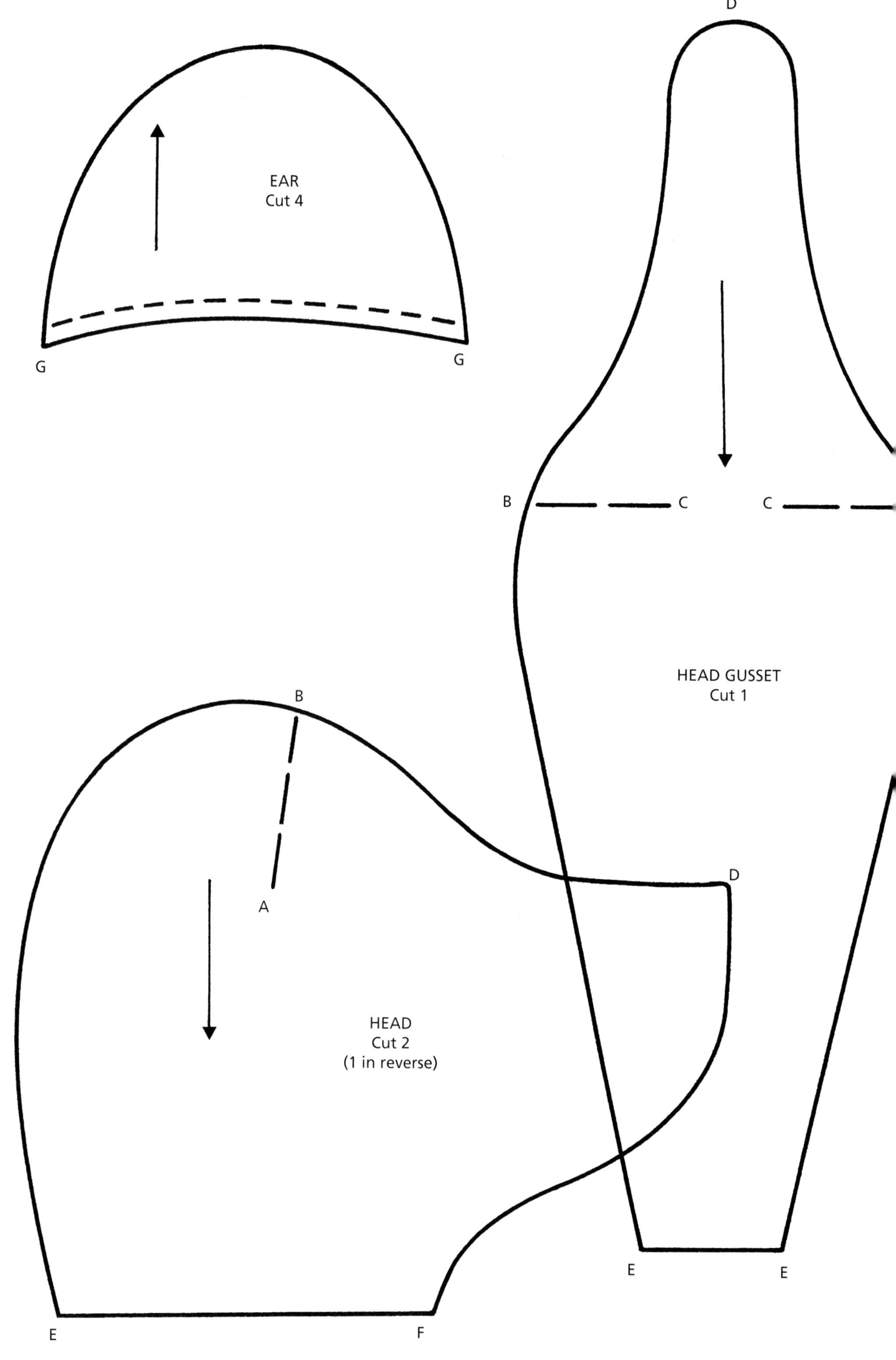
EAR
Cut 4
G
G
D
B
C
C
HEAD GUSSET
Cut 1
B
D
A
HEAD
Cut 2
(1 in reverse)
E
E
E
F

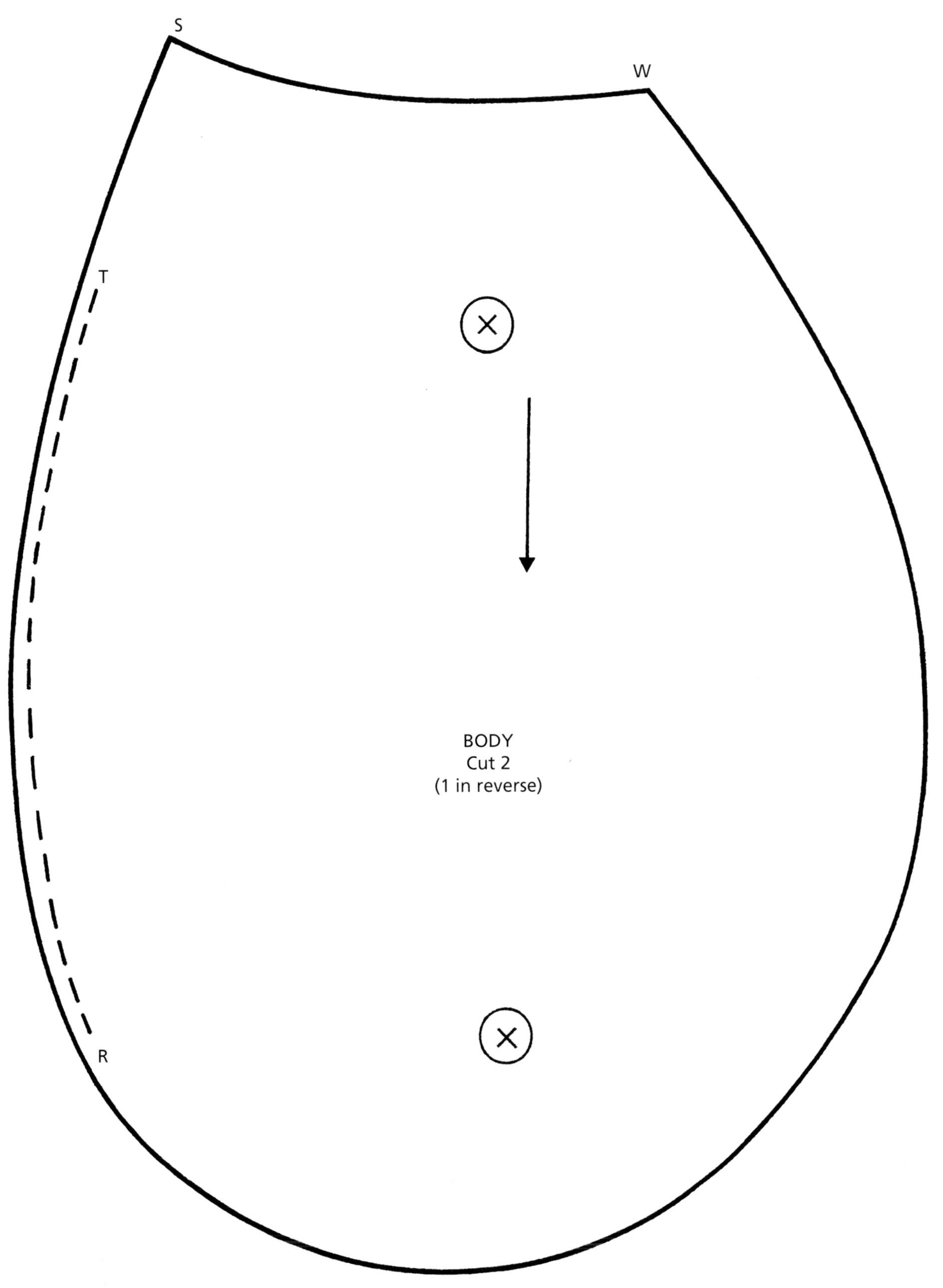
S
W
T
R
BODY
Cut 2
(1 in reverse)

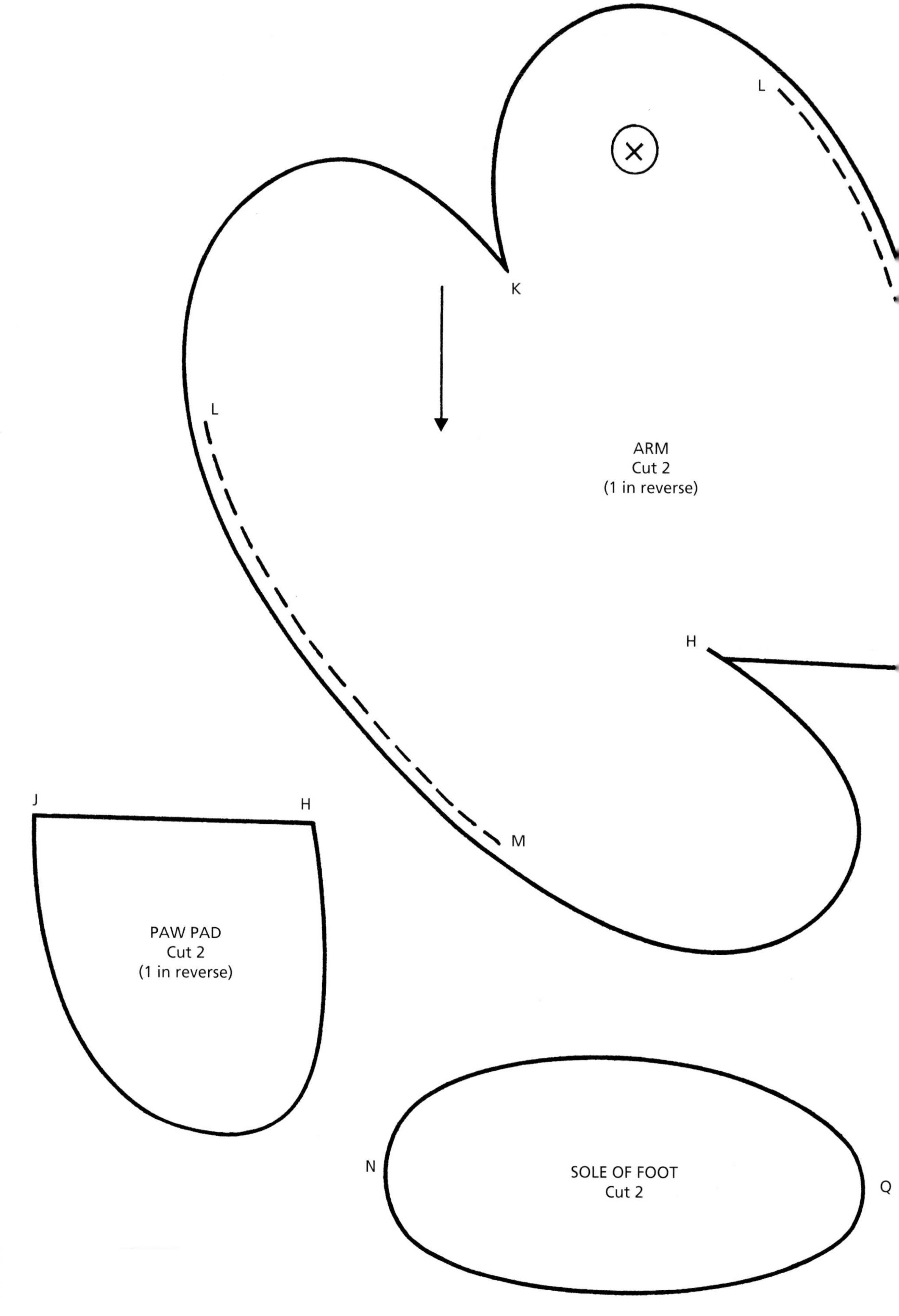
L
K
L
ARM
Cut 2
(1 in reverse)
H
J
H
M
PAW PAD
Cut 2
(1 in reverse)
N
SOLE OF FOOT
Cut 2
Q

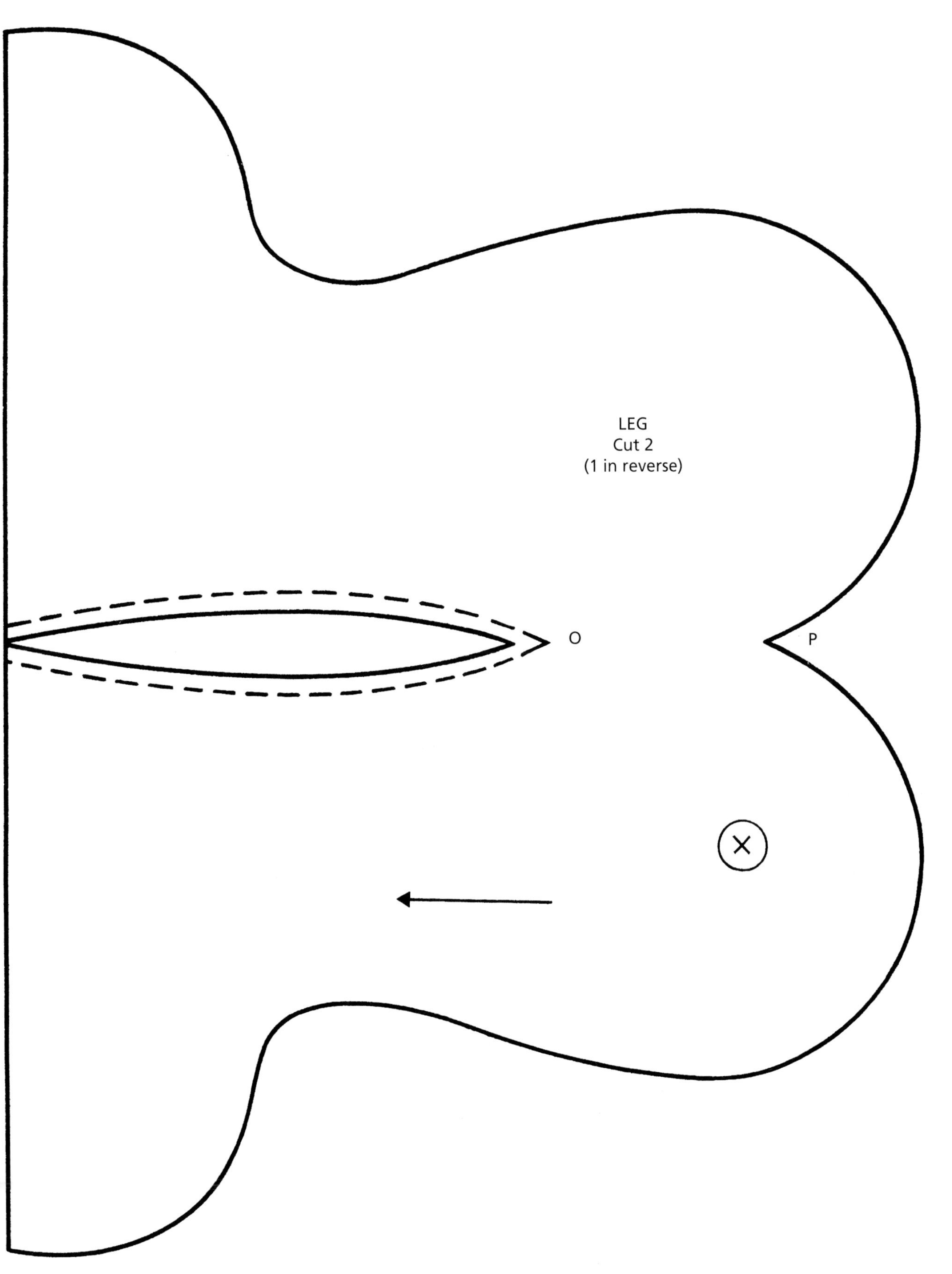
LEG
Cut 2
(1 in reverse)
O
P

B

A

HEAD
Cut 2
(1 in reverse)

E

F

E E

D

B C C

HEAD GUSSET
Cut 1

D

G G

EAR
Cut 4

J

PAW PAD
Cut 2
(1 in reverse)

H

L

K

L

ARM
Cut 2
(1 in reverse)

M

H

J

M

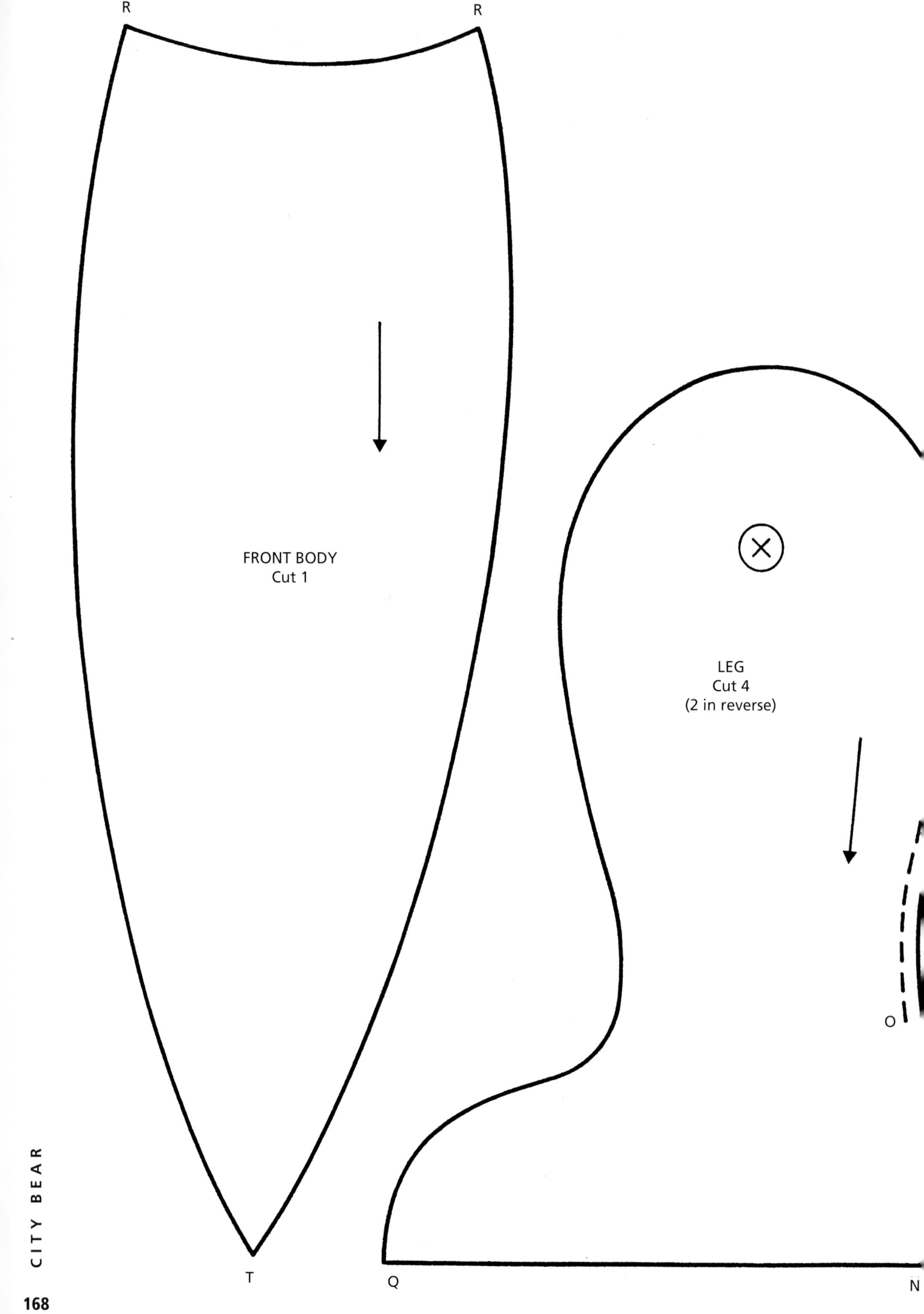
R
R
FRONT BODY
Cut 1
T
LEG
Cut 4
(2 in reverse)
O
Q
N

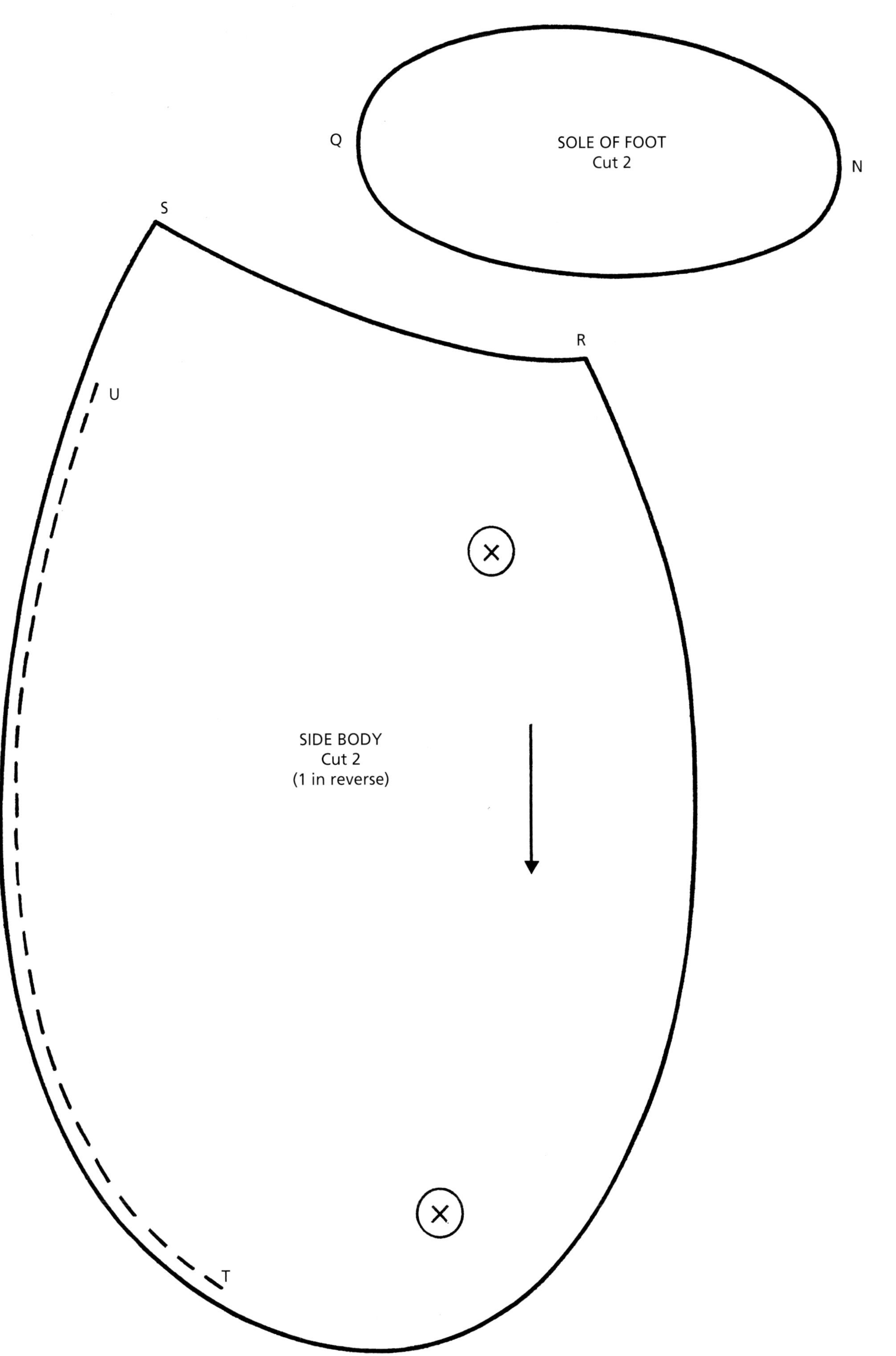
SOLE OF FOOT
Cut 2
Q
N
S
R
U
SIDE BODY
Cut 2
(1 in reverse)
T

B

D

A

HEAD
Cut 2
(1 in reverse)

E

F

P

LEG
Cut 4
(2 in reverse)

EAR
Cut 4

G

G

J

H

PAW PAD
Cut 2
(1 in reverse)

O

Q

N

D

INNER ARM
Cut 2
(1 in reverse)

H

K

L

J

C

C

B

HEAD GUSSET
Cut 1

K

OUTER ARM
Cut 2
(1 in reverse)

L

E

E

N

SOLE OF FOOT
Cut 2
(1 in reverse)

S

W

T

BODY
Cut 2
(1 in reverse)

V

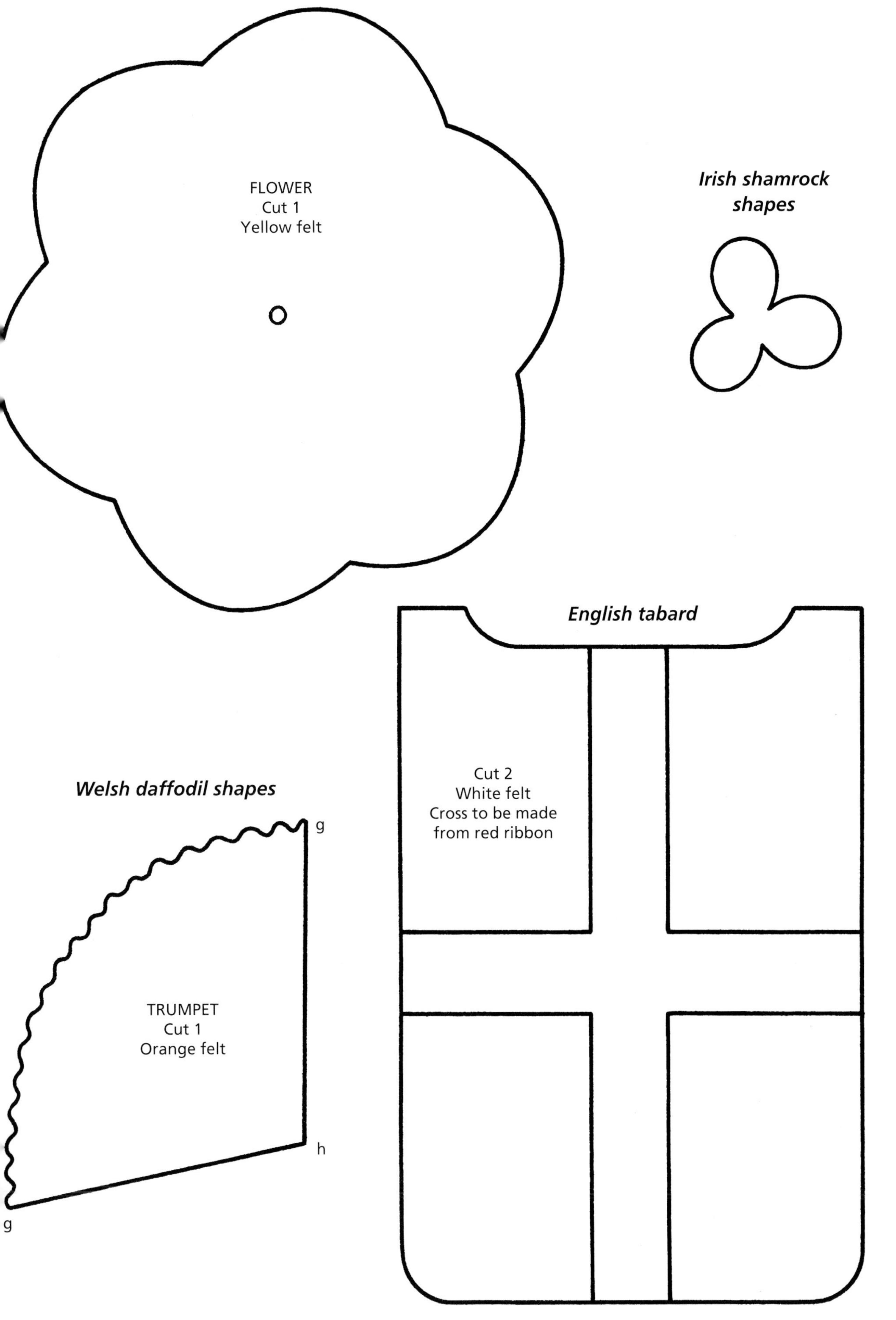
FLOWER
Cut 1
Yellow felt
Irish shamrock
shapes
English tabard
Cut 2
White felt
Cross to be made
from red ribbon
Welsh daffodil shapes
g
TRUMPET
Cut 1
Orange felt
h
g

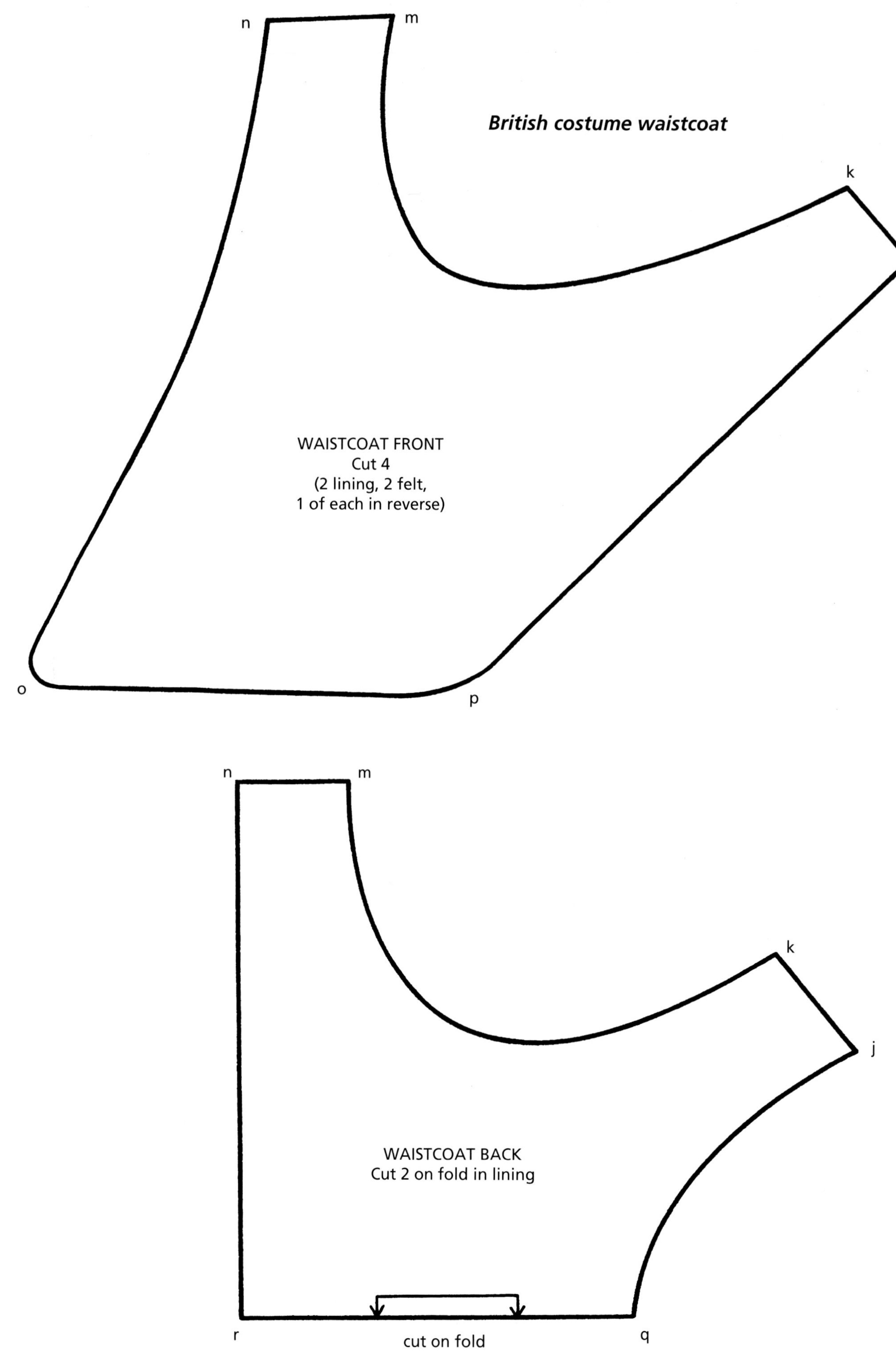
n
m
British costume waistcoat
k
j
WAISTCOAT FRONT
Cut 4
(2 lining, 2 felt,
1 of each in reverse)
o
p
n
m
k
j
WAISTCOAT BACK
Cut 2 on fold in lining
r
cut on fold
q

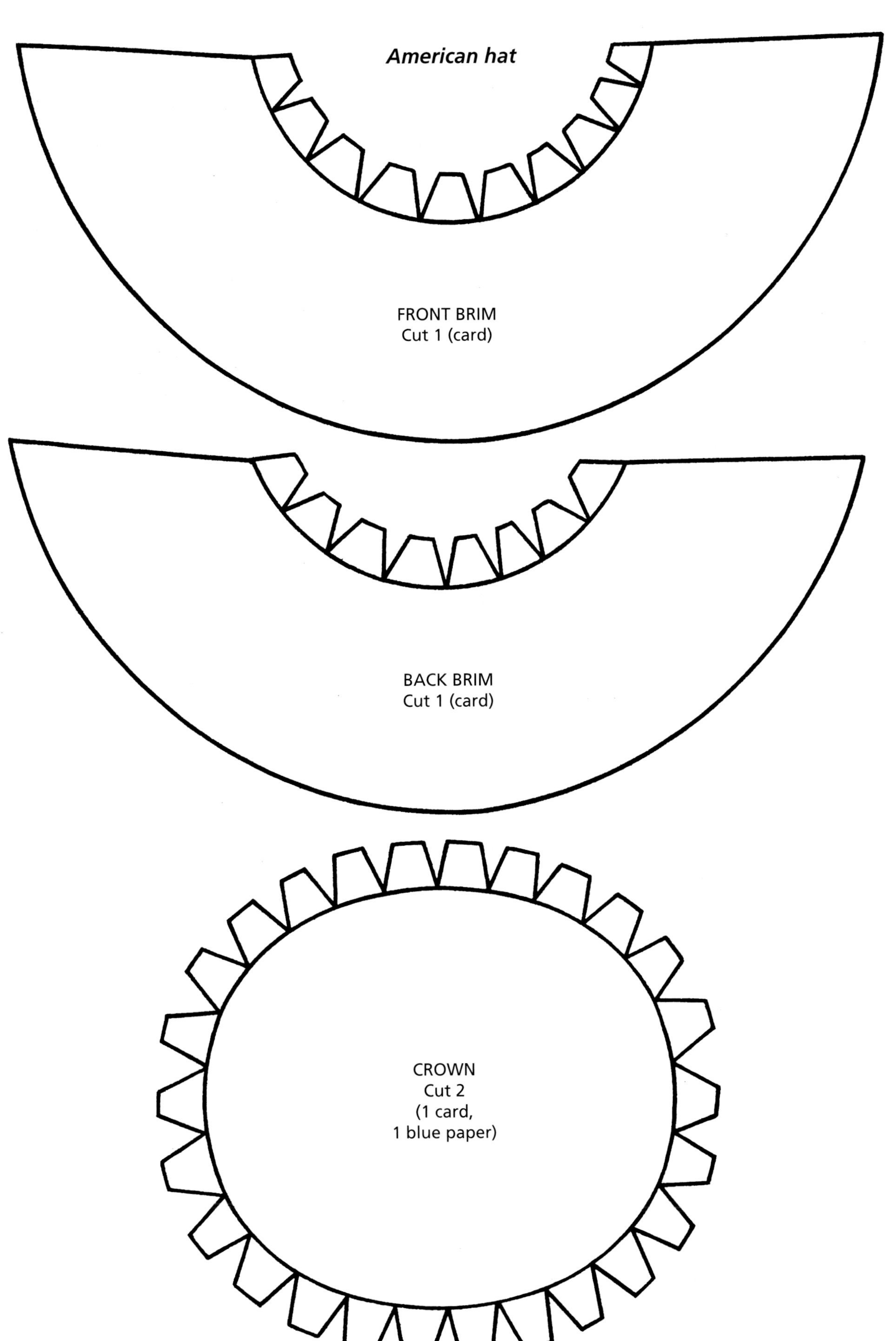
American hat
FRONT BRIM
Cut 1 (card)
BACK BRIM
Cut 1 (card)
CROWN
Cut 2
(1 card,
1 blue paper)

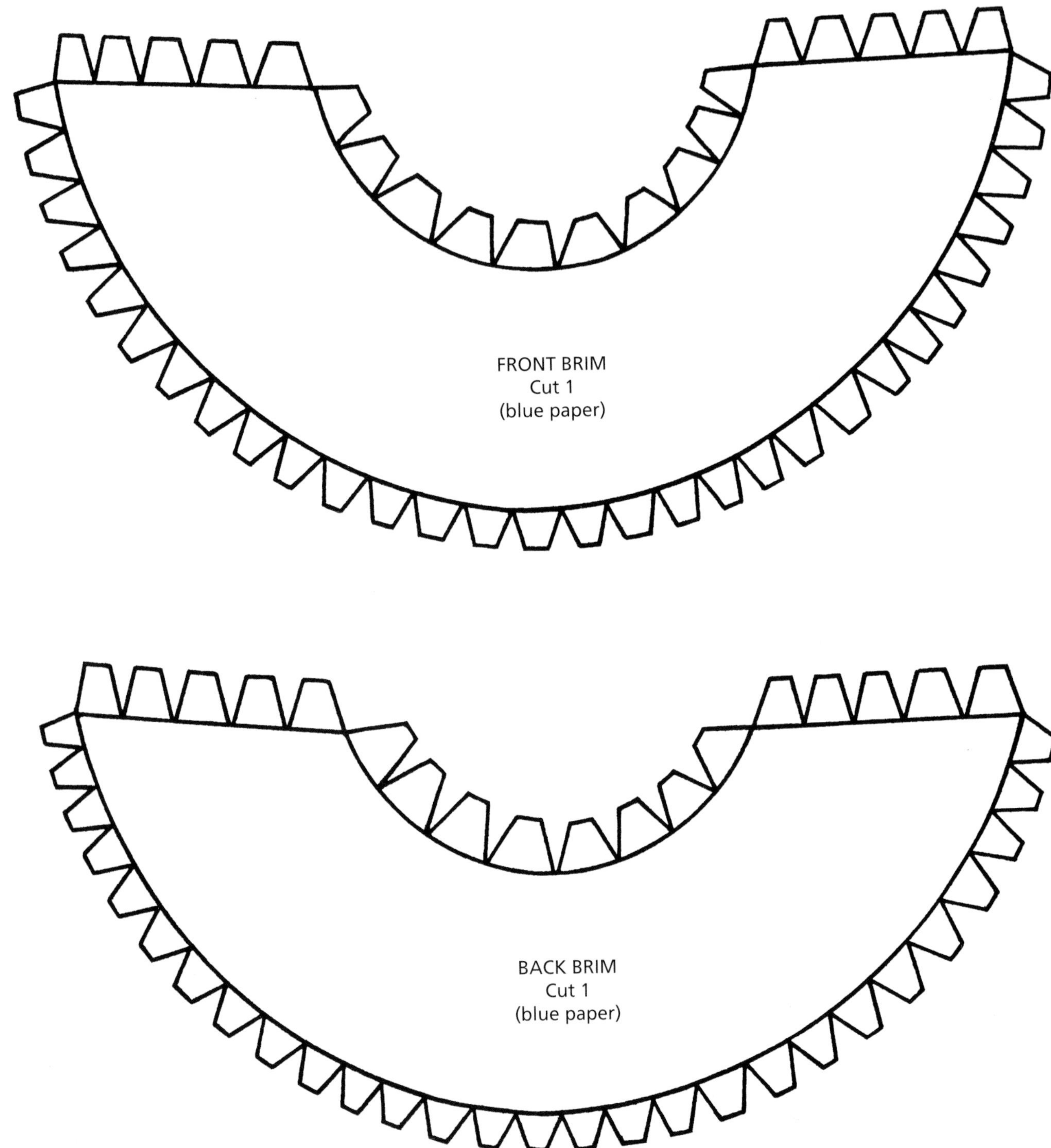
FRONT BRIM
Cut 1
(blue paper)
BACK BRIM
Cut 1
(blue paper)

Australian hat

t

s

BACK BRIM
Cut 1
(double felt)

FRONT BRIM
Cut 1
(double felt)

MAIN PIECE
Cut 1
(double felt)

t

s

CROWN
Cut 2
(1 card, 1 double felt)

t

METRIC CONVERSION TABLE

INCHES TO MILLIMETRES AND CENTIMETRES

MM = MILLIMETRES CM = CENTIMETRES

in	mm	cm	in	cm	in	cm
1/8	3	0.3	9	22.9	30	76.2
1/4	6	0.6	10	25.4	31	78.7
3/8	10	1.0	11	27.9	32	81.3
1/2	13	1.3	12	30.5	33	83.8
5/8	16	1.6	13	33.0	34	86.4
3/4	19	1.9	14	35.6	35	88.9
7/8	22	2.2	15	38.1	36	91.4
1	25	2.5	16	40.6	37	94.0
1 1/4	32	3.2	17	43.2	38	96.5
1 1/2	38	3.8	18	45.7	39	99.1
1 3/4	44	4.4	19	48.3	40	101.6
2	51	5.1	20	50.8	41	104.1
2 1/2	64	6.4	21	53.3	42	106.7
3	76	7.6	22	55.9	43	109.2
3 1/2	89	8.9	23	58.4	44	111.8
4	102	10.2	24	61.0	45	114.3
4 1/2	114	11.4	25	63.5	46	116.8
5	127	12.7	26	66.0	47	119.4
6	152	15.2	27	68.6	48	121.9
7	178	17.8	28	71.1	49	124.5
8	203	20.3	29	73.7	50	127.0

About the Author

Valerie Tyler has had a lifelong love of crafts. As well as making bears, clothes and soft furnishings, she also makes bobbin lace, spins, weaves, knits, embroiders and enjoys working with stained glass. With her young daughter she creates salt dough models, glass paintings and anything else which happens to attract their creativity.

In a varied career as a teacher, Valerie has taught children aged from five to eighteen. She is now an education consultant and a professional storyteller, and she lives in Kent with her husband and four children.

TITLES AVAILABLE FROM
GMC Publications

BOOKS

WOODWORKING

40 More Woodworking Plans & Projects *GMC Publications*
Bird Boxes and Feeders for the Garden *Dave Mackenzie*
Complete Woodfinishing *Ian Hosker*
Electric Woodwork *Jeremy Broun*
Furniture & Cabinetmaking Projects *GMC Publications*
Furniture Projects *Rod Wales*
Furniture Restoration (Practical Crafts) *Kevin Jan Bonner*
Furniture Restoration and Repair for Beginners *Kevin Jan Bonner*
Green Woodwork *Mike Abbott*
The Incredible Router *Jeremy Broun*
Making & Modifying Woodworking Tools *Jim Kingshott*
Making Chairs and Tables *GMC Publications*
Making Fine Furniture *Tom Darby*
Making Little Boxes from Wood *John Benn*
Making Shaker Furniture *Barry Jacks*
Pine Furniture Projects for the Home *Dave Macken*
Sharpening Pocket Reference Book *Jim Kingsh*
Sharpening: The Complete Guide *Jim Kingsh*
Space-Saving Furniture Projects *Dave Macken*
Stickmaking: A Complete Course *Andrew Jones & Clive Geo*
Test Reports: *The Router* and *Furniture & Cabinetmaking* *GMC Publicatio*
Veneering: A Complete Course *Ian Hos*
Woodfinishing Handbook (Practical Crafts) *Ian Hos*
Woodworking Plans and Projects *GMC Publicatio*
The Workshop *Jim Kingsh*

WOODTURNING

Adventures in Woodturning *David Springett*
Bert Marsh: Woodturner *Bert Marsh*
Bill Jones' Notes from the Turning Shop *Bill Jones*
Bill Jones' Further Notes from the Turning Shop *Bill Jones*
Colouring Techniques for Woodturners *Jan Sanders*
The Craftsman Woodturner *Peter Child*
Decorative Techniques for Woodturners *Hilary Bowen*
Essential Tips for Woodturners *GMC Publications*
Faceplate Turning *GMC Publications*
Fun at the Lathe *R.C. Bell*
Illustrated Woodturning Techniques *John Hunnex*
Intermediate Woodturning Projects *GMC Publications*
Keith Rowley's Woodturning Projects *Keith Rowley*
Make Money from Woodturning *Ann & Bob Phillips*
Multi-Centre Woodturning *Ray Hopper*
Pleasure and Profit from Woodturning *Reg Sherwin*
Practical Tips for Turners & Carvers *GMC Publicatio*
Practical Tips for Woodturners *GMC Publicatio*
Spindle Turning *GMC Publicatio*
Turning Miniatures in Wood *John Sainsbu*
Turning Wooden Toys *Terry Lawren*
Understanding Woodturning *Ann & Bob Philli*
Useful Techniques for Woodturners *GMC Publicatio*
Useful Woodturning Projects *GMC Publicatio*
Woodturning: A Foundation Course *Keith Row*
Woodturning: A Source Book of Shapes *John Hunn*
Woodturning Jewellery *Hilary Bow*
Woodturning Masterclass *Tony Bo*
Woodturning Techniques *GMC Publicatio*
Woodturning Tools & Equipment Test Reports *GMC Publicatio*
Woodturning Wizardry *David Spring*

WOODCARVING

The Art of the Woodcarver *GMC Publications*
Carving Birds & Beasts *GMC Publications*
Carving on Turning *Chris Pye*
Carving Realistic Birds *David Tippey*
Decorative Woodcarving *Jeremy Williams*
Essential Tips for Woodcarvers *GMC Publications*
Essential Woodcarving Techniques *Dick Onians*
Lettercarving in Wood: A Practical Course *Chris Pye*
Practical Tips for Turners & Carvers *GMC Publications*
Relief Carving in Wood: A Practical Introduction *Chris Pye*
Understanding Woodcarving *GMC Publications*
Understanding Woodcarving in the Round *GMC Publicatio*
Useful Techniques for Woodcarvers *GMC Publicatio*
Wildfowl Carving - Volume 1 *Jim Pear*
Wildfowl Carving - Volume 2 *Jim Pear*
The Woodcarvers *GMC Publicatio*
Woodcarving: A Complete Course *Ron Butterfie*
Woodcarving: A Foundation Course *Zoë Gertr*
Woodcarving for Beginners *GMC Publicatio*
Woodcarving Tools & Equipment Test Reports *GMC Publicatio*
Woodcarving Tools, Materials & Equipment *Chris P*

UPHOLSTERY

Seat Weaving (Practical Crafts) *Ricky Holdstock*
Upholsterer's Pocket Reference Book *David James*
Upholstery: A Complete Course *David James*
Upholstery Restoration *David Jam*
Upholstery Techniques & Projects *David Jam*

TOYMAKING

Designing & Making Wooden Toys *Terry Kelly*
Fun to Make Wooden Toys & Games *Jeff & Jennie Loader*
Making Board, Peg & Dice Games *Jeff & Jennie Loader*
Making Wooden Toys & Games *Jeff & Jennie Loader*
Restoring Rocking Horses *Clive Green & Anthony De*
Scrollsaw Toy Projects *Ivor Carl*
Wooden Toy Projects *GMC Publicatio*

Dolls' Houses

Architecture for Dolls' Houses	*Joyce Percival*
Beginners' Guide to the Dolls' House Hobby	*Jean Nisbett*
The Complete Dolls' House Book	*Jean Nisbett*
Dolls' House Accessories, Fixtures and Fittings	*Andrea Barham*
Dolls' House Bathrooms: Lots of Little Loos	*Patricia King*
Easy to Make Dolls' House Accessories	*Andrea Barham*
Make Your Own Dolls' House Furniture	*Maurice Harper*
Making Dolls' House Fireplaces and Stoves	*Patricia King*
Making Dolls' House Furniture	*Patricia King*
Making Georgian Dolls' Houses	*Derek Rowbottom*
Making Miniature Oriental Rugs & Carpets	*Meik & Ian McNaughton*
Making Period Dolls' House Accessories	*Andrea Barham*
Making Period Dolls' House Furniture	*Derek & Sheila Rowbottom*
Making Tudor Dolls' Houses	*Derek Rowbottom*
Making Unusual Miniatures	*Graham Spalding*
Making Victorian Dolls' House Furniture	*Patricia King*
Miniature Bobbin Lace	*Roz Snowden*
Miniature Embroidery for the Victorian Dolls' House	*Pamela Warner*
Miniature Needlepoint Carpets	*Janet Granger*
The Secrets of the Dolls' House Makers	*Jean Nisbett*

Crafts

American Patchwork Designs in Needlepoint	*Melanie Tacon*
A Beginners' Guide to Rubber Stamping	*Brenda Hunt*
Celtic Knotwork Designs	*Sheila Sturrock*
Collage from Seeds, Leaves and Flowers	*Joan Carver*
Complete Pyrography	*Stephen Poole*
Creating Knitwear Designs	*Pat Ashforth & Steve Plummer*
Creative Embroidery Techniques Using Colour Through Gold	*Daphne J. Ashby & Jackie Woolsey*
Cross Stitch Kitchen Projects	*Janet Granger*
Cross Stitch on Colour	*Sheena Rogers*
Designing and Making Cards	*Glennis Gilruth*
Designs for Pyrographers	*Norma Gregory*
Embroidery Tips & Hints	*Harold Hayes*
An Introduction to Crewel Embroidery	*Mave Glenny*
Making Character Bears	*Valerie Tyler*
Making Greetings Cards for Beginners	*Pat Sutherland*
Making Hand-sewn Boxes	*Jackie Woolsey*
Making Knitwear Fit	*Pat Ashforth & Steve Plummer*
Making Model Theatres in Paper and Card	*Robert Burgess*
Needlepoint: A Foundation Course	*Sandra Hardy*
Pyrography Handbook (Practical Crafts)	*Stephen Poole*
Tassel Making for Beginners	*Enid Taylor*
Tatting Collage	*Lindsay Rogers*
Temari: A Traditional Japanese Embroidery Technique	*Margaret Ludlow*

The Home

Home Ownership: Buying and Maintaining	*Nicholas Snelling*
Security for the Householder: Fitting Locks and Other Devices	*E. Phillips*

VIDEOS

rop-in and Pinstuffed Seats	*David James*
tuffover Upholstery	*David James*
lliptical Turning	*David Springett*
Voodturning Wizardry	*David Springett*
urning Between Centres: The Basics	*Dennis White*
urning Bowls	*Dennis White*
oxes, Goblets and Screw Threads	*Dennis White*
ovelties and Projects	*Dennis White*
lassic Profiles	*Dennis White*
Twists and Advanced Turning	*Dennis White*
Sharpening the Professional Way	*Jim Kingshott*
Sharpening Turning & Carving Tools	*Jim Kingshott*
Bowl Turning	*John Jordan*
Hollow Turning	*John Jordan*
Woodturning: A Foundation Course	*Keith Rowley*
Carving a Figure: The Female Form	*Ray Gonzalez*
The Router: A Beginner's Guide	*Alan Goodsell*
The Scroll Saw: A Beginner's Guide	*John Burke*

MAGAZINES

Woodturning ◆ Woodcarving ◆ Furniture & Cabinetmaking
The Dolls' House Magazine ◆ Creative Crafts for the Home
The Router ◆ The ScrollSaw ◆ BusinessMatters

◆

The above represents a full list of all titles currently published or scheduled to be published.
All are available direct from the Publishers or through bookshops, newsagents and specialist retailers.
To place an order, or to obtain a complete catalogue, contact:

GMC Publications,
Castle Place, 166 High Street, Lewes, East Sussex BN7 1XU, United Kingdom
Tel: 01273 488005 Fax: 01273 478606

Orders by credit card are accepted